PRAISE FOR *PRIMATES*

"Picture *Real Housewives*, add in pop sci . . . Martin's new book."

—*Publishers Weekly*

"Recalls Betty Friedan's *The Feminine Mystique* . . . *Primates* is pacy and skillfully weaves cultural insight with personal anecdote. . . . This is an intriguing insight into a closed world. It is easy to dismiss the subjects as frivolous and mean, which many seem to be. But our envy and schadenfreude makes the rich a compelling curiosity."

—*Financial Times*

"Martin puts her academic background (anthropology classes and a doctorate in cultural studies) to witty good use in describing this wealthy tribe's extremes. . . . It became clear to me, reading Martin's book, that our Bay Area tribes aren't so different from those of New York."

—*San Francisco Chronicle*

"A very funny, and slightly scary, look at the denizens of Manhattan's Upper East Side."

—*Connecticut Post*

"If anthropologist Jane Goodall had landed on Park Avenue with a Birkin bag instead of in the wilds of Tanzania with a notebook, this is the book she would have written. *Primates of Park Avenue* is a smart, funny, and original dissection of the tribal rites of rich and striving New Yorkers as they migrate between Manhattan's Upper East Side and the Hamptons."

—Steven Gaines, author of *Philistines at the Hedgerow*

"A Jane Goodall wielding an American Express Black Card, the author leads readers through the hierarchical benchmarks of Upper East Side mothers. This anthropological journey into the wilds of New York City's most exclusive zip code could have easily devolved into condescension, but instead it proves that mothers everywhere want the same thing: health and happiness for their progeny."

—*Library Journal* (starred review)

"I am a huge fan of everything Wednesday Martin writes—her astute observations are filled with wisdom and humor, and more than once have helped me see the world through different eyes."

—Jane Green, *New York Times* bestselling author of *Saving Grace*

"Dr. Wednesday Martin is a genius. This book is a must for anyone fascinated by people, trends, and tribes."

—Lucy Sykes, coauthor of *The Knockoff*

"People aiming to study primates in the wild are carefully taught to avoid anthropomorphism. Reading human motivation into the behavior of free-living primates is a no-no. But what about using information from primate field studies to interpret human behavior 'chimpomorphically'? Confronted with the need to cope with sociopathological conditions on New York's ultrawealthy Upper East Side, Wednesday Martin delved deeply into her knowledge of primate behavior. The result is this book, in which primatology leads to a deeper understanding of the human hearts that beat beneath designer-clad exteriors. A tour de force."

—Robert Martin, PhD, professor of biological anthropology; Curator Emeritus at the Field Museum of Chicago; and author of *How We Do It: The Evolution and Future of Human Reproduction*

"When mean girls and wannabes grow up, they become the women so perfectly depicted in Wednesday Martin's funny and intelligent memoir. How wonderful that she survived the jungle of Park Avenue with strong female friendships intact."

—Rosalind Wiseman, author of *Queen Bees and Wannabes*

PRIMATES
of
PARK
AVENUE

a memoir

WEDNESDAY MARTIN, PHD

SIMON & SCHUSTER PAPERBACKS

New York London Toronto Sydney New Delhi

Simon & Schuster Paperbacks
An Imprint of Simon & Schuster, Inc.
1230 Avenue of the Americas
New York, NY 10020

Author's Note: This work is a memoir. It reflects my experiences over a period of several years. Some names and identifying details have been changed, and some individuals portrayed are composites. For narrative purposes and to mask the identities of certain individuals, the timeline of certain events has been altered or compressed.

First Simon & Schuster trade paperback edition June 2016

SIMON & SCHUSTER PAPERBACKS and colophon are registered trademarks of Simon & Schuster, Inc.

For information about special discounts for bulk purchases, please contact Simon & Schuster Special Sales at 1-866-506-1949 or business@simonandschuster.com.

The Simon & Schuster Speakers Bureau can bring authors to your live event. For more information or to book an event, contact the Simon & Schuster Speakers Bureau at 1-866-248-3049 or visit our website at www.simonspeakers.com.

Illustrations by Andreas Gurewich

Manufactured in the United States of America

1   3   5   7   9   10   8   6   4   2

The Library of Congress has cataloged the hardcover edition as follows:

Martin, Wednesday.
  Primates of Park Avenue : a memoir / Wednesday Martin, PhD — First Simon & Schuster hardcover edition.
      pages cm
  Includes bibliographical references.
  1. Martin, Wednesday. 2. Upper East Side (New York, NY)—Biography. 3. New York (NY)—Biography. 4. Mothers—New York (State)—New York—Biography. 5. Mothers—New York (State)—New York—Social life and customs. 6. Primates—Behavior—Miscellanea. 7. Interpersonal relations—New York (State)—New York. 8. Upper East Side (New York, NY)—Social life and customs. 9. New York (NY)—Social life and customs. I. Title.
  F128.68.U63M37 2015
  974.7'1—dc23

                                       2014041481

ISBN 978-1-4767-6262-3
ISBN 978-1-4767-6271-5 (pbk)
ISBN 978-1-4767-6272-2 (ebook)

For Blossom and Daphne. And for all the mommies.

CONTENTS

INTRODUCTION

ONE OF the first gifts I received after my older son was born was a baby book from an old friend, a mom of two who still lives in the small Michigan town where she and I grew up. The gift both welcomed my son and acknowledged that I was living in New York City now, a place very different from the one where she and I spent our childhoods. *Urban Babies Wear Black* is a whimsically illustrated board book that lists, with the succinctness of a five-minute sociology lecture, exactly how urban babies are different—starting with their outfits (black and stylish versus pink or blue and cutesy-pie), going on to what they eat and drink (sushi and lattes versus hot dogs and milk) and how they pass the time (going to operas and art galleries versus the playground). I'm pretty sure I loved this book more than my baby did. In our first weeks at home together, I read it to him over and over. Sometimes, I even found myself reading it while he napped.

Eventually it dawned on me that the appeal of the book was that it also had things to say about the babies' *mothers.* These creatures were visible only in small, alluring pieces—a high heel here, a fancy dog leash there—as they strolled and jogged and taxied

1

and toted their tots across the pages of the book, making their babies chicly urban, being chicly urban themselves. I scrutinized the manicures and the fur baby carriers closely as I read aloud to my son. Who were they really, these glamorous, stylishly turned out women with sophisticated babies? What did they do? And how did they do it?

I wanted to see more of these mommies of urban babies because I wanted to know more about my peers, other Manhattan mommies. Because I was a woman with kids in the industrialized West, I was mothering utterly unlike the people I had studied and written about for years in my work as a social researcher focusing on, among other things, the history and evolutionary prehistory of family life. Hunter-gatherers and foragers, living as our ancestors once did, raise their babies communally, in a rich social network of mothers, sisters, nieces, and other conspecifics who can be counted on to care for (and even nurse) the infants of others as if they were their own. My mother had a version of this support system when my brothers and I were growing up in Michigan: a dozen or so other women in the neighborhood who mothered full-time were fictive kin she could call on to watch us when she needed to run an errand or take a nap, or simply craved some adult company. Meanwhile, we got to hang out with other kids. Backyards connected homes, mothers, and children in a web of reciprocal altruism: You help me, I'll help you. I'll watch the kids from my back window today, you do it tomorrow. Thanks for the flour; I'll bring you a slice or two of cake when it's baked.

In stark contrast, my New York City baby and I lived in an intensely privatized way, in spite of our proximity to so many others. I seldom even *saw* my hundreds of downtown Manhattan neighbors, who were busy with their own lives. Everything they did transpired in spaces—offices, apartments, schools—sequestered from public view. Having left my natal group, living far from my natal land, I had no nearby kin to call on. My closest adoptive relatives were elderly in-laws, enthused to see us but unable to lend a hand. And, as we live neolocally in the United States—leaving extended family to form our own separate households upon marriage—they were a half hour's journey from us, anyway.

Meanwhile my husband, like my own father and so many fathers in the West, and particularly the ones in Manhattan—an extraordinarily expensive town, where the pressure on wage earners with dependents is tremendous—went back to work after just a week home with the baby and me. For a time we had a baby nurse, a fixture of Manhattan babyhood who is hired through word of mouth to help with the type of baby basics our mothers and grandmothers used to teach us. She arrived cheerily every morning to lend a hand and remind me of what I had learned from the hospital maternity ward's brief baby-care classes, and from babysitting so long before. Aside from her and the friends who visited, though, I was mostly alone with our neonate, and with my anxieties about getting mothering right, day after day.

I was also something of a shut-in. We had a lovely little jewel of a backyard garden where I loved to sit with the baby. Other than that, I had very little desire to leave the house. The kamikaze cabdrivers, throngs of rushing people, jackhammers, and car horns made the town I had loved for over a decade feel newly inhospitable, even dangerous, to my son. A good friend, who had given birth just before I did, was so disenchanted with big-city motherhood that she fled to the suburbs. And I hadn't made friends at the Mommy & Me yoga studio around the corner. Although none seemed to be working, the downward-dogging new moms scattered with polite nods each day after class, presumably to shut themselves up in their individual homes with their individual babies and do their individual things.

Who, I frequently wondered, was going to teach me to be the urban mommy of an urban baby?

A Midwesterner born, I had a slow and relatively traditional childhood. I walked to and from school with a pack of mixed-age neighborhood kids every morning, then played kick the can and mucked around our backyards and the nearby woods with them, unsupervised, into the early evening. Weekends, we all rode bikes and did Girl or Boy Scouts. When I was older, I babysat some evenings and weekends, too, a logical first job for a hands-on big sister and a popular pastime among the young pre-reproductives in our neighborhood.

Probably the only notable thing about my background, the thing that could help me find my footing now, was my mother's fascination with anthropology and the then-nascent field of sociobiology. Margaret Mead's *Coming of Age in Samoa* was one of her favorite books. Mead's suggestion that Western-style childhood and adolescence wasn't the only or right way, and that Samoans arguably did it better, scandalized the country when the book came out in 1928, and all over again when it was reissued in 1972. Mead, my mother explained, was an anthropologist. She studied people in different cultures, learning about them by living among them and doing what they did alongside them. Then she wrote about it. Being an anthropologist struck me as an impossibly exotic and glamorous and appealing job, growing up as I did surrounded by mothers who were mostly housewives and fathers who were mostly doctors and lawyers.

This was also the era of Jane Goodall, a beguiling, ponytailed blonde in khakis and a pith helmet who became the public face of primatology. Goodall—who observed and protected her brood of Gombe chimps in Tanzania, introducing them to the world via *National Geographic*—was my idea of a rock star. Over dinners at our house, we talked about my father's day, my mother's day, what my brothers and I had done at school—and Mary Leakey, a cigar-chomping mom of three whose fossil discoveries in Olduvai Gorge and Laetoli, Tanzania, were forcing everyone to rethink human prehistory.

When my younger brothers bickered at dinner, my mother invoked Robert Trivers's theories of parental investment and sibling rivalry. When they were nice, she talked about kin selection and altruism. Wasn't it odd, she mused one day when I was around ten years old, E. O. Wilson obviously on her mind as she folded the laundry, that if I were about to get hit by a car and she pulled me out of the way, she would be doing it to protect not just me but also her own genes?

This unsentimental (if oversimplified, circa 1975) take on the sociobiology of motherhood, this entirely novel theory of relationships between parents and children, got my attention. Along with my mother's book collection—Mead sat alongside Colin Turnbull's books about the Ik of Uganda and the Mbuti Pygmies of Zaire, Betty Friedan, *The Hite Report, Silent Spring*, and towering piles of *Natural History Magazine*—it also likely set me on a course to study biological and cultural anthropology, with a focus on the lives of women. Nothing fascinated me more than grooming, friendship, and struggles for dominance among savanna baboons. Or the strangeness of worlds within worlds like my college campus's Greek system of sororities and fraternities, with their choreographed pledge-week rituals and passionate loyalties and rivalries. I studied Old World and New World monkeys and *Homo habilis* and *Homo ergaster* brain sizes, and wrote about how sorority girls weren't so different from great apes.

In my twenties, seeking excitement, I moved to New York City to pursue a doctorate in cultural studies and comparative literature. Manhattan changed everything about me—my goals (I finished my doctorate but decided I didn't want to be an academic after all), my fashion sense (clothing, always an interest, became a near fixation in a town of beautiful and beautifully turned out women), even who I was on a cellular level (the sheer excitement of being in a big city altered my cortisol levels and metabolism, transforming me into a stereotypically skinny Manhattanite with insomnia). Energized, I wrote and edited for magazines and taught a few courses in my discipline to pay the rent.

In my midthirties, having delayed marriage and childbearing as highly educated women living in affluent metropoles tend to do, I married a wry native with deep professional and emotional roots in his town. He was born and raised here, a reality as exotic and appealing to me as, say, being from Tahiti. Or Samoa. He had a pleasingly nerdy microknowledge of the city's history and seemed to have a personal anecdote about nearly every street corner, building, and neighborhood. If I had any hesitation about making a life for myself in New York City, he swept it away with his passion for the place. It was appealing that his parents and brother and sister-in-law were here, with his teenage daughters from his previous marriage living with him on weekends. His was a cozy, ready-made family for me, with my own family so far away.

New York City had the added benefit of being one of the few places a writer like me could thrive, in ecological niches as diverse as advertising, publishing, and teaching. Teeming and vital, the city reminded me of a rain forest, the only other habitat that could support such extreme and robust variation among life-forms. At one point I had lived in an Indian neighborhood abutting a Peruvian one, then moved near an enclave called Little Sweden. My husband wasn't budging, and I was fine with that. We settled downtown, and six months after marrying, I was pregnant. We never thought about leaving New York City. My husband had been raised here, after all, and I had gone to the significant trouble of moving to Manhattan from halfway across the country. Why wouldn't it be good enough for our offspring, too? And so our moment of discovery—*We're having a baby!*—was not just personally joyful. It was also the beginning of something much bigger than me or my marriage or my background or my feelings about being a mother. It marked a transition, I realized only later: my initiation into another world—the world of Manhattan motherhood.

This book is the stranger-than-fiction story of what I discovered when I made an academic experiment of studying Manhattan motherhood as I lived it. It is the story of a world within a world, a description I do not use lightly. We moved to the Upper East Side just after 9/11, craving both physical distance from the tragedy and closer proximity to my husband's family. This felt especially important now that we had a child. We longed, at a moment when the world seemed so dangerous and our town seemed so vulnerable, to give ourselves and him the comfort of a tight band of loving relatives. That would be the easy part. There were also the other mommies to learn about and live among.

We eventually settled on Park Avenue in the Seventies. From my base camp, I went to Mommy & Me groups, applied to exclusive music classes, wrangled with nannies, coffee'd with other mothers, and "auditioned" at preschools, for my firstborn son and then his little brother.

In the process I learned that motherhood was another island upon the island of Manhattan, and that Upper East Side mothers were, in fact, a tribe apart. Theirs was a secret society of sorts, governed by rules, rituals, uniforms, and migration patterns that were entirely new to me, and subtended by beliefs, ambitions, and cultural practices I had never dreamed existed.

Becoming an Upper East Side mom, one day and interaction and trip to the playground at a time, was an experience I undertook with some trepidation. The überwealthy and status-conscious neighborhood where we landed, and the frequently smug-seeming mommies dressed to the nines around me, felt foreign and intimidating. But, like a higher-order primate and like humans everywhere, I longed to fit in, for my own good and, even more, for my son's, and eventually my other son's, too.

I knew well from my studies of literature and anthropology alike that, without a sense of belonging, and actually belonging, we great apes are lost. Outcasts in literature and the real world may be interesting antiheroes we can root for, but they are usually miserable. From Odysseus to Daisy Miller, from Huck Finn to Hester Prynne, from Isabel Archer to Lily Bart, social outsiders and pariahs, particularly female ones, do not fare well. Unprotected, unsupported by a network, they die figuratively and sometimes literally, not only on the pages of books but also in society and the wild, as field biologists have amply documented. And there is no one more at risk than a female primate transferring to a new troop with a neonate. Primatologists tell us, for example, that mother chimps who attempt to join a group of strangers are frequently subjected to harassment and harrowing physical violence by established females; sometimes they and their infants are even killed by the very peers from whom they seek community.

Of course, nobody was out for my blood as I sought to find my place on the Upper East Side, at least not literally. But finding a way in and gaining acceptance felt important, even urgent. Who wants to be on the outside? Who doesn't want friends to have coffee with after morning drop-off? Who doesn't want her child to have playmates and playdates? My in-laws and my husband helped me along, telling me where to shop for groceries and explaining the byzantine rules of the galas, over-the-top bar and bat mitzvahs, social clubs, co-op boards, and other strange-to-me rites and practices specific to our new home. But Upper East Side mommy culture was a thing in itself, my own puzzle to solve, since I was a mommy who wanted—needed—to play ball. Yes, I had made plenty of forays to the Upper East Side over the course of my time in New York. I knew it was glossy and moneyed and privileged. I knew understatement was not an Upper East Side thing. I knew the uniform and philosophy and ethos were different from downtown's. But there was no getting a purchase on the secret world-within-a-world of Upper East Side *motherhood* until I entered into it. Without children, I might never have noticed it, this parallel universe of privileged parenting and privileged childhood. With children, though, I was more than compelled by it—I felt obliged to understand it, infiltrate it, crack its cultural code. Getting to know the mommies all around me and learning to do it their way, becoming an Upper East Side mother, was a journey so strange and so unexpected that nothing I had studied or experienced—not the cow-jumping and blood-drinking rites of the Masai, or the ax fights of the Yanomami in the Amazon, or the ritualized bacchanalian rites of sorority rush at a Big Ten school—could rival it, or prepare me for it.

Childhood on the Upper East Side is unusual by just about anyone's standards. There are drivers and nannies and helicopter rides to the Hamptons. There are the "right" music classes for two-year-olds, tutors for three-year-olds to prep them for kindergarten entrance exams and interviews, and playdate consultants for four-year-olds who don't know how to play because they don't have time to play because they have so many "enrichment classes"—French, Mandarin, Little Learners, and cooking classes, as well as golf, tennis, and voice lessons—after preschool. There are wardrobe consultants to help moms buy the right clothes for themselves for school drop-off and pickup. There are teetering high heels and breathtaking J. Mendel and Tom Ford furs at playgrounds and at birthday parties that cost $5,000 and up in apartments so big and with ceilings so high that they can and do have full-size bouncy castles inside.

If childhood is unusual here, motherhood is beyond bizarre. I learned firsthand about the "gets" that define life for the privileged and perfect women with children I lived among. Their identities, I discovered, are forged through cruel, Upper East Side–specific rites of passage: the co-op board interview and school "exmissions"; the cults of Physique 57 and SoulCycle, where the highly educated, frequently underemployed, and wealthy women I have come to think of as Manhattan Geishas pour their vaunted career ambitions into perfecting themselves physically. There are obsessional quests for nearly-impossible-to-procure luxury items (like my own, once I had "gone native," for a Birkin bag) and "insider trading" of information, such as how to hire a black-market Disney guide with a disability pass in order to circumvent all the lines. An Upper East Side mommy's identity also emerges from the fraught, complicated relationships between herself and the women she hires to help her raise her children and run her home (or homes). Learning about Upper East Side motherhood west of Lex, living among and learning from Upper East Side mommies, opened up a world that titillated, fascinated, educated, and occasionally appalled me.

The women who taught me how to be an Upper East Side mother could be ruthless in their advocacy for their offspring—and themselves. Sure, they were loving mommies, but they were also entrepreneurial dynasts dead set on being successful and, therefore, having "successful" kids. None of them admitted to having prepped their three-year-olds for a standardized kindergarten exam called the ERB, for example, even to their best friends. But they all did it—finding the tutors through word of mouth and sometimes shelling out thousands of dollars for the lessons—out of equal parts love, fear, and dry-eyed ambition. Just as many scheduled their children's playdates with the "alpha offspring" of the rich and influential, in a bid to move up the invisible but pervasive and powerful hierarchy that organizes life here, strategically avoiding the kids of "lower-tier" parents as they would a used Band-Aid. It struck me that, for some of the women I lived near and chatted with in the school halls, children were another way to "live high"—more like baubles than babies, someone for whom to buy the right things, lavish with the right kind of attention from the best experts, feed the best and healthiest foods, and help get into the most prestigious schools. I'll admit it: sometimes my adventure made me cynical.

The flip side of these women's ambition and aggression, I found, is extraordinary anxiety. The pressure to get it right, to be a perfect mother and a perfectly fit, perfectly dressed, perfectly sexy woman as well, and the time and energy devoted to it, seems to stress many to the breaking point. To remedy this they turn to alcohol; prescription drugs; "flyaway parties" with girlfriends to Vegas, St. Barths, and Paris on their private planes; compulsive exercise and self-care (Flywheel, bone broth, and raw, organic, cold-pressed juice fasts are big); jaw-dropping clothing and accessory purchases (among the women I know, "presale" is a verb, and dropping $10,000 at Bergdorf Goodman or Barneys in a day is not necessarily a huge deal); and lunch and a blowout or spa days with their oftentimes equally anxious girlfriends, and sometimes envious "frenemies."

My goal, initially, was to assimilate while keeping a distance from the stress and madness and competitiveness of Upper East Side mommy culture. My background in social research and anthropology, I figured, would help me stay sane and grounded as I made a place for my children and myself in a world that sometimes felt inhospitable. But, like anthropologists the world over, I eventually found myself "going native." This is the term for what happens when the field scientist slips from objectivity into identification with the people she is studying, crossing the line from understanding to essentially "becoming" them. My connections to my friends downtown fraying as I applied myself to work and motherhood and cultivating mommy friendships uptown, I slowly but surely, without even realizing it, began to dress and act and think more like the women around me, and to care about what they cared about. Their world was equal parts alien, alluring, and alienating to me, but the imperative I felt to find a place among them was surprisingly strong.

Thankfully, I eventually made friends among the tribe of rarefied Upper East Side women with children I met. Deep, nurturing friendship is no easy thing in a rigidly hierarchical social environment where jockeying, competition, and pervasive insecurity and stress are the rule. Their rituals, the rules and practices of their tribe, were mostly strange to me, and frequently off-putting. So was the attitude of superiority and indifference I encountered initially. These things set these women apart. But they had, I learned, much in common with women with children all over the city, and all over the world. In times of hardship they frequently bond with and look out for others in ways that are unexpected and extraordinary. The worldwide, eons-old evolutionary imperative of our species and of so many primates to cooperate and care runs through and informs and defines female friendship and motherhood everywhere. Even on the glossy, well-toned, hypercompetitive, and megamoneyed Upper East Side.

What I noticed—what I still notice—as most unusual among these particular friends was their generosity and eagerness to translate for me the world they understood better than I did, their enthusiasm for sharing insights about their universe, their sense of irony about the lives they themselves and others around them led. And their sense of humor. "Anybody who doesn't get how ridiculous and over-the-top our lives are, and how funny and nuts it is, isn't anybody I want to be friends with anyway," one mother told me when I only half-jokingly expressed concern that, once word of my project got out, she might get in trouble for being seen with me. I was afraid to write this book. But she and others put me at ease by showing me that even in the strangest, most off-putting contexts and oddest-seeming worlds, there is a fair amount of normalcy to be found, and reminding me that even in apparently inhospitable, unfriendly climates, there is real warmth and kindness to be celebrated.

In my years of studying and living among them as a social researcher and mommy, I learned that women with children on the Upper East Side want what mothers everywhere want for their children—for them to be healthy and happy, to feel loved, to thrive, and, one day, to make something of themselves. But the similarities end there. Unless you were raised in Manhattan, and perhaps even if you were, nothing about Upper East Side childhood seems natural. And, by extension, unless you were raised by an Upper East Side mommy yourself, nothing about motherhood here feels logical or straightforward or common-sensical. Upper East Side mothers are not born when their babies are, I learned the hard way. They are made. This is the story of how I was made, and remade, and how it often felt like my un-doing. It is a consideration of one narrow sliver of motherhood on one tiny island, and a meditation on what it might mean for everyone else.

CHAPTER ONE

Comme Il Faut

Fieldnotes

Environment and ecology

The island is a geographically, culturally, and politically isolated landmass roughly seven times longer than it is wide. The climate is temperate, with relatively harsh winters and extremely hot and humid summers that, in recent years, approximate tropical conditions due in part to two centuries of intensive land clearing and industrial practices. The island's longitude is 40°43'42" N, and its latitude is 73°59'39" W.

Island dwellers live in a state of ecological release—resources such as food and water are abundant and easily procured; disease is minimal; there is no predation. Living in a niche characterized by literally unprecedented abundance, untethered from hardship, the wealthiest islanders are able to invest heavily in each and every offspring and to invent elaborate and complex social codes and rites, the observance of which are time-, labor-, and resource-intensive.

In spite of the extraordinary abundance of food, water,

and other resources island-wide, there is persistent and marked poverty in some areas. The isolation, extreme population density, and vast discrepancies in wealth, as well as traditionally gender-scripted roles and behaviors around child rearing and work, may inform and in part account for many of the strange-seeming behaviors of the wealthiest island dwellers, discussed in the following pages.

Island dwellings

The island's inhabitants are primarily vertical dwellers, making their homes directly on top of one another in structures of finely ground stone. Living in these "vertical villages" allows inhabitants to maximize physical space, a precious commodity in short supply on their tiny and remarkably densely populated island. In some locations, particularly where the wealthiest islanders reside, these vertical villages are notably restrictive, with a secretive "council of elders" presiding over who will and will not be allowed to live there. Scouting out a dwelling is one of the most labor-intensive practices of the female members of the tribe I studied—most often the task is undertaken by primaparas. Almost without exception, "dwelling shamans" guide these women in their quests for homes—which are also quests for identity. The shamans offer specialized knowledge, counsel, and emotional support throughout this costly, protracted, and painstaking initiation process.

Geographical origins of islanders

Island dwellers have heterogeneous geographical origins. Many dispersed at sexual maturity from their natal groups

in distant, smaller, and even rural villages, immigrating to
the island for enhanced professional, sexual, and marital
prospects. Other island dwellers are indigenous; their status is higher than that of the nonautochthonous residents,
particularly if they were raised in certain corners of the island or attended particular "learning huts" while growing
up there.

Beliefs of and about islanders

Whether they are autochthonous or émigrés, island dwellers are believed by outsiders, many visitors, and their
countrymen to harbor haughty attitudes about themselves
and their island. They are known throughout the land for
their brusqueness; intellectual gifts; dazzling adornment
practices; and acumen in barter, trade, and negotiation. Increasingly, their trade is in invisible ideas and abstractions,
enhancing the sense that they have privileged knowledge
and even "magical" powers. The journeys and tribulations
of those who move to the island and struggle to succeed
there are the stuff of legend, literally—there exists a long
oral and written tradition about the supposedly indomitable
and unique spirit of people who are able to "make it there."
Once they have established themselves on the island, it is
said, they can "make it anywhere."

Resource acquisition and distribution

On the whole, the island dwellers are the richest in the entire
nation, living untethered from the environmental constraints
that have such a profound impact on life-history courses in
other habitats worldwide. Obtaining adequate calories for

themselves and their children, the main ecological challenge to parents worldwide and throughout our evolutionary prehistory, is a simple given for wealthy island dwellers. However, as in many industrial and postindustrial societies, fathers of the very traditionally gender-scripted tribe I studied tend to focus on the job of provisioning their wives and families with less-tangible resources, including financial, social, and cultural capital. While many island-dwelling females work outside the home, during the childbearing and child-rearing years, many wealthy female islanders believe it is their "role" to remain home with their children, where they are often assisted by alloparents—individuals other than parents who take on parental roles. They call these alloparents "housekeepers," "nannies," and "caregivers."

Island organization
The island is organized, in the minds of island dwellers, into four quadrants: Up, Down, Right, and Left. The "Up" and "Down" areas are believed to be markedly distinct—with Up being preferable for raising children and Down being considered primarily a place for pre-reproductives, cultural "outsiders," feasting, and ecstatic nighttime rites. Islanders further divide their island into left and right hemispheres. "Left" and "Right," like "Up" and "Down," are believed to have different—even polar opposite—characteristics. Left is believed to be more casual and progressive, in contrast to Right's perceived formality and conservatism.

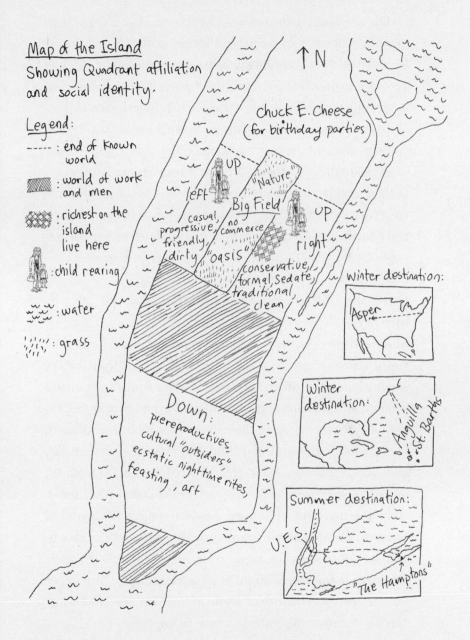

Map of the Island
Showing Quadrant affiliation and social identity.

Legend:

- - - - - : end of known world

▨ : world of work and men

▨ : richest on the island live here

🧍 : child rearing

〰 : water

⸝⸝⸝ : grass

↑N

Chuck E. Cheese (for birthday parties)

UP

left "Nature" Big Field UP right

casual, progressive, friendly, dirty "oasis"
no commerce

conservative, formal, sedate, traditional, clean

Winter destination:
Aspen

Winter destination:
Anguilla St. Barths

Down:
prereproductives,
cultural "outsiders",
ecstatic nighttime rites,
feasting, art

Summer destination:
U.E.S.
"The Hamptons"

For islanders, Up/Down and Right/Left are more than mere directions or coordinates; they are powerful and deeply felt oppositions that organize an island dweller's identity and everyday experience. Fittingly, islander subtribes are defined by their quadrant—e.g., Right Siders, Left Siders, Updwellers, Downdwellers. Island dwellers are largely indifferent to residents of adjacent areas of the archipelago, rarely going there or even speaking of them. "Crossing over" to outlying parts of their own landmass and to other islands in the archipelago requires complex transportation, insider knowledge of routes, and a tariff, further reinforcing not only islanders' intense xenophobia but also their literal geographical separateness.

Quadrant affiliation and construction of social identity

Many islanders express trepidation and experience anxiety and distress when they travel from their quadrant of the small island to another, considering such transitions inconvenient, time-consuming, difficult, and even unlucky. Superstitiously, some organize their lives and appointments (with their medical, financial, and child-care shamans) so that they only rarely have to leave their immediate area. Quadrant identity also informs practices such as dress and adornment, child rearing, and voluntary seasonal migration patterns (western zone inhabitants are more likely to seek out mountain ranges in summer, while residents of the eastern zone, particularly the Upper Right zone, have a marked preference for one specific, elite ocean destination. There are also zone-specific warm-weather destinations in winter).

There is a broad belief on the entire island that two zones are "best" for child rearing and family life. These two zones, Up Right and Up Left, flank the massive, fetishized, and aptly named "Big Field," proximity to which is highly desirable. This may stem from the islanders' collective history and pre-history; as savanna dwellers who took to trees for safety and eventually as propertied agrarians who needed to be on the lookout for hostile intruders, they may value and feel most comfortable when viewing a cleared expanse from a "safe" height. Thus, a dwelling with a view of Big Field is desirable and costly, and confers and reinforces high social status. Big Field is also believed to be ideal for children, who play there under the supervision of teachers, parents, and mostly, allo-parents. No industry is allowed in Big Field; there is minimal commerce. It is a sacred zone, and believed to be a powerful health tonic: gazing at Big Field and walking in it are said to have restive and fortifying effects. Those who live closest to Big Field in the Up Right (or Upper East Side) quadrant are the richest on the island, with some of the most distinctive, entrenched, and bizarre-seeming tribal practices, rituals, and beliefs. These inhabitants are the subject of our study.

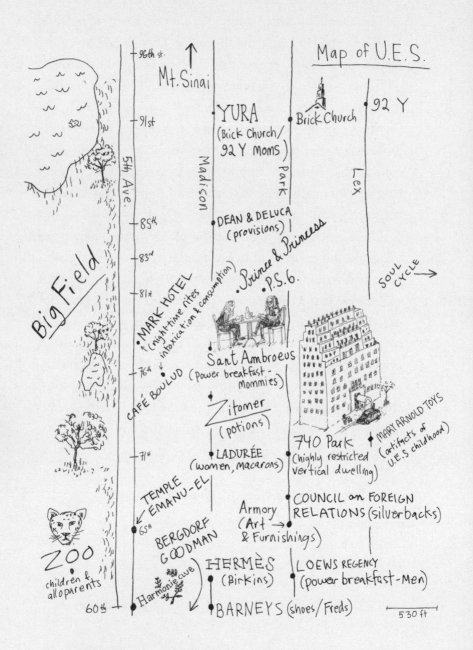

Map of U.E.S.

96th st. ↑ Mt. Sinai

91st • YURA (Brick Church/ 92 Y Moms)

Brick Church • 92 Y

5th Ave.

Madison

Park

Lex

Big Field

85th • DEAN & DELUCA (provisions)

Prince & Princess

83rd

81st MARK HOTEL (night-time rites ↑ intoxication & consumption) • P.S.6

SOUL CYCLE →

Sant Ambroeus

76th CAFÉ BOULUD (power breakfast-Mommies)

Zitomer (potions)

71st • LADURÉE (women, macarons)

740 Park (highly restricted vertical dwelling) • MARY ARNOLD TOYS (artifacts of U.E.S childhood)

COUNCIL on FOREIGN RELATIONS (silverbacks)

TEMPLE ← EMANU-EL

65th BERGDORF GOODMAN

Armory (Art → & Furnishings)

ZOO children & alloparents

HERMÈS (Birkins)

LOEWS REGENCY (power breakfast-Men)

Harmonie Club

60th • BARNEYS (shoes/Freds)

530 ft

W E HAD decided to move uptown in search of a "better childhood" for our son. Uptown has Central Park, after all, an oasis of sorts wedged between the Upper East and Upper West Sides, and lots of good public and private schools. At the time it also had the things it was so hard to find downtown—kid-friendly restaurants, clothing stores for kids, and places to take your kid for a haircut where he could watch a Wiggles video while sitting in a chair shaped like a fire engine. We wanted some respite from the constant reminders of 9/11, which still hung over downtown, nearly a year later, in so many ways—poor indoor air quality, unremitting anxiety, and palpable sadness. We wanted access to playgrounds and a family-focused neighborhood in an excellent public school district. And we wanted to be near my husband's parents, as well as his brother and his family, a web of loving cousins and grown-ups who would lend a hand and prop us up when we were sleep deprived and dealing with teething or temper tantrums. With our commitment to staying in Manhattan, this meant one thing: the Upper East Side.

Whenever I mentioned to our downtown friends that we were moving uptown, they looked at me as if I were excitedly divulging plans to join a cult. "At least a downtown trophy wife has glasses, a PhD, and her own nonprofit," a girlfriend's husband observed as we discussed it over drinks one night. It went without saying that we all knew an Upper East Side trophy wife had blond hair and breast augmentation. And stayed home with the kids. And the staff. Right? I wasn't sure. I hadn't ventured above West

Twenty-Third Street for years, except to visit my in-laws and go
on the occasional museum excursion. At such times I could not
fail to notice the lacquered, polished looks of the people and the
stores and every single surface and outfit and bit of brass. But the
mommies never particularly caught my eye. After all, I had never
really known any Upper East Side mommies. How would that
be? How would they be? "Be sure to budget the money for a fur
coat," my girlfriend smirked. I laughed, and my husband choked
on a cashew. There was no shortage of stereotypes about uptown
versus downtown, and I was eager to see for myself how true or
false they were.

    First, though, I had to find us a place. And I do mean *I*, because
my husband promptly delegated the apartment-hunting project
to me. This was ostensibly logical since, as the mother of a very
young child, I had rearranged my work schedule as a writer to
be "flexible" and "freelance"—I could put it on hold for days or
weeks at a time. We also had a part-time nanny who could watch
my son while I searched. But there was a deeper cultural logic
at work, too: in Manhattan, the woman is in charge of finding a
place for the family to live. She might also pay for it, or for half of
it. But in heterosexual marriages, regardless of who does what, it's
usually the woman who finds the apartment. I had puzzled over
this plenty, and in the end chalked it up to agriculture. While our
hunter-gatherer ancestors had roamed and ranged with the food
supply, setting up and breaking down camp with little attachment
to place or possessions, the transition to a crop-based economy
changed everything. With it came the notion of property—
"These fields are mine!"—and increased fertility for women, who
were now relatively sedentary, and so ovulated more frequently.

Before you could say "millet," women were transformed from gatherers—with all the clout, influence, and freedom that came with supplying their bands with nearly all their daily calories—into keepers of the hearth and home, with little say beyond what time the dinner they had spent the day making would be served, and little prestige other than as baby vessels. I didn't mind that I was the one taking care of the baby and tending to our home and finding us a new one. It made sense, given that my husband's career was more lucrative than mine, and given my intense desire to be with our little son. But there were days when I wondered whether what my girlfriend and her husband had said over drinks was true: that, compared with downtown, Upper East Side gender politics were even *more* markedly agriculturalist Bantu than freewheeling, downtown-ish, hunter-gatherer !Kung San.

Meanwhile, I suspected that it couldn't be too hard to sell our town house and settle on an apartment uptown, even for someone as clueless as I was. After all, in New York City, town houses are status symbols of the first and highest order. For Manhattanites, having your own stand-alone dwelling, with no one above or below you, is an unusual, highly prized, and highly desirable way to live. It is supposed to confer privacy, which we prize in the West, and a certain spatial grandeur in a town where you pay by the square foot. And so, in spite of our place being relatively modest—the kitchen was small, and there was no elevator—prospective buyers were lining up to see it. I was forever making it look pristine and then rushing out the door so a broker and client could "view" it.

I used this time in exile to call brokers from a nearby café. Most were women. They would keep me on the phone for a while, somehow peppering *me* with questions—about my husband's job, my job, where I was from, where I went to school, even our net worth—rather than the other way around.

Manhattanites also do a version of this at parties and other gatherings, with all the subtlety of census workers, in order to peg who you are. The first time it happened to me, I was bewildered. "Oh, they did Jewish Geography with you," my Jewish husband observed. "They wanted to know where you stood." As far as I could see, though, the game knew no religion. In a huge town, knowing whether and how you might be connected to someone, whether they know someone you know or want to know—the Chinese call it being *guanxi*, a system of connectedness in a country of billions—makes a certain amount of sense. Even if it seems a little (or a lot) mercenary.

After each inquest, the brokers would inevitably tell me they didn't have the *specific* listing I was asking about, but they had some *other* things to show me. In fact, it seemed that *none* of the beautiful apartments I saw online or in print advertisements actually existed—phone calls revealed that they were "already sold" or "in contract" or were listed as available because "the website needs to be updated." When I told my husband about this, he pronounced it a typical bait and switch and suggested we needed a "buyer's broker" of our own. "Sort of like a native informant? Or a guide?" I wondered excitedly, and my husband affirmed that she would be just that. Like the loyal trackers who helped Dian Fossey find her gorillas day after day, and the Inuit people of Baffin Island who took it upon themselves to explain their ways to Franz Boas, the father of modern anthropology, when he alit among them, I needed an insider to advise and enlighten me.

My husband gave me the number of a woman who had helped him sell his small Upper East Side studio years before—and the

next day I gave her a ring, introduced myself, and told her I'd like
to see some apartments. I thought that, having someone on my
side, it would all be easy. I was so naïve. I had merely opened the
door. Now the real work began.

Inga had a glamorous accent—my husband told me she was
Danish, and a former model—and was brisk and businesslike.
"First of all, you have someone selling your town house, right?
Because I don't usually work downtown." She explained that uptown and downtown real estate were vastly different worlds. And
that the Upper *West* Side wasn't her strongest suit; she was primarily an Upper *East* Side broker.

"Okay, well, yes, we want to live on the East Side." I stumbled
a little here, taking in the apparently immense, insuperable differences between the neighborhoods as far as brokerage practices were
concerned. "And"—I found my footing now—"we want a place
in the good public school district." There was a long pause. Then
came the curt pronouncement: "That's not going to be easy." I had
disappointed her somehow with my requirements, and I found myself suddenly crestfallen and hopeless. *This was not going to be easy.*

"But"—Inga spoke in a Scandinavian singsong I already found
endearing—"we're going to try. I have things to show you." Here
I brightened and felt a rush of optimism and relief. She had things
to show me! Yes, I had a guide! Inga wouldn't just help me find
a place to live, I had a feeling as I hung up the phone. She would
also teach me the grammar of the Upper East Side. Every anthropologist needs at least one reliable, insightful native informant
who is willing to show the way, translate the language, explain
the customs, and spill his or her culture's dirty secrets and tacit
social codes. In short, informants help you find a way in. And I
was pretty sure I had found mine.

"Is your boss coming today?" the well-dressed woman with an Hermès scarf tied around her neck asked me doubtfully. Her shiny, Botox-frozen brow telegraphed a faint shadow of what must have been confusion as I showed up in an ornate lobby on Park Avenue before Inga for our first day of apartment hunting.

"Um . . . I don't . . . have a boss . . ." I managed, extending my hand and introducing myself. She had obviously taken me for Inga's client's assistant, based on my casual "nerdy hipster" Marc Jacobs outfit, all the rage downtown. Here was my first clue that women without jobs in my town had personal assistants to scout apartments for them. And that I needed a new apartment-hunting uniform. Inga showed up just then, a tall, razor-thin, beautiful brunette in an exquisite and stylish off-white suit, and I discerned that the other broker admired her, which put me suddenly at ease about everything—what I was wearing, our move, and the entire process of finding a place. It was like magic.

I wasn't so far off the mark. The brokerage business in Manhattan—apartment buying and selling—is an ecological niche by, for, and about women. This is especially true on the Upper East Side. Brokerage's language is clothing. The seller's broker dresses to channel the respect she wants to garner for her seller; the buyer's broker dresses to impress and intimidate the seller's broker, and to project an image on behalf of her prospective buyer, who in turn dresses to convey her seriousness to both brokers (if she is extremely rich, she can dress down, thus conveying that she knows that they know that she doesn't need to play this game; they are dressing up for *her*). It all culminates in a kind of dress-off in lobby after lobby, showing after showing, day after day. Imagine Sergio Leone music and women bedecked in Brunello Cucinelli and Loro Piana at dawn.

Bags seemed especially important; many of the brokers I saw that first day, when we "viewed" four or five apartments, had purses by Chanel, quilted and lustrous, with chains and heavy flaps and interlocking Cs. Or rectangular calf affairs with open tops and handles, the Cs just under them, easy and elegant. "If we're going to find an apartment, I need a new bag," I half-joked to my husband after I arrived home in the early evening that first day. I was shot from the walking (had I been a different kind of client, one more in tune with the practices of the Upper East Side, I would have arranged a driver for me and Inga) and also the unexpected psychological gymnastics, the emotional exertion, of looking at the apartments and interacting with the brokers and contorting my standards and desires to whatever each place presented, wondering whether it could work.

Every morning for the next several weeks, I would don my Upper East Side apartment-hunting uniform: demure sheath dress, Agnès B. or French Sole flats, and the most ladylike bag I owned—no slouchy satchel would do for my errand. The final touch was a sleek (I hoped) ponytail. After all, I was headed up to the Land of the Sleek. Thus attired, I would hail a cab and, after what was usually a half hour's ride north and east, meet Inga in a given lobby of a given prewar building, almost always west of Lexington Avenue. Our search area was dictated by the boundaries of the excellent public school district, so, basically, we were looking in the most expensive neighborhood in all of Manhattan. In order to eventually send our kid to school there for free. The irony of this was not lost on me, my husband, or Inga, who quickly became the third person in our marriage. "We

could really see a lot more things if you were flexible about the
school district," she suggested diplomatically to me once we had
gotten to know each other. "But I know what you and your husband want," she added quickly when I shot her a look. "So we'll
keep going in the district."

It seemed to take forever to find an apartment. After all, this
was during the boom, and the real estate market was tight. Sellers were asking for sky-high prices; buyers were at their mercy.
The spot we wanted to be in, Inga intimated over and over, was
the toughest nut in the city to crack. We looked and looked and
looked.

We looked at "classic sixes" and "classic sevens" and "classic
eights" in "nice buildings" and "good buildings" and even "white-
glove buildings," where the staff literally wear white gloves. All
the buildings had doormen to greet you and many had attended
elevators, meaning someone to push the buttons for you. But
they were all different from a "great building," which might be on
the same block and look exactly the same from the outside, yet
demand a massive down payment, refuse mortgages, and require
the prospective buyer to prove she has three or five or even ten
times the apartment's value in liquid assets. Great buildings can
ask for these things, and also make certain exceptions for certain
people if they feel like it, Inga explained early on, because they
are essentially private clubs, run by boards of residents who make
and enforce rules as they see fit. These are the types of buildings that routinely refuse the applications of wealthy celebrities,
buildings that sent Richard Nixon and Madonna alike down the
path of town-house living, no doubt disgusted and wounded by
their rejection. Great buildings are inhabited by titans of industry and their socialite wives and are known by their addresses:

740 Park. 927 Fifth. 834 Fifth. 1040 Fifth. Others have names: The Beresford. The San Remo. The Dakota. River House. They are made of limestone and designed by architects of note, such as Rosario Candela and Emery Roth. These buildings were not for us, but neither, apparently, were the "family" buildings, which sounded perfect to me. "No," Inga explained patiently when I asked, "that *doesn't* mean they have playrooms. It means they allow ninety percent financing. We can do better." Just as Inga's outfits—Jil Sander, Piazza Sempione, Prada, she told me when I asked—were a reflection of my status, so would the building I wound up in be a reflection of hers. She wanted the best for us—because she had skin in this game, too.

I wasn't fussy about these distinctions—we just needed a good enough place in the right school district. But to my surprise and eventual frustration, being flexible didn't make finding a place or the process of looking any easier. There just wasn't a lot of "inventory," brokers told us over and over. And it was overwhelmingly, unexpectedly strange to enter people's lives and spaces in such an intimate way—to see their things and their habits, or, for that matter, to see the absence of any traces of people in perfectly pristine places. I noticed the particular style of decoration on the Upper East Side. There was lots of toile. And yellow. And blue. Again and again. It was hard to imagine what I would do differently, how our furniture would fit here, how we would live in every one of these apartments, my husband and son and I. Which corner would be best for the toddler bed? If we decided to have another child, where would he or she go? Could I work from home in this apartment? And so on.

If the apartment passed muster initially—in the right school district, with the right number of bathrooms and some nice light and views—then the next day my husband, like all husbands, would come have a look, and the women (Inga and I, the seller's broker, perhaps the seller, too) would be infused with another kind of energy, an anxious attention, an eagerness to please. I felt like Vanna White, ridiculous, as the other women and I "demonstrated" the apartment, opening doors and showing linen closets. It was not like me to simper and serve, but here I was doing it, as if we were all in a play and knew our roles. In further adherence to this apartment-hunting script, my husband would sniff around, the brokers hanging on his every word and gesture, looking for the subtlest clues to his dis/pleasure. He tended to be polite but by no means overly friendly in these situations. He gave nothing away in front of the brokers, and after a quick circle of the premises, would soon head back to the Important World of Men's Work. Then he would call me and tell me what he thought.

It all would have made me feel like Marion Cunningham on *Happy Days* but for the fact that I knew I was ultimately the one deciding where we would live. It was a woman thing, the home sphere. That's why all the brokers and potential buyers were women. The men were there to provide gravitas and a bit of frisson, and then disappear, and then sign off. Or not. After which we would do whatever we wanted. Welcome to the Upper East Side.

As I pondered these gendered divisions of work and meaning in what would be my new habitat, I couldn't help but focus on more practical matters as well. Namely, in spite of a budget that in Atlanta or Grand Rapids would get us a mansion with a pool, many of the apartments were disappointments. There was a pattern: a gorgeous, gilded, attended lobby at a "prestigious" address on Park or Madison or Fifth. We went up, entered the apartment . . . and I thought I might faint. *Is this where all the well-turned-out women of the Upper East Side were living?* I frequently wondered in disbelief. Some of the places were immaculate, even "triple mint," but many if not most were in a state of gentle or not-so-gentle neglect. Frayed rugs and old carpeting. Worn kitchens. Yellowed paint. And, almost always, a maid dusting or polishing the silver or folding laundry.

And then, every time, without fail, the framed photos and mementos in the living room told the same story. I was transfixed by them, in apartment after apartment: a picture of a young woman next to a diploma from Brearley or Spence. A young man in his graduation photo . . . near a framed diploma, all gold-leafed letters and Latin script, from Horace Mann or Buckley or St. Bernard's. The perfect hair. The unlined young faces. The airbrushed smiles and teeth adjusted to perfection by orthodontia. It hit me like a sledgehammer one day at a place on Madison Avenue in the low Eighties—these people were downsizing or selling because they had to. Their kids, in whom they had invested so much, so intensively, had finally graduated and fledged. The parents had pushed themselves to their outer financial limit for . . . housekeepers and private schools. They'd rather move than give up either. So now they would sell and move into a smaller place. And bring the diplomas and housekeepers along.

"Can you believe it?" I said to my husband on the night of my big realization as I flopped into bed, exhausted and depressed from seeing four consecutive apartments with gilded lobbies, frayed carpets, and fancy diplomas.

"I can," he said with a sigh. A Brooklynite who had moved to the Upper East Side as a teen, he was a New York but not a Manhattan native, fluent in the desires and beliefs and strivings and anxieties and priorities of the people whose apartments I was in every day, yet also able to see the strangeness of it all. "All that stuff, the housekeepers and private-school diplomas—isn't just window dressing," he told me now. "It's who they are."

He yawned, but I was suddenly wide-awake. I remembered an anthropology professor trying to help us understand the concept of honor among the tribe he studied in Yemen. "It's not an abstract idea," he explained to the roomful of us in the undergraduate seminar that day so many years before. "When someone sullies your honor, you can't ignore it and go on, just feeling embarrassed." No, he told us, it's like someone has hacked away a piece of your flesh. Something is missing, and you are damaged and injured. Private school diplomas and housekeepers, I realized now, were clearly not just fetishized markers of status, not merely something to wear or have or display with pride. They were also utterly intrinsic to one's identity on the Upper East Side, so crucial, so fundamental, that you would forgo fresh sisal and a kitchen redo and an apartment in "triple-mint" condition to hold on to them.

So that explained it, then. The way, all around me, women—brokers with kids, women whose apartments I was looking at, friends of friends on the Upper East Side—talked about where their kids went to school, and used their children's ages and school affiliations during introductions. Yes, it was a way to describe themselves and do a little coalition building in the process. But it was also who they were. Period. "Hi, I'm Alicia. My kids Andrew and Adam go to Allen-Stevenson—I think yours do, too?"

"No, my kids go to Collegiate [Bam! Here she establishes superior rank owing to her children's enrollment in a TT—top tier—school] but my friend Marjorie's four boys are all at AS.

[Subtext: My friend Marjorie is really rich—you have to be to have four kids—and by association, so am I.] Maybe you know her. How old are your kids?"

"Oh, wait, really? My nephews are both at Collegiate. [Here she reveals that she is a mere degree from TT school status herself, since her *sister's* kids go to a TT school, and thus she is something like an equal.] They're twins, in second grade: Devon and Dayton?" And so on.

Private-school affiliation was so important that, without exception, these women seemed dumbfounded that I planned to send my son to the neighborhood's excellent public school, PS6, when the time came. They might raise their eyebrows and say politely, after a pause, "Yes, you'll see at the time where he ends up." Others were more blunt. "*Come on,*" one broker said with a forced smile, sounding a little exasperated, as she opened kitchen cabinets to show me they were lighted inside. "You're going to send your kid to private school like everybody else. You'll drop him off with your driver. Like everybody else. So you can buy *anywhere.*"

But my husband and I were adamant. We had gone to public schools, and so could our son. It seemed normal and sensible, and we continued to push for a place near the excellent public school on East Eighty-First Street between Madison and Park. This is an area brokers refer to as "Upper East Side Prime." Which just made our quest that much harder.

Now that we had come this far, I needed some tutoring from my husband and Inga. I knew I had bridged the first, fundamental divide in Manhattan real estate social identity, the one that separates "renters" from "owners," when I got married. My husband put me on the deed to his house, and it became ours, and that was that, but apparently it meant a lot in our town. Many people who rent in Manhattan keep it a secret, or at least don't talk about it, owing to some sense of inferiority, a feeling that renting is second-class and contingent. "You own, correct?" was one of the first questions brokers asked me (or, more often, asked Inga *about* us before agreeing to show us apartments), wanting to make sure we weren't presenting them with an additional hurdle, pleased to have it confirmed that we were already members of the tribe of owners.

An additional distinction was prewar versus postwar buildings. Sure, I thought, it would be nice to live in a beautiful old building with beautiful original details, built by an architect of note, storied and historic. But I wasn't going to make a federal case out of it. Now came another essential distinction, one that largely broke down along the prewar/postwar distinction: co-op versus condo. Living in a house downtown, I was untutored regarding this particular binary opposition, one of the fundamental distinctions that organizes Manhattan buildings and Upper East Side identity.

In a co-op, Inga and my husband explained, board members decide who gets to live there and who doesn't, and what the rules are. Some of the rules are straightforward and logical. For example, "summer rules" ensure that apartment renovations take place only in summer, when it's easier to escape the noise by going outside or even to your country place for the whole summer. We live right on top of each other and under each other in Manhattan, so construction can wreck your quality of life. Summer rules are "very Upper East Side," Inga informed me; almost no Upper West Side co-ops have them. And they make sense.

Other co-op rules are more arbitrary, more cultural than

functional. For example, in a co-op you can't just sublease your apartment or let your twentysomething move in. The board has to approve such things. And a particular building's co-op may require that an applicant document astronomical liquid assets. Or not. They "require" this (when they choose not to overlook the requirement) as a kind of "insurance," in spite of the fact that they essentially have a lien against every apartment in the building. That's because in a co-op nobody owns an actual apartment. He or she owns "shares"—a bigger apartment generally means more shares. Shares are power. People who want to buy a co-op apartment almost always have to be interviewed by the board. And at a board interview, my husband and Inga warned me, the board members could ask you anything at all. Or decide not to let you move in for any reason at all. So *that's* why the rare apartments in co-op buildings on Park and Fifth we looked at that advertised "No board approval" were mobbed, I realized, wondering whether owning shares in a co-op felt like having a housekeeper and a child in private school.

Condos are a little more expensive, I learned, generally allow more financing, and you really own them. They are also a little more free-and-easy. You can sublet your place, or use it as a pied à terre, if you choose. And in a condo, a management company scrutinizes your application, which feels less personal and invasive, somehow, than a bunch of your possibly future neighbors poring over every detail of your financial and personal life.

Whether it was a co-op or a condo, prewar or postwar, I considered as I made my way from the West Village to the Upper East Side daily, it was time to settle on a place. The cab fare was killing me. We had to move uptown so I could stop getting there every day.

And then one day, I found a place I thought would do. It was a modern building on Park Avenue, not a "prestigious" prewar building by a famous architect. I didn't care—after all, it was less than two blocks from Central Park. The apartment itself initially seemed a little dark. But that was just the paint and I could "see through it." The kitchen was "top-of-the-line," as brokers say, if on the small side. There were "open city views," meaning there was no view of the park, but there were no buildings right in front of your window, either; they were all a good distance off, giving you plenty of light and a pleasant feeling of space and company at the same time. It had the right number of bedrooms, one of them with a cute little table and chairs and an arts-and-crafts project in progress—buttons and pieces of dried macaroni and glitter on pink construction paper. This little girl's room could easily be my little boy's room, I realized, taking it in. The warm feeling of the kid-friendly mise-en-scène overrode my dislike of the lowish ceilings, busy street-corner location, and less-than-ideal layout.

I walked through the place a second time and a third, my excitement growing. "The broker couldn't be here," Inga explained—I knew it was a diss of some sort in the world of brokers and buyers and sellers, a communication that Inga and I didn't merit her time, she was busy elsewhere or something—but I didn't care. A second visit was arranged with all possible haste, so the broker—harried, indifferent, unfriendly—could meet and approve of me. Once she had, we scheduled yet another viewing, this time with my husband in tow.

My first clue that the owner was home, as we opened the door for our couple's "viewing," was the sound of her admonishing her daughter. Peering down the hall, I could see she was blond, like me, and about my age and build. She was saying, "Leda, if you're eating, offer some to the other people in the room first!" Apparently she was referring to her broker, a large woman with short reddish hair whom I had met briefly on my previous visit, and who now stood between us and the family like a Jean Schlumberger–accessorized pit bull. Rings and bracelets flashing, she literally tried to block me as I walked toward the owner, who had her hand extended and gave me a friendly smile, to introduce myself. "I'm Allie," she said, sounding harried and polite at once, a cadence and way of being that was becoming familiar to me as I met Upper East Side women on the street and in their apartments. Apparently it was important to Allie to set her eyes on the person or persons who proposed to buy the space she was trying to sell, and I was glad I had dressed nicely, relatively speaking. Her outfit was beautifully chic—fitted black capri pants, a snug lavender blouse, and a perfect, glossy light pink pedicure on her bare feet. From the looks of it, she had a hair and makeup artist. And this was just a Wednesday afternoon. "This is Sharon," Allie told me, and the broker took my hand limply, looking past me. "Hello. We meet again," I offered in a voice I hoped was pleasant.

It wasn't the first time I had seen a broker be overtly and theatrically protective of her clients and strangely hostile toward a potential buyer. Sellers' brokers were the self-appointed guardians of the families in transition, I had come to understand, their guides through a liminal state as they segued from owners to sellers to buyers to owners again themselves. Brokers wanted to be in on all points of these big transitions because they were also big transactions, with large commissions hanging in the balance. They were petrified of anything messing up a deal in the works, including contact between an owner and a potential buyer. And of being cut out. But there was something else, too, something stranger about brokers and clients on the Upper East Side, and I saw it now, as Allie told me she had to go check on her daughter, who had wandered down to her bedroom. I turned to Sharon and, just to be polite, asked her little Leda's age.

"She's three, and she goes to Temple Emanu-El Nursery School," she responded shortly, and as haughtily as if she were reporting that she herself had just won a Nobel Peace Prize. I had noticed the tendency of brokers, architects, and nannies on the Upper East Side to act as though their status and that of their clients or bosses were one and the same—here it was again. When I asked if Temple Emanu-El was nearby, giving clue to the fact that I didn't know anything about it, Sharon gaped at me in disbelief. I smiled, hoping to soften the blow of my obvious ignorance and indifference. But internally I was rolling my eyes and thinking, C'mon, lady. This isn't your house. Or your family. She wanted the commission, no doubt, but she likely had several other interested parties lined up to buy the place. Sharon was a rich lady, like so many Upper East Side brokers. Her commission on every sale was 6 percent, and her personal take was 3 percent. In the midst of an economic and real estate boom, I was nothing to her, and it showed. I disliked her. We just stood there.

Thankfully, Allie soon returned, offering apologies and a sparkling water. We talked about our children—her daughter was a bit older than my son—as she walked me around the apartment, chatting about what she liked and what she didn't with a straightforwardness I found winning. Sharon had fallen back behind us. She was no match for mommy talk. Inga, who told us my husband had called to say he was held up in traffic, had known to hang back all the while and now made parallel chit-chat with her colleague, who, I thought with a bizarre flash of pride, could never hope to be in her league. Inga was the better broker in every way—poised, socially and professionally skilled, beautiful. Ha!

"The people who work in the building are *okay*," Allie told me as she led me down the hallway toward the master bedroom, "not *great*, but okay." She explained that they were staying in the building but moving up to the penthouse, which had one more bedroom than this one did, and park views. I felt a little jolt of embarrassment—she was moving into a better place, and we were moving into her castoff—and then I pushed it away. Who cared? I surmised she was pregnant when she told me the plan, but didn't ask. Instead I murmured something about how I'd just be relieved to have a lobby and an elevator—life in a town house, all those stairs and so on, was not easy with a little one and a stroller. She lit up. "You live in a *town house*? That's my dream!" she pronounced emphatically. Somehow, I felt I had now righted myself from the injury of moving into her discarded husk of a house, like a needy hermit crab. Here we reached the bedroom and she began opening cupboards and closets, narrating them to me. These cubbies were for purses—I saw flashes of Gucci and Louis Vuitton and Goyard—and here were the shoe shelves, row after row of them.

"Do you want to keep the safe?" she asked me, leaning down to show me how it worked. I paused. *What would I put in a safe?* I wondered. I wasn't much of a jewelry person. On our first vacation together, my husband had wanted to buy me some jewelry and I told him, "Thanks, but I don't really like . . . gems." It was true. He had to talk me into even a relatively modest diamond engagement ring, which initially struck me as an odd and entirely unsubtle and distasteful semaphore: I am someone else's property. Eventually I capitulated because it was just easier that way and because it gave me a certain sense of security to be part of the tribe. And because, well, it was pretty.

"Sure." I fumbled now, somehow not wanting to let on to Allie that I wasn't like her in this or any other regard, and she quickly explained, "It's good for the basics. Your big stuff you can have stored at the private bank on the corner; that's what I do." I took in the stilettos and the carefully folded cashmere sweaters arranged by color as she went on.

"I had the closet customized but I made some mistakes," she summarized, standing up again. "I can show you how I'd do it again if you want, so it's more efficient." Here she sighed and apologized for the "mess," though I couldn't see one. In fact, it was something all the women I met on the Upper East Side always did—apologize for a mess that wasn't there. Note to self: figure that one out.

Allie was smiling and extending her hand again. "Well, I'm really glad I got to meet you." She explained that she had to run out with Leda and was sorry not to be able to meet my husband just then. "But I hope it all works out," she pronounced meaningfully. "And . . . I'll look for you in Palm Beach. You're going, right? We'll be at The Breakers."

I was confused. "Um . . ." I cast my eyes about the room, letting them rest on the blue toile wallpaper as if it might hold some type of explanation. "We're going . . . but not until May," I said finally, recalling on the spot that in the late spring we were going to a conference my husband had there, wondering how on earth she knew about it.

She looked a little taken aback. "Oh, well . . . I guess it's . . . I *guess* it's still nice there then," she faltered. Now she tilted her head and nodded and said, "Aspen, then!"

She said it so confidently, as if everybody saw everybody in Aspen, that I thought for a brief moment that she knew something I didn't know about my travel plans, and we were in fact going. But of course I hadn't skied in years and told her that no, we'd be having Christmas in New York. Her eyes widened. "Oh right," she said, "getting ready for the move and everything, I guess?" I nodded and smiled, as if to leave open the possibility that, yes, next year we'd be right back to Palm Beach for Thanksgiving and Aspen for winter break. *Definitely.*

Apparently I had confused her as much as she had confused me. Clearly, I had to get a grip on the migration patterns of the Upper East Side. I was a bird of a different feather.

The apartment we hoped to buy was one of the only condos on Park Avenue, making it particularly desirable for people who didn't want to have to deal with a co-op and all its rules and regulations and restrictions, or who feared they wouldn't measure up. And for people who really cared about a Park Avenue address. And so here was the rub—the building was actually a "condop," a hybrid beast that was technically a condo but "acts like a co-op." Oh Lord, I thought when Inga delivered the news. There's a *word* for that?

Whatever it was, the application was long and detailed, demanding we disclose everything from our credit-card numbers and college GPAs to every school we, our parents, and our children had ever attended. "Why don't they just ask us how often we have sex?" I nearly wailed to my husband as we talked it over. A circumspect Midwesterner in my heart, I was outraged and deeply offended by the idea of all this poking and prodding from total strangers.

I was coming to understand that the "purchase application process" was one of the most humiliating hazing rites imaginable, after which, everyone said, you could not shake the feeling that a lot of people you don't know well know way too much about you. Because they do. And that, I realized, as we contemplated our next move and our application, is one of the ways hierarchies are established and maintained in Manhattan, where buildings comprise unrelated strangers living in close physical proximity and a fragile but utterly imperative mutual dependency prevails. We engineer relationships and a sense of obligation to do right by exchanging information, just as women gossiping over fences or sitting next to each other washing clothes on river rocks do.

Of course, the exchange is unequal. As supplicants (I preferred the term to *applicants* because it felt more honest) abasing ourselves for access, we were at a disadvantage, and at the mercy of our potential neighbors. By showing our carotid artery, or our belly, as dogs do when they lie on their backs in a fight, we demonstrated a willingness to submit, to cede power, to make ourselves utterly vulnerable. As with punishing hazing rituals and rites of passage the world over, we would emerge on the other side utterly exhausted and spent, with a newly minted identity: residents of XYZ Park Avenue. Or so we hoped.

I was in the very early stages of a complicated pregnancy and on mandated bed rest when it was time to do our board interview. No problem, the board representatives said—they would come to us. And they did. There we were, just us and seven total strangers. In our bedroom. I wore pearls and a jacket on top and pajama bottoms under the covers. We served cheese and crackers and wine. They had to stand up. They commented awkwardly on our book collection and asked about our son and whether we had plans to renovate.

It seemed our answers and application were good enough. We moved into our new home on Park Avenue at the very height of the economic boom, a moment when incomes, investment portfolios, and egos were surging all over the city, and nowhere more so than in our newly adopted, elite zip code. If we thought we were done, that after having completed this particular bruising and humiliating rite of passage we were home free, or even home, and that we could finally let our guard down a little and just relax, we were wrong.

Oh my God, I realized one afternoon with a start as my toddler and I sat on the new sofa in our new living room reading a story about a teacher and her students on a magic school bus. *I totally forgot to apply to nursery school.*

CHAPTER TWO

Playdate Pariah

G EOGRAPHICALLY SPEAKING, the Upper East Side is only a few miles from the West Village. We had merely moved from one corner of town to another, which sounds like no big deal. But in social and emotional and cultural terms, it was another world. There were changes big and small, such as getting our son accustomed to his new bed and the noise the bathtub made. And then there was the process of acclimating, all of us, to our new neighborhood. The whole place felt starchier and more formal than I had imagined it would. On my first runs to the corner for groceries, I felt terribly underdressed in my jeans and clogs; the women around me were decked out, dressed and groomed to the max even at 10:00 a.m. on a Tuesday. Everything about them—their demure, costly looking boots and cashmere pea coats with gleaming buttons, their shiny blowouts and gorgeous bags—looked lavishly expensive and meticulously tended to. All the world was a stage in our new ecological niche, it seemed, each day an opportunity for a fabulous, carefully curated change of wardrobe, as well as painstaking attention to hair and makeup.

The inside of our new building was not any more relaxed or casual. Or friendly. Just as we moved in, a debate was raging among residents over whether people with babies and toddlers in strollers should be required to take the service elevator, normally used for ferrying deliveries and garbage. The passenger elevators, some of our neighbors apparently believed, should be reserved for everyone except children, including dogs. These were dressed in cashmere and leather finery, accessorized with bejeweled leashes clutched in the hands of decidedly ungrandmotherly dowagers sporting massive diamonds. "Is that thing real?" I whispered to the elevator attendant after a soignée older woman wearing the biggest bauble I'd ever seen stepped off one afternoon. "I think so," he whispered back, eyebrows raised in astonishment. "She has a few of them, actually."

I marveled, day after day, at the *abundance* all around me. It wasn't just that the neighborhood and the neighbors were rich. Through the lens of anthropology, I saw that they lived in a state of what one could only term *extreme ecological release*. Every living thing is tethered to its surroundings. Environmental conditions—climate, flora and fauna, predation—all help determine the daily course and overall life cycle and evolution of every population of every species. In much of the world, humans still struggle to ward off predators and disease, and work hard to provision themselves and their families in unstintingly difficult environments—the savanna or the rain forest or a shantytown in Brazil. It is nothing new to say that things are different for the well-off in the industrialized West, where our dinners come prepackaged from stores, we get vaccines, and, in the words of primatologist Sarah Hrdy, there are no jaguars lurking outside our nurseries. In short, many of us live unconstrained by our environment in unprecedented ways. But nowhere, I considered as I walked from here to there every day, foraging for crisp Frette sheets and shiny All-Clad pots and pans and the perfect sconces, are we as radically and *comprehensively* released as on the Upper East Side of Manhattan. It was the land of gigantic, lusciously red strawberries at Dean & Deluca and snug, tidy Barbour jackets and precious, pristine pastries in exquisite little pastry shops on spotless, sedate side streets. Everything was so honeyed and moneyed and immaculate that it made me dizzy sometimes.

What really caught my eye, though, was the profusion of indescribably lovely *children's* stores. There were nearly a dozen of these within a few blocks of our new home, and they specialized in the kind of classic, beautifully crafted clothing for tots you never saw downtown—little wool shorts and kneesocks, navy blue shoes with beige leather soles, white blouses with Peter Pan collars and red rickrack trim, and fuddy-duddy argyle cardigans for mini-me boys. It was all made in Italy or France. Except the pajamas, which were always made in Portugal. My favorite of these upscale children's boutiques was called Prince & Princess. "No, we're not having any sales, we *never* do. But we can give you a perfect *size*," a saleswoman told me when I asked whether there was a markdown in the future of a tiny powder-blue cashmere sweater I coveted for my tyke. Living in a state of ecological release, I surmised, must have an impact on parenting. But other than paying retail for fancy kids' duds, what precisely did it mean to be a child, and a mommy, living on the floridly, exotically plentiful and bounteous Upper East Side? What did it do to mothers and children to live in this world—and what, I wondered with a pulse of anxiety, would it do to my child? And to me?

Things weren't equally Edenic for everyone, even here; this

I knew. For Eden was segmented into the Haves and the Have-Mores and the Have-Mosts. You could tell the difference pretty easily—the Have-Most women looked the *most* carefully put together and the *most* beautifully turned out, and generally had the *most* children. The first time I witnessed a perfectly coiffed, perfectly dressed petite brunette and her two nannies hauling her brood of half a dozen into an upscale kiddie-clothing boutique, it was so unlike anything I'd seen before that I could hardly process it. Was she a stepmother to a few of them? I wondered, staring as the kids wiggled and protested in and out of precious outfits whose price tags presumably ran into the thousands of dollars. She must be. Right? Oh no, she wasn't, the saleswoman later told me. She was a stay-at-home mother whose husband owned a whole lot of businesses and buildings and concerns. And she wasn't a rarity in my new niche, not by a long shot.

I quickly became desensitized to massive families—they were everywhere. Three was the new two, something you just did in this habitat. Four was the new three—previously conversation-stopping, but now nothing unusual. Five was no longer crazy or religious—it just meant you were rich. And six was apparently the new town house—or Gulfstream. The culture war in our building between the older residents and families with children—the retirees who owned yippy little dogs and believed that babies in strollers belonged on service elevators versus the couples with young kids pressing for a playroom off the lobby—mirrored a larger trend in the city. People with children were staying, rather than fleeing for the suburbs as the previous generation so often had. The superheated economy meant that the rich—whether they were newer, hedge-fund wealthy or inherited-wealth wealthy—were snapping up town houses, or two or more apartments at a time, connecting them and creating three- and four- and six-bedroom spreads with space you could previously find only in Westchester or Wyoming.

The change was creating pressure in two places: the real estate market—where, as I had just learned, there was not enough inventory to keep up with demand—and Manhattan private schools. I knew there had been a time when, if you could pay private-school tuition—the price tag had now climbed to something like $25,000 per year for nursery school and $35,000 or more for "ongoing"—your kids could go. Getting into Brearley was just a matter of affording it. But now, I kept reading in the newspapers and hearing moms around me whisper over coffee on the park benches, with so many families deciding to make a life here, and so many of them able to afford private school, everything was different.

So many kids. So much money. And only so many school spots. In this land of plenty, it seemed, some things were very, very hard to get. The specter of failing to land one's child in an elite school—in the altered ecology of the Upper East Side, this was the terrifying predator to be outwitted and bested. It was our jaguar.

"You *forgot?*" the woman demanded, the second word a register higher and a measure harsher than the first.

Her voice conveyed disbelief, disapproval, and more than a hint of the haughtiness of someone who has something she knows someone else wants very badly. Our son would be attending public school eventually, we were sure. So we didn't need to find him a spot in a preschool that was a "feeder" for a prestigious private school. But getting into *any* nursery school up here at all—"top tier" or not—was a cutthroat endeavor. What with all the parents committing to raising all those kids they were having in the city, spots at nursery schools previously considered "safety schools" were now coveted and nearly impossible to come by. Manhattan was bursting at the seams with children and their anxious, ambitious-on-their-behalf parents. But the nursery schools themselves had not yet caught up with demand. They hadn't expanded their class sizes in any real way, most of them. And there were not any "new" nursery schools.

Meanwhile, not sending your kid to nursery school just wasn't done. The vast and overwhelming consensus was that children did better with some formalized preparation and socialization before kindergarten. And so the woman on the phone had me where I lived—at the intersection of ambition and anxiety about my little son's well-being. I wondered briefly about my blood pressure—it felt as if my heart were trying to pound its way out of my eyes—and took a deep breath before pleading my case. Again. It was my third call of the morning. Yes, I knew it sounded strange, but we had recently moved from downtown, where things were different and deadlines were later, and if she could just *possibly* tell me whether it was worth my while at all, I would be really, *really* grateful. And if it was, and she would deign to let me, I would dash *right over* to pick up the Envelope from her—the large manila mailer with an application, parent-essay form, and, in some cases, forms for letters of recommendation inside. I *so* appreciated her time, I really did, and I apologized for the trouble.

But what I really wanted to say to her, to all of them, was, *"Why are you so unfriendly?!"* We were talking about nursery school, after all. Sure, there were too many kids and too few slots. I got that. But c'mon, this was about graham crackers and finger painting and circle time. Warm, fuzzy, hands-on fun. Making friends and reading stories. Wasn't it her job, as the school's liaison to the outside world, to be helpful and polite, no matter how clueless the caller and how naïve her questions? Up here on the Upper East Side, though, child's play was apparently a deadly serious business. And a lot of work. There was a right way to do it—applications, playdates, all of it. When it came to school, I had things to learn.

A few music-class moms and my sister-in-law, an Upper East Side mother of four teens, were in charge of my education and filled me in about the school drill. Certain nursery-school directors, they explained, have relationships with certain "ongoing" (that is, K–8 or K–12) school directors who do, in fact, based on their relationships, have better and worse track records getting kids into "good colleges"—which in a superheated, übercompetitive environment no longer means Ivy League schools but basically any US college with decent teaching and research facilities. Moreover, many nursery schools and "ongoing" schools have agreeable "sibling policies"—once you have a child in that school, the next one's admission is pretty much a given. Between the nursery school playing a role in where your kid winds up for college and the likelihood that if you play your cards right, you have to apply to K–12 only *once*, preschool mattered a lot more than you might think. And preschool directors were very, very powerful people. Yes, we were sure the neighborhood public school would be good for our son, and our family. But what if, down the line, we wanted the option to send our son to private school? What if the class size in public school was too large for him to learn effectively? What if the public school went down in quality while he was there (it was not unheard of, when a school got a new principal) or before he even arrived? What if the trend of "teaching to the test," a practice that seemed to be burning out and stressing public-school teachers, kids, and parents alike, continued, and created problems for my son as it did for so many kids in public school? What if, for *whatever* reason, we wanted him to be in private school at some point? That meant we needed a great preschool director now, so she could pull strings for us later. Lesson learned.

I sighed as I held the line. I was a supplicant again, and this time around, I gathered, I was at an even more distinct disadvantage than I had been in my housing quest, because, unlike all the other mothers on the Upper East Side, I hadn't received the Memo. The one that apparently read: "Always plan way, way, *way* ahead." One of the tribal ways, I was learning from my chats with other moms on playgrounds and at the park, was to always be doing what you were supposed to be doing *long* before you thought you should be doing it. For example, before nursery school, your toddler was supposed to take classes at Diller-Quaile School of Music. Before Diller-Quaile, you were supposed to do a certain baby group. Everything, it seemed, fed into everything else, and having this knowledge, exchanging it, and acting on it in a timely fashion was something like insider trading. It affirmed that you were part of the tribe of Upper East Side mommies.

It was also an anxiety-provoking way of living, parenting, and being, because it meant you could never let your guard down and relax about *anything at all*. When these moms shook their heads upon hearing that my kid "took music" at the pedestrian Gymboree, I could not help but think of Jane Goodall's matriarchal chimp Flo, the entrepreneurial dynasty whose canny advocacy, sheer ambition, and skillful coalition building on behalf of her offspring Fifi, Figan, and Faben catapulted them to the top of the dominance hierarchy of their troop in Gombe, Tanzania, making the family's reign something previously unheard of: an intergenerational affair. Just getting by up here, it seemed, required Flo-like perseverance, cleverness, forethought, and strategy.

Other times, as these women imparted information to me, they seemed to sprout the darkened feathers and sharp beaks and compassionless, glinty eyes of birds—David Lack's bird mothers, to be specific. Lack, a British ornithologist, blew apart our cherished assumptions about motherhood and maternal love in his post-WWII study of brooding behavior among birds in the English countryside. He noticed that some bird moms were better than others, fledging more chicks who then went on to fledge chicks themselves, and wanted to get to the bottom of it. Why did some bird moms succeed where others failed? Lack wondered. The birdbrained mothers, he eventually discovered, were the ones who went all out every time, laying and tending to as many eggs as they could, going gung ho for each and every hatchling, in every breeding season, depleting themselves in the process. Tired and worn down by their efforts, with bigger broods to defend and provision, they were more likely to die—and so were their chicks. These "selfless" avian moms didn't have nearly as much success as did the cooler, more calculating bird dames who ran the numbers *before* they threw themselves into hatching and provisioning their young. "Looks like it's going to be a crappy, cold, late spring, probably very few worms. Should I hatch these eggs, or let them go, and lay more next time around, when ecological conditions might be better? Or just hatch a couple?" Once the chicks were hatched, the game of playing the odds, Lack discovered, went on. A not-so-wise mother bird would feed her whole brood. A smarter one *might* do the same. But depending on circumstances, she might just as easily let the biggest chick push the littler ones out. Or peck its younger sibs to death. Or she might fly the coop entirely, calculating that she could do better next time around, in another breeding season with more potential mates and more abundant berries. Such "retrenchments in maternal care," Lack discovered, were as important to being a successful mother as the willingness to nurture and sacrifice. Smart bird moms played the odds and made informed "maternal trade-offs" every day. It didn't take long for evolutionary thinkers and primatologists like Sarah Hrdy to figure out that primates—both the human and nonhuman variety—do exactly the same thing.

Sure, with the advent of birth control, and in this environment of affluence and extreme ecological release, these moms on the Upper East Side were utterly unlike bird mothers in that they could afford each and every child and could lavish them *all* with food, attention, and clothing from Bonpoint. But that didn't mean there wasn't strategy in their game. One example: the matter of conception. Do you like the idea of having your baby in warm, lazy summer, when Dad can more easily take a paternity leave? Does a yearly outdoor kiddy birthday party with cake at the picnic table sound nice? *Not up here, sister!* Summer birthdays, it turned out, were just no good. Especially if you had a boy. Boys, the thinking went, were more rambunctious, less compliant, and slower to develop fine motor skills—hence they needed to be "older" once they started school. In the South, such "redshirting" had begun so that boys would be bigger for sports teams. But in New York, it was for brains and development and that killer cognitive edge. Schools wanted boys to start each grade having had their birthdays not later than August, they said. In which case my son, born in July, barely made the cutoff. But they *actually* meant May, my sister-in-law explained. And they would prefer, say, an October birthday. Moms who became pregnant in January, February, or March won the Flo prize—and, if all else went well, the coveted school spots. The rest of us had kids who went through life and the Manhattan private-school system with the black mark of a June, July, or August birthday. A friend joked that Upper East Side IVF clinics should post warnings in September, October, and November: *Skip this cycle.*

So, it dawned on me, not only was I slow on the preschool application uptake but I had also conceived a child of the wrong gender at the wrong time. "Oh no, you didn't even apply yet and he also has a *bad birthday?*" the moms I was getting to know exclaimed without fail when I appealed for advice. One said it in front of my son at the playground and he began to sob. "What's bad about my birthday, Mommy?" "Nothing, honey," I comforted him. But I was lying. I had moved us to a place where birthdays could, in fact, be "bad." The gist of it was that I had to get on the phone *right now.* So here I was.

"I'm sorry," the woman told me now. She had picked up the line again with an alarming clatter and didn't sound sorry at all. "There are no more applications." She hung up without a goodbye, before I could thank her. Presumably, she was in a hurry.

We could just buck all this nonsense, I thought, putting the phone down as calmly as I could. It was stressful and silly. Who cared where our son went to nursery school, or if he even went at all? Weren't kids all over the world doing just fine without nursery school? I hadn't gone, I reasoned, and I was okay. But the Upper East Side was not West Africa or the Amazon basin or

Grand Rapids. No, I couldn't check out of this game if my child's future was even potentially at stake. What kind of mother would that make me?

Thus began my disorienting slide from bystander to total buy-in: with fear. I had been seized by the culturally specific and culturally universal anxiety of not being a good enough mommy, of being a mommy who does less than enough for her children.

Prolonged childhood sets us primates apart. While other mammals go from newborn to weaned juvenile to sexually mature adult with startling (to us) speed, we humans and our closest relatives take our time. Primatologist and Saint Louis University associate professor of anthropology Katherine C. MacKinnon observes that "most primate species spend 25–35 percent of their life span in a period of juvenility." She cites the example of orangutans, who are classified as "infants" for the first five years of their lives, and juveniles for ten to twelve or so years. "A prolonged juvenility, relative to overall life span and body size, is true for all apes and most monkeys," she says.

It's a gradient, she points out. But of all primates, we are born the most dependent, and stay that way the longest. It begins when we enter the world essentially as fetuses, half-baked, neurologically unfinished, uniquely needful and dependent. Unlike nonhuman primates, we can't even cling at birth; others have to hold us. That's just for starters: "altricial" or highly dependent offspring, and neoteny, the retention of youthful traits for a prolonged period, affect parents and kids in many and profound ways, for many years. As anthropologist Meredith Small observes, "Human childhood makes human parenthood longer and more complicated." We are physically and psychologically en-twined with our offspring, and they with us, often for a lifetime. We clothe, feed, and pay to educate our kids into adulthood. At that point we may underwrite the cost of their housing and even-tually contribute emotionally and financially to *their* kids' well-being. How can we, as a species, justify this costly, never-ending investment in our children?

As it turns out, for many millennia, we *couldn't*. Our early an-cestors, it seems, did not likely tarry between infancy and inde-pendence as we do now, but rather got right down to the business of becoming sexually mature. And then, as science writer Chip Walter puts it, "around a million years ago, the forces of evolution inserted an extra six years between infancy and preadolescence—a childhood—into the life of our species." Why? For decades experts believed that this change came about because young, early homi-nins needed an additional period to learn skills such as language and tool use. Childhood, in this view, got stretched like taffy in order for us to impart all the necessary lessons of humanity. Being so special, we needed something special—a childhood.

There were flaws in the theory, though. Natural selection would not likely favor the emergence of an idyll period that was burdensome for parents and risky for parents, dependent off-spring, and entire groups alike, just so some kids could learn to start fires and talk pretty. In order to figure out the *real* reason for childhood, thinkers had to stop presuming that childhood had always been the way it is now. Maybe it *wasn't* originally a time of playing and learning at all. Maybe childhood evolved not for children but for *adults*, and was *beneficial for them*. Indeed, the only scenario that makes sense, anthropologists such as Barry Bogin, Kristen Hawkes, and Anne Zeller say, is that childhood came about to shift the burdens of reproduction off reproducing adults, so they could reproduce again. They suggest that kids were helpers, babysitters who allowed their mothers to rest and get nourished, which in turn allowed them to provision the kids they had, and have more. It was kids, not male partners, who turned us into "cooperative breeders," helping us thrive where other *Homos* bit the dust. Childhood was about work, not play.

The proof is in the contemporary human pudding. In most cultures, children are net contributors to their households by age seven. They tend livestock, clean the kitchen, and fetch firewood; they cook, do laundry, and sell stuff in markets. But mostly, they are babysitters for their younger sibs and, sometimes, their cousins. In fact, in a survey of 186 societies worldwide, UCLA anthropologist Thomas Weisner found that, in most places, mothers are *not* the principal caretakers or companions of younger children. Older children are. Kids, those who study them tell us, are wired to help out, to spend their days in multiage groups of other kids, caring for one another, absorbing and passing along the skills they have learned from observing and working alongside adults.

This order of things seems to work well for everybody, especially in contexts of low-skill work where children's contributions are meaningful. In traditional Mayan villages in Mexico, for example, kids essentially run households and market stalls. These children, anthropologist Karen Kramer found, have high levels of self-confidence: they know exactly what they're supposed to do, master it, and feel important. And their parents do not report stress, depression, or fatigue as so many parents in the industrialized West do. In West African countries where children begin helping out as early as age three, people often say, "A man with children can never be poor." Children are assets, loved and valued as such. Kids, in these contexts, bring real joy because they really contribute. They make their parents rich.

But in the industrialized West, we have turned childhood on its head. Our children are expected to do next to nothing until late in the game. They are taken care of and tended to. Rather than hanging out in language- and skill-rich multi-age groups with lots of older and younger sibs and cousins, where they learn to talk and contribute to the home economy, they go to school, sometimes as early as age two. There, they are sequestered from the rest of society with kids their own age (the most efficient way to create groups of kids when birthrates are low) and unrelated adult strangers called teachers, who may or may not have their best interests at heart. Deprived of a group of older relatives who can teach them practical skills and impart language simply by speaking all around them all day long, they have to learn it in a labor-intensive dyad ("Da da da da" we say, and "cat cat cat," over and over). This is just one example of how, in our world, kids are *work*, and our lives are arranged around their needs, rather than the reverse. You can feel it every time you make your child's bed or tidy up the kitchen after making her a special, kid-friendly meal. Or pay someone else to.

Meredith Small famously observed that children of the Anthropocene, our current geological era, are "priceless but useless." We value them in our own way, practicing what we might think of as "descendant worship," the same ways other cultures practice ancestor worship. But we also complain that kids are terribly costly and tiring—which they are, because they do very little to earn their keep. This reversal of the evolutionary order of things creates unique ecological, economic, and social circumstances for *mothers*. If the idea that childhood is a carefree idyll is a modern Western invention that comes from affluence, so, too, is the notion that mothers should be their children's principle caregivers and companions, mainly, if not solely, responsible for not just their survival through infancy but also their well-being over the course of their entire childhood, even their success over a lifetime. In changing childhood, we have changed motherhood as well, until it is virtually unrecognizable compared with what it used to be, and what it is elsewhere.

Nowhere is this change in childhood and motherhood more the case, more in evidence, or more intensified than on the Upper East Side of Manhattan. In a niche of extreme ecological release, in a highly competitive culture, "successful" offspring are status objects—and mirrors. Promoting them, working assiduously on their behalf, is a vocation. Being a mommy here is a cutthroat, high-stakes career, stressful and anxiety-producing precisely because it is ours alone to succeed or fail at, leading to the success or failure of our offspring. And ourselves. The circuit is seamless— and, I was learning, nearly inescapable.

This explained why Upper East Side mothers all wore tiny medallions engraved with their children's initials around their necks. And stacking rings, one for each child, on their fingers. And entered the names of other mothers in their contacts under the names of their *children*, so that, on so many of my new friends' phone and email lists, I came up not as "Wednesday Martin" but as "Eliot M/ mother, Wednesday M." We were our children, utterly merged together. The message came home every time I saw a woman wearing her child's school badge on a lanyard around her neck: "So and So, Parent, Such and Such School." In emails we introduced ourselves, or signed off, as "Pierce's mom" or "Avery's mom." In conversation we said, "Did you ask Schuyler's mom?"

These women had become their offspring, and vice versa. As my friend author Amy Fusselman wrote, "It was as if I had no life or identity before them, as if my children had given birth to me."

Anyway, were these other kids, the ones whose mothers had already applied, somehow better than mine? I fretted as I considered the ever-contracting range of options we faced on the nursery school front as every day slipped by without our submitting an application, and the spots filled up in a game of musical chairs I was on some level increasingly anxious not to lose. Were they any smarter or cuter than my kid? Were their parents any nicer than my husband and I were? *I doubted it*. I was going to get those applications if it killed me. I was going to call my sister-in-law. And my native guide, Inga. I was going to ask for a favor. They didn't have kids the same age as mine. Neither did their friends. So they could afford to be generous. I was getting the hang of it. Or losing my perspective entirely. It depended on how you looked at it.

Inga was game, and wired. She knew literally dozens of people with kids at fancy nursery schools, having sold many of them their apartments over the years. My sister-in-law was happy to help, too. But there was a catch: the First Choice Dilemma. In Manhattan, after going through the school application process and calculating the odds and calibrating your desires, you send a letter to or have a conversation with a school that is your "first choice." In this document or chat, you use the language of monogamy and commitment, promising, essentially, that if they accept your child, he or she will go there. If your child should get into a school on a friend's recommendation but then go elsewhere, your friend will look bad. And you can consider the bridge to that school burned in perpetuity, and a friendship lost. When my sister-in-law's four kids attended their nursery school, it was just the friendly neighborhood preschool around the corner. But by the time we were applying, with all the new money in town and the director's strong record of getting kids into highly desirable ongoing schools, it was the most prestigious pre-K in Manhattan. Indeed, it had recently weathered a scandal in which a master-of-the-universe type tried to pave the way for a client's child's admission with a million-dollar donation. The child was not admitted.

Before we got our son in anywhere at all, there were applications and parent interviews and child "playdates" at the schools. The applications were easily procured, in spite of our tardiness, once Inga and my sister-in-law called their friends who could get the schools to hand them over. I scampered across the Upper East Side picking up manila envelopes for days, then got down to work writing essays about what made my toddler special, what his strengths and weaknesses were, what kind of learner he was. Sorely tempted to write, "I really don't know yet, since he's *two*," I instead banged my head against the wall until I came up with what I hoped were some good-sport responses. Next came the playdates, which I grumblingly referred to as "auditions" because it felt more honest. They were generally scheduled during nap time, unfathomable until you consider that the schools were basically trying to exclude as many "nonsibling" kids as they could. Overtired kid had a meltdown in the play kitchen? Or smacked someone at the craft table? Or just wasn't paying attention during story time? Better luck at another audition at another school. I will never forget the "playdate" where there was a single desirable toy—a brightly colored play oven with knobs and lights and buttons—surrounded by a few other, lesser toys. It was the center of a game of musical chairs rigged by admissions people who wanted to see how a bunch of tired toddlers would respond to the stress of confronting exactly what they were incapable of handling at that point in their development—the need to take turns and delay gratification and manage their own frustration under unusual circumstances. With no reward.

After waiting and waiting, my son grew visibly upset. Other kids were shoving one another, and him. The "playdate" was devolving into chaos. I was disgusted and angry, and as my son burst into tears, I got up from my spot on the floor to comfort him (they never told you where to sit or how to be at these idiotic "playdates," because watching you wonder and try to figure it out was part of their "assessment"). And I hoped then, as I still hope today, that the director of that school would end up in a special circle of hell, one reserved for people who stress out two-year-olds and their hopeful, tense, and vulnerable mothers for no good reason.

All around me at every one of these misery sessions, mothers were beautifully dressed and groomed, tightly wound, ready to melt down if their children did. We were all being tested. And we knew it. Often you got the sense that some of the administrators enjoyed watching us squirm, enjoyed making relatively rich, privileged women feel small by wielding their own cultural capital, their power to pick and choose families, to include or exclude little children. It was not unusual to see a mommy crying on the street as she bundled up her child and headed off. I cried myself when my son "flubbed" an audition by eating a handful of sand from the sand table and yelling "GIVE IT BACK!" when a little kid grabbed a book from him. At another nursery school, this one in a church, he walked in and announced, "Damn it all!" and I knew, from the narrowed eyes of the administrators, that they were not amused. The cruel ritual was played out over and over, for weeks. To me it seemed like institutionalized sadism, and I heartily resented it.

But what could I, or any of the other mothers, do? The nursery schools had all the power, and many of them, you could tell, believed that the fact we were all there begging to be admitted attested to their excellence. Really though, none of them was so excellent; it was a numbers thing. There just weren't enough schools. And given the hordes applying to the school my husband's nieces and nephews had attended, many of them with their own strings to pull and connections to play, we had to try *everywhere*. So I kept going, kept dragging my son to auditions. One day, holding my hand as we were about to enter yet another "playroom" full of kids he didn't know, he looked up at me and said, "Mommy, I can't do this," and I wanted to weep.

We thought it best to let my husband, a calm and collected fellow, take our son to the audition at the fancy preschool his nieces and nephews had gone to. He pointed out that this particular director was probably one of the most powerful people in the city, and hence, the world. We had a good chuckle about that, but he wasn't entirely kidding. I tapped my fingernails on my desktop waiting to hear from him after the audition. When the phone rang, I nearly fell off my chair. "I'm going to jump out of a window," my husband whispered. My heart did a dive down to my feet. "Why?" I asked, struggling not to sound as hysterical as I felt.

It turned out that the school's director was in the room for my son's audition. As she talked and rolled Play-Doh and pasted and drew with my son and the other kids, he wanted her attention.

He called her name several times and when she failed to respond in the noisy classroom, he punched her (albeit lightly) in the arm and said, "Hey, I'm talking to you!"

I have no idea why my son was admitted to the school. I never asked. We chalked it up to my sister-in-law's influence and the fact that the school, so desirable, was also deeply tribal. If you were family of someone who had gone, perhaps especially someone who had sent four kids there and donated a fair amount of money and was pleasant to deal with, you were at a distinct advantage. You were, in their view, vetted, and a relatively safe bet. Even, apparently, if your son punched the boss lady in the arm. And here we were, with a child at the "best" nursery school in the city. I was learning how to reap the benefits of tribal membership. Now I would learn that there were disadvantages as well.

We were euphoric when our son landed at a "good" nursery school. It felt like a slam dunk, a real accomplishment, and while I knew better than to talk about it much, for fear I would seem to be gloating, I was not above relishing the envious looks of other mothers when they asked where he would go to nursery school and I told them. Like a town house, a big diamond, or waterfront in the Hamptons, a spot at this nursery school, reflecting as it supposedly did one's social connectedness and influence, and increasing the likelihood that your child would go on to a "top tier" grammar school, was a coveted Manhattan "get." Mostly, though, it made me feel like a "good" mother. Like Flo.

But, once again, our sense that we had crossed the finish line and were "done" was an illusion. Because aside from a shrinking water hole in the Serengeti during the dry season, there is

no place more desperate, aggressive, dangerous, and inhospitable than the halls of an exclusive Manhattan private school at
morning drop-off and afternoon pickup. Those corridors make
the conference rooms at Goldman Sachs (where, an investment
banker acquaintance once observed, "They don't bother to stab
you in the back, they just stab you in the front and step right over
your body") seem like nice, friendly places to stroll with Aunt
Bea from Duluth. I had landed at the fanciest school in the snob-
biest zip code in the wealthiest town in America, where everyone
was advocating for and living through their offspring. So maybe I
should have seen it coming. But I didn't.

My son started nursery school at the height of the boom.
There was adrenaline in our blood and hope in the air. People
were closing deals. People were buying second and third and
fourth homes. Everyone in Manhattan seemed manic with happiness. And every day after dropping my son off at school, I cried.
Not because it was touching and sweet to watch him cross the
threshold of the classroom. Not because letting him go was
some metaphor for watching him grow up. Not because being a
mother is poignant and painful sometimes.

No, I cried because the other moms were so mean. I called
them the Mean Girl Moms when describing them to my husband
and my friends from downtown.

They gathered in the hallways in clusters and cliques, heads
bowed, murmuring, laughing, whispering. They all seemed to
know one another somehow, "from before." Their uniform telegraphed that they were one tribe united—their identical Burberry
raincoats on rainy days and their chic puffers on cold days. Their
crinkly Lanvin flats, or the high heels that screamed, "I have a
driver." They might have lifted their heads from their huddle to

return my hello as I walked by—but that almost never happened. I arrived early at school every day to avoid the feeling—that sensation of falling through space—I got when they looked right through me. Standing awkwardly on the edge of the group, alone, I would usher my son into his room the second the door opened, say good-bye, and scurry away. Outside on the sidewalk my arms felt empty and on the worst days my stomach churned. Because it was unsettling to feel invisible. And because, for the life of me, I couldn't get any of these women to agree to make a playdate for our children.

This I knew: our children request that we arrange for them to play with someone after school, and we arrange it. We arrange it by text or email or phone. I knew the drill from other moms and other schools. But my texts, emails, and phone calls to the mothers of my son's classmates went unnervingly unanswered. Even worse, when I followed up in person with the moms in the hallways, they frequently put me off or changed the subject. Sometimes, when I asked, they shot alarmed or sly looks at their friends, as if to telegraph, "Oh my God, is she actually *doing* this? Can you believe how *awkward*?!" My son and I, I realized as the other moms continued to look through me every day, were playdate pariahs. I was uncharacteristically distraught.

The fate of those female chimps playing in my head, I assessed the playing field. Being shunned was not a pretty picture, nor a fate I wanted for me or my child. The women who were ignoring me seemed nasty and off-putting, yes. I wanted to poke a few of them in the eye, yes. But on some level, I needed them, and I needed to fit in, and my kid needed a playdate or two, and some friends. Schlepping him downtown was not an option—and anyway, our friends there didn't have kids his age, or any kids at all, in some cases. Spontaneous meet-ups with new kids at the park or playground up here, just making friends on the spot, sounded like a nice idea, but in a town where kids are hyperscheduled from drop-off to dropping off to sleep at night, that was extremely unlikely. Besides, the moms at the playground seemed to regard me as a stalker at worst or someone with poor boundaries at best when I approached in a friendly way. It was clear that on the Upper East Side, moms and toddlers had their pecking order worked out and their places set and their dance cards full long before the wee ones were out of their Robeez. I was late to the ball, and it made me feel desperate. My poor kid. And yes, poor me. I didn't want drop-off and pickup to feel so bad. I needed to like and be liked by the moms at school.

During this period I wasn't feeling well physically—I had a spaced-out, derealized feeling many days, a sense of being dissociated from my body and the people around me. Describing it to my husband at dinner one night, I realized it was a clinical condition I had read about before in my studies. I had culture shock—a syndrome of unfamiliarity and alienation that bedevils anthropologists and foreign-exchange students and poor kids who get into elite colleges. By this point in my life I had spent time in many foreign cultures and always found a way in. I had worked briefly at the UN, writing speeches and attending functions with diplomats from all over the world, so I knew I had not entirely inconsiderable social skills. I was well dressed, relatively speaking, and friendly. What the hell else did these women want from me? Was there something I wasn't doing? Something I was supposed to say? Trying hard to shake off the feeling that I was being judged and found wanting, or that it mattered to me much, I vowed to stop trying to find a way in, and simply watch. I was a struggling, insecure mom, but I was also a social researcher. So I'd act like one.

Observing was easy, since no one really wanted to speak to me. The first thing I noticed was that outside, the Escalades with drivers were piled three deep and the moms were dressed to kill, though none of them seemed to have jobs. They were on their way to I didn't know where, but obviously to them it mattered. Often the most overdressed ones—tipping in their platform boots and sky-high stilettos—would call out, "See you there!" after dropping their kids at the classroom door. "There" must be dreadful, I found myself thinking. In the elevator, the rule was more or less total silence. One morning when I had a meeting and eschewed my jeans and thermal shirt and ponytail for something more fashionable, sleek hair, and a bit of makeup, two immaculately groomed women watched, glowering, as I left the elevator. One hissed, "Who was *that*?" and my hairline prickled. The world of the school was turned inside out—it was all about the moms. The moms air-kissing and hobnobbing and chitchatting and sometimes backstabbing. The kids, in this reordered world, were part of a fashionable ensemble, dangling from the impressively toned arms of their mommies like ornaments or accessories. Motherhood, I gathered, was another outfit. And friendliness and chitchat were hoarded, bestowed upon only a few.

I also noted that on most mornings, if a mom did deign to speak to me, she gave a curt hello, after which she performatively turned her back and began to speak to someone else. The head of the school's PTA—a woman I had come to think of as the Queen of the Queen Bees—was the first person to do this to me. Mistakenly thinking, on one of the first days of school, that I was in a world where the rules approximated those of, say, a work environment or friendly cocktail party, I approached her—the parent liaison to the school, after all, and so someone more or less officially representing it—and introduced myself. She looked at me as if, in saying hello and outstretching my hand, I had committed a faux pas like drinking the contents of my finger bowl at a dinner party and then removing all my clothing. "How gauche and presumptuous of you to greet me," her sneer and raised eyebrows said. Then she simply turned away without so much as a hello. I was shocked. But eventually, I realized this was just an extreme version of what nearly all the women at my son's school did. They conserved their hellos for a select few and expended just about nothing on most others.

This sort of refusal to greet and dramatic back-turning most often took place, I realized, when the hoped-for interlocutress was a socialite, someone I recognized from the pages of a glossy magazine, or the wife of a wealthy man whose name I knew from the newspaper or from my days in advertising. Yes, I figured out pretty quickly, these women were not talking to one another so much as they were jockeying for position *to talk to one or two or three particular moms*. They had a laser-like focus, it became obvious, on what I came to think of as the highest-ranking females—those who were, it seemed, richer, prettier, more successful or, most important of all, married to someone more successful than anyone else—someone who, apparently, mattered more.

Often I'd call my close friend Lily, the calmest mother and most gracious hostess I knew, whose daughter was my son's age, to tell her the latest, and she would gasp. "That can't be true! That they think it's all right to be so awful!" she would shout into the phone, and just imagining her as she said it, downtown in the studio where she worked as a fashion designer, reminded me there was a world outside the one I was trying to break into, a world I understood. It was a place where women worked and there were gay couples and straight couples and there wasn't always enough money for every single thing you wanted and not everyone had a car and a driver. "I hate them," my friend Candace would say, urging me to act out a shunning scenario from the day before while we had coffee. And then she would remind me what writer Wendy Wasserstein, whose children had gone to the same school mine went to, had said about the experience: "So many skinny women, so many gigantic bags." And we would laugh. It helped, but the next day I still had to go back to the school.

My husband thought it was all ridiculous girl stuff and that I was overreacting. "C'mon, it can't be that bad," he told me when I shared the details of yet another morning drop-off drama. So I let him do drop-off the very next day. "What the hell is wrong with those women?" he asked after his first misadventure. "They wouldn't even respond when I said 'Good morning'!" *I told you so*, I smirked. We marveled that these women had determined that even the most basic and commonly observed tenet of the social contract—returning a greeting—was for chumps. They were above it.

Not long after my husband's experience, our son came home from school one day and excitedly announced that he had been invited to a playdate by his friend Tessa—on her family's private plane. It was a strange and fanciful invitation, I thought, until our nanny, Sarah, told me that everybody at the school had a private plane and all the kids had been discussing the relative merits of their particular planes when our son said we didn't have one, and Tessa took pity on him and invited him to play on *hers*. I felt nauseated, but it was a start. He was doing better than I was.

As I sat on the bench watching morning drop-off, longing for a real playdate for my son and me, I didn't just think of vulnerable female chimps and their babies. I also recalled what I had learned years before about *Papio anubis*, or olive baboons, in seminars on primate social behavior. Olive baboons live in troops of up to 150 members, with males dispersing at sexual maturity, so that the groups are composed of female baboons who are usually related, form tight cooperative networks, and essentially run the show. The troops are rigidly hierarchical, with the highest-ranking female baboons getting all kinds of benefits—better food, safer sleeping spots, nicer male "friends" and protectors (who have to emigrate from other troops and pass muster before they are accepted), lots of opportunities to copulate, and higher rates of reproductive success—that is, more offspring that survive into adulthood and reproduce themselves.

Lower-ranking females obviously want some of this sweet life as well. One strategy they may use to "pull themselves up" in *Papio anubis* society is attempting (often repeatedly) to groom the alpha females—and care for their babies. High-ranking females may rebuff these attempts over and over, with swats and slaps and even frequently vicious attacks on the would-be babysitters, but eventually a high-ranking female may allow a lower-ranking one to become what she desperately wishes to be—an "allomother," or an extra caregiver to the alpha's infant or junior offspring—for limited periods of time. This gives the lower-ranking female an "in"; after all, she is increasing the boss lady's fitness by allowing her more opportunities to forage for herself and her baby, unfettered. And the prestige of her affiliation with the mom, via the child she is hauling around and tending to, can afford her more power and security in the troop over time. Powerful olive baboon moms have the power to empower less-powerful ones by proxy.

Far from the savanna, in the halls of an Upper East Side nursery school, during an economic boom, my husband and I were low-ranking primates, and it showed. The kids were all extensions of their parents, it seemed, used in bids for upward social mobility. "Maybe if we befriend Ari, whose dad is a hedge-fund manager, we'll become friends and Ari's mom will tell Ari's dad about my husband's start-up and . . ." Other times, it seemed, these lower-ranking moms just wanted to bask in the glow of the fantastic wealth of others and warm their children there. We were new to the scene, and my husband couldn't really help anyone's career, so we were an unknown quantity, slow to be welcomed. On the Upper East Side, there is a sense that one's child's friends and playmates can set your position in a hierarchy, bumping you up or dragging you down. You are only as fabulous as the playdates you procure on behalf of your progeny, and if you don't rate, neither does your cherub. This precarious and anxiety-inducing order of things, I was learning, turns mothers into powerful gatekeepers . . . and hopeful supplicants.

As happens for so many nonhuman primates who transfer into a troop, I was stuck at the bottom of the dominance hierarchy, regarded with suspicion, alternately ignored and harassed. How I wished, some days, that I were a howler monkey—*those* young females who immigrate jump to the top spot, pushing more established females down the hierarchy. But no, I was a baboon in this instance. There is no one lower-ranking than a new female in a baboon troop, and if she fails to build coalitions with the mid-level and top females, her life circumstances and those of her offspring can be dire. I knew this: if my son and I were ostracized, that status would be hard to shake as long as we stayed here. I didn't want my son to be the kid with no friends at school. I didn't want us—him—to be shunned. So I schemed and smiled in the hallways even though it was killing me. And, in spite of all the hours of observation, I wondered what to do.

My salvation was unexpected, but had I remembered my studies better, I might have hoped for or even tried to engineer precisely the circumstances that turned my fate around. It came the same way it does for so many nonhuman female primates in my predicament: through the attentions of an alpha male. At a "class cocktail party" hosted by the "class mom," I got into a vaguely flirtatious conversation with the father of a boy in my son's class. He was polite, clever, and slightly rakish, unusual among the straitlaced Upper East Side finance guys I was still trying to get used to. He was easy to talk to, and since my husband had stayed home with our son and the moms were busy talking to one another in a clump I had no hope of breaking into, he and I chatted. I later learned he was the scion of some sort of Manhattan banking empire, the son of a powerful and wealthy matriarch like Flo, and so very "top tier" in the school and our class. The next day at drop-off he suggested, in front of a group of moms, that our boys should play. "How about this Friday?" he asked, and I agreed.

"How did you do *that*?" one of the friendlier moms asked in a whisper, her eyes wide as he headed off. "I've been trying to get him to make a playdate for weeks and he won't! Even though my parents knew his parents when they all lived in Westchester." I shrugged and suggested that next time, she might try having a glass of wine with him.

From that day forward the playdate tide turned dramatically. My son had a regular weekly playdate with the alpha's son, which paved the way for playdates with the kids who were friends with his kid, and whose parents—rich and powerful as he was—were friends with him. When these mothers saw me engaged in friendly conversation with Alpha Dad in the hallway, they took note, it seemed: their body language and newly friendly smiles suggested that they felt I had been vetted and approved. Talking to me, they could now rest assured, wasn't necessarily going to pull their own rank down or be a total waste of time. And the more these mothers acknowledged and returned my hellos in the halls, the harder it was for them to ignore my emails and playdate pleas.

When I stood back from it, the playdate hierarchy high jinks struck me as strange and unsavory. Their seamy underside was the notion that some parents and some children were more worth it than others. This was repellent, but it was also the name of the game. If my son was finally playing with schoolmates and was happy, I was happy. And I felt very indebted indeed to Alpha Dad, even if Candace and Lily agreed that it was a bad idea to count on him for anything. *Wasn't he married to one of these unfriendly women? Could he be much better himself?* they asked. I wasn't sure. I just knew that in this upside-down world, where the parents lived through the kids, it was sort of like being a teenage girl again, and having the attentions of the high school football team's star quarterback. His casual friendliness had utterly transformed my son's social life and my rank, which I now realized were unquestionably and inextricably linked. Like Candace and Lily, I didn't trust the state of affairs to last for long, and I was right—Alpha Dad moved on, as alphas do. By that time, though, my son had what he needed, which meant I did, too. Maybe this wasn't going to be so hard after all.

CHAPTER THREE

Going Native:
Mommy Wants a Birkin

W HEN I STUDIED anthropology in college and graduate school, I was fascinated by descriptions of the anthropologist who "goes native"—merging with the culture she was supposed to be studying, slipping into *being* one of those she had set out to examine and analyze. With Bronislaw Malinowski, about whom I wrote my doctoral dissertation, it was a gradual process. He became increasingly fed up with his informants in the Trobriand Islands, who were not as forthcoming as he wanted them to be, and eventually commenced having sex with Trobriand women. In another case, a professor of Middle Eastern culture of my acquaintance revealed he had "gone native" at dinner one night when he greeted his graduate students dressed in traditional garb from Yemen, where he had done fieldwork, and proceeded to conduct himself as an indigenous Yemeni tribesman for the course of the evening (sabers were involved). In *Reflections on Fieldwork in Morocco*, Paul Rabinow made an entire narrative out of losing it—and himself—there.

Going native is today viewed by anthropologists as equal parts inevitable and instructive, a dynamic process that happens as fieldworkers get to know their subjects, and come to understand, value, and internalize some of their beliefs. First, typically, a fieldworker may feel at sea, alienated, overwhelmed by the unfamiliarity all around her. Bit by bit, however, she gains her footing and eventually, without even noticing it is happening, begins to "think Samoan." Or Aka. Or Upper East Side.

But in the field, "going native" was long tainted with shame. This is because anthropology struggled for so long to distinguish itself as a "science" separate from and superior to its actual historical roots in missionary work, Victorian "armchair science," and plain old imperialism. Slipping from scientist to "one of them" is messy and unscientific, to say the least. So, for a long time, anthropologists prided themselves on their "objective distance" from the cultures they studied and lived in, staving off "going native" like a case of malaria. "Going native" has always carried with it a whiff of impropriety, and a menacing, thrilling sense of losing one's very self.

As a self-designated participant-observer of privileged Upper East Side motherhood, an interloper in the Upper East Side mommy tribe, I frequently felt conflicted about my relationship to the women and culture around me. On the one hand, I longed to fit in, to become one with and one of them, and felt I *had* to, mostly for the sake of my child (and, later, child*ren*). But I also struggled to keep my sense of apartness or separateness—some semblance of analytic distance—as I watched and took part in the frequently insane-seeming doings and goings-on about me. The back-turning, the dozens of illegally parked Escalades, one of which nearly plowed into my son one day as we struggled to get a cab after pickup. *Who the hell wanted any part of this selfish, entitled world?* I sometimes asked myself.

Ultimately, though, the drop-off dramas and experience of being a playdate pariah—which made me feel so vulnerable, sad, and rejected—actually drew me deeper into the world of my son's school. They hardened my resolve to assimilate and win acceptance. I wasn't going to let anybody reject me, or my kid. Screw them. And once he (and I) had playdates and a school-based social life, these "triumphs" drew me further into the world I was observing, rendering my foothold in the world outside it more tenuous. I called and saw my downtown friends less and less, given the rigors and demands of work and keeping my hand in the game and maintaining friendships for my son and me uptown. Before I knew or realized it, I had surrendered to this new world in a real way, and there was no going back.

My final undoing was a powerful talismanic object with nearly magical and certainly mesmerizing powers—an Hermès Birkin bag.

The first time I really noticed it happening, I was headed back home after a quick trip to the corner market. Swinging a plastic bag of bananas and a carton of milk by my side as I made my way from Madison toward Park on East Seventy-Ninth Street, I felt expansive and happy. The sun was out and the wide sidewalk was remarkably uncrowded. It was a lull period—morning rush hour over, not yet lunchtime—and there was hardly anyone out and about in our normally bustling neighborhood. For a Midwesterner accustomed to space and quiet, it felt, momentarily, a little bit like home—only with elegant prewar buildings and doormen in upbeat moods saying hello as you walked by. My son was in a good school. He had school chums, a social life, if you will, and so, by extension, did I. Sure, I wished the moms were a little friendlier, and I still felt distinctly on the outside most of the time when I dropped my son off and picked him up. But I was a good-enough mother of one, with another on the way. I was finally finding my way and my place on the Upper East Side, it seemed, and on this day I was pleased.

Half a block ahead I saw a solitary, well-dressed woman striding purposefully toward me. We walk briskly in Manhattan, and in no time she (perhaps in her midfifties) and I (late thirties) were closing the space between us. In keeping with Manhattan sidewalk etiquette—more like a traffic law, really—I did as cars and New Yorkers do and kept to the right. So why was this well-dressed, well-coiffed woman drifting to her left, directly into my path, with every step? Were we in England?

I adjusted to the right again, and yet again, to give her even *more* room as she continued her course toward me. If I kept moving to the right as she was quite clearly forcing me to do by bearing down on me in this way, I realized, I would walk directly into the big orange metal trash can now several steps in front of me. This was *ridiculous*, I thought, surveying the entire wide, empty sidewalk and slowing down. Just before the trash can, I came to an abrupt halt (what choice did I have? Dart in front of her to the other side of the sidewalk entirely?) and looked at her, for she was a mere six inches away from me now, in spite of the vast expanse to her right. She caught my eye and held my gaze while she deliberately and not at all gently grazed my left arm with her magnificent bag. Then she smirked—she actually smirked!—and continued her purposeful brush past me. I turned around to watch her back recede down the sidewalk, breathless with surprise that she had done what she had done. Whatever it was. What *was* it?

I had been charged. At least that is how it felt to the anthropologist in me, who in my undergraduate days had watched hours of documentary footage of chimps coming toward one another with aggressive bearing and intent—arms swinging, teeth displayed, emitting screeches and guttural vocalizations. Unpacking my groceries, I played back the encounter in my mind, feeling uneasy, irritated even. What the hell was going on? I realized, now that I thought it through, that this kind of thing had happened before—a woman taking the measure of me and then crowding me—but never quite as explicitly. It was time to start paying attention, *really* paying attention, to Upper East Side primate social behaviors.

Sure enough, I began to notice similar encounters unfolding all around me. In uptown crosswalks and upscale boutiques and the waiting room of a famous cosmetic dermatologist, I perceived that, subtly and not so subtly, women dressed to the nines not only took the measure of but also "charged" other women. Not infrequently, one of those other women was me. Sometimes, in these encounters, I actually had to step aside toward the curb or flatten myself against the wall of a building to allow a woman to stride by me, so adamant was she in her refusal to budge or swerve a fraction of an inch from her course, a course that had been altered as if to tell me . . . something. What, I wondered, did the woman who charged want the woman she was charging to do?

My previous territory, the West Village, was mere miles away, but another country, apparently, when it came to uniforms, customs, and warfare between women. Sure, I recalled now, once in a while down there you would encounter a blank-faced, freakishly tall supermodel striding down the narrow, buckling strip of concrete that ran alongside Bleecker Street as if it were her own personal catwalk. But that was just a professional narcissist doing what she did. Stepping out to run a quick errand on the Upper East Side, on the other hand, you could find yourself embroiled, unwittingly, in a remarkably antagonistic and neatly gendered game of chicken, in which one apparently high-functioning, well-dressed and otherwise-normal-seeming woman asked another, *Who's going to move first?*

After a few weeks of watching and walking about while tuned in to the charging phenomenon, the female pedestrian in me was thoroughly inside the experience, constantly alert and ready to joust when out for a walk or en route from one place to another. But my inner social researcher wanted more data. And so, early one morning, having dropped my son off at school, I bought a coffee and parked myself in front of a doorman building in my neighborhood, and I watched. The next day and the next and the next I stood outside a store, and then near an intersection with real foot traffic. A few times I actually made observations inside buildings frequented by women, or rather the entrances to them, since entering and exiting seemed to be highly fraught and contentious moments when charging was likely to happen—high-end retail shops, a restaurant known to be the native habitat of a cross section (age-wise) of ladies who lunch, and a few lobbies.

Eventually, I observed nearly a hundred of the type of encounter I had that day on East Seventy-Ninth Street. My research was informal, of course, but I did come to some conclusions. Chief among them: women on the Upper East Side, particularly women in their thirties and women on the downhill slope of middle age, are utterly attuned to and obsessed with power. In many but not all of the encounters I observed, it was an older woman who "charged" a younger one, moving toward her until a kind of social crisis point was reached, when actual impact was avoided—often at the last second—as the younger woman quickly moved aside. The actors in these scenarios then unfailingly continued as if unaware of the (non-)exchange that had taken place between them. It was as if both players were complicit in some deep sense, agreeing to agree that what had just happened hadn't.

Over and over, I watched encounters unfold, until an explanation began to take shape about women and their bids to assert their dominance over other women. It was their right, they said as they charged, to expand their space by forcing others to give it up. Their message, when I had observed enough of these encounters, was pretty clear. It was not simply "Get out of my way" but something more pointed: "I don't see you. *Because you don't even exist.*" Their handbags—heart-stoppingly beautiful and expensive-looking affairs slung across or hanging from their shoulders or dangling from their hands, quilted and dyed, snakeskin and lambskin and ostrich, with interlocking Cs or Fs or intricate buckles and locks—apparently had a lot to do with it. They were armor, weapons, flags, and more, it seemed: everyone who charged someone seemed to have a fantastic bag, and to revel in brushing her opponent with it. This was the coup de grace.

The late Nora Ephron wrote that people in LA have cars, and we in Manhattan have our handbags, and these encounters between women brought new meaning to this analogy for me. If handbags are our cars, as Ephron suggests—at once functional and utterly symbolic, our attempt to get ourselves and our stuff from point A to point B and also to be seen as we hope to be seen as we traverse the town—then, it seemed to me, all along the uptown avenues of affluence there was plenty of road rage. With nothing but a plastic bag from the grocery store on my arm, I had been asking for it.

I thought, too, of the dominance displays of Mike, a chimp in Jane Goodall's Gombe troop. Mike is legendary among primatologists and students of anthropology for having shown the kind of remarkable resourcefulness that can reorder the world, or at least upend an entire, well-established social hierarchy. Small and low ranking, Mike was a relatively new transfer to the troop when Goodall arrived in 1960; she observed that he often took a beating, literally, from the older and bigger chimps of Gombe. His life was that of a miserable, stepped-on outsider, an ostracized newcomer to the party.

And then, Mike got himself a beautiful purse.

Actually, he discovered a couple of empty, discarded, lightweight metal kerosene canisters with handles. And brilliantly, he realized he could incorporate these props into his dominance displays—choreographed performances in which male chimps seek to intimidate and impress the chimps they live with, without actually harming them. Usually in a dominance display chimps chase or body check one another, further making their point by shaking branches, slapping the ground, and throwing rocks, all the while issuing loud pant-hoot calls and excited screams.

Primatologists and wildlife photographers have frequently been on the receiving end of such dominance displays and report that they are startling, even terrifying. So imagine the surprise of the Gombe troop members when Mike came running at them dragging big, noisy unfamiliar *things* by their handles, banging them and swinging them through the grass like scepters. And then *further* enhanced his display by standing tall in the middle of the group and crashing the mysterious objects together, making an unholy, previously unheard-of racket that seemed to say, *Now I own you!* This groundbreaking social spectacle sent even Goliath, the reigning alpha male, into a cowering panic. The researchers of Gombe quickly removed the canisters, to little effect. The other chimps remained in utter awe of Mike, who rapidly dethroned Goliath in spite of his high-ranking supporter, the former alpha male David Greybeard, to become alpha chimp himself. For five entire years. Such was the powerful half life of a great handbag.

I could not change or beat them, and no, I certainly could not and did not want to join these Mean Girl Moms west of Lex. Or maybe I did and could, kind of. What I needed was a kerosene canister of my own. Yes, something about these arrogant women, who pushed and crowded me as though I didn't exist, let alone matter, made me want a beautiful, expensive bag. Like a totem object, I believed, it might protect me from them, these ladies who were everywhere in my adopted habitat and who said so much without a word, using only their eyes and their faces and, always, their handbags. Perhaps, I thought, a nice purse like the ones they had might trick them, mesmerize them into believing that they oughtn't challenge me to sidewalk duels and all the rest. That it would be worth it to say hello, when we saw one another at a party or in the school halls or at a restaurant, without giving me a disdainful once-over. Plus, I reasoned, it might annoy them. With a gorgeous bag, I thought, I would not just have a sword and a shield. I would have something that they did not have, or something that they wanted, or something that they *did* have and didn't want anyone *else* to have. I imagined the Queen of the Queen Bees trying to brush by me and getting stuck in her gut with my boxy Birkin. Really, you couldn't put a price on that.

I had caught my first glimpse of an Hermès Birkin bag in Paris, in the late eighties. The bag the woman in jeans and a little *tailleur* was clutching was Perfect. It was red: not a predictable scarlet, not some insipid pinkish red. It was an insouciant, self-confidently uncommon brick red, the lipstick color you had been looking for for years and never found, the platonic ideal that drove you to buy tube after tube of not-right reds in pursuit of The One. The shape, too, was just right—just off the visual map of things you were used to, provocative in its subtle difference from a purse or a messenger bag. There were file folders in there, barely peeking out, suggesting a life of work *and* beauty. I actually followed the woman for a few blocks through the Eighth (of course it was the Eighth, the arrondissement of all things starchily, sexily French), stalking her handbag, trying to figure out what it was.

Later, I breathlessly sketched it for a friend of mine who squealed when I gave her the key/lock detail and said, "Oh, you mean a Birkin! An Hermès Birkin bag! Of course, *everyone* wants one!" She went on to extol the bag's beauty and rhapsodize over the casual yet reverent ways Frenchwomen carried their Birkins, often with their worn *Guide Rouge* inside, or a baguette poking out. It was so . . . French. And so expensive, she explained.

I sighed, feeling pained and jet-lagged as I translated the francs into dollars, sure at first that I must have made a mistake. I was a graduate student at the time, and given my budget, wanting a Birkin was about as reasonable as wanting to be the president of France.

The Hermès Birkin bag is storied, and the story of its origins is, like the *clochette* that dangles from it, inextricable from its aura, its Birkin-ness, its irresistible appeal. Legend goes that in 1981, free-spirited English actress and singer Jane Birkin—she of the decades-long romantic and artistic collaboration with Serge Gainsbourg—was boarding a plane with a straw weekend bag whose contents scattered to the floor as she tried to load it into the overhead compartment. Like a rarefied knight in shining armor, Jean-Louis Dumas, then chief executive of the world's preeminent and most exclusive leather maker, Hermès, was there to help her pick up the pieces. Thanking him, Birkin explained that she simply didn't have a bag that did the trick for her jaunts between London and Paris, and that, so the story goes, got him thinking. And, apparently, designing.

In 1984, Hermès first offered a black leather tote of remarkable craftsmanship, refinement, and tact that somehow managed to hit a few pitch-perfect bohemian notes as well. A scaled-down version of a bag Hermès originally created to hold horse saddles a hundred years before, it had history, *two* handles, and a top you could choose to leave folded back and open or buckle closed. Sure, you could hook it over your arm, but you could also just swing it in your hand. Or sling it over your shoulder—the handles (two make it feel somewhat young and free-spirited, more like a cool socialite with a career than those one-handled lady-bags-who-lunch) were just about that long. It was something between a pocketbook and a weekender in its size and its look and its very essence, chicly functional. It was the opposite of the Kelly, that other iconic bag designed by the house of Hermès specifically for Princess Grace to help hide her pregnancy. The Kelly bag is all propriety, all matronly, blushing correctness. The Birkin, in contrast, makes no excuses for being pregnant before she is married. She is the Kelly's younger, wilder, more fun sister.

That doesn't make her cheap or easy—*mais non!* From the very beginning, the Birkin was made in extremely limited quantities—only 2,500 per year. This is at least in part because making a Birkin is so labor-intensive, requiring close to fifty hours of attentive, detailed, and exacting work from start to finish. Birkins are made almost entirely by hand, by workers who must apprentice with Hermès's senior leather craftsmen for at least two years to qualify for the job. Birkins are works of art in this sense, and to shore up that notion, each Birkin is made by a single artisan who "signs" and dates his creation with a special stamp denoting the year and his initials. The Birkin's proportions are strict—whether the Birkin is of the 25-, 30-, 35-, 40-, or grandiose 55-cm variety, the ratio of length to width to height is precise, its silhouette unmistakable and beyond reproach. Only the French could marry the Enlightenment and the sexual revolution as Hermès managed to in the Birkin. It is the modern little black dress of handbags.

Today, you can get a Birkin in Blue Jean (no, it is not the color of dark denim or any denim for that matter, but a whimsical, summer-perfect summer-sky shade). Or gold. This is a "beginner's Birkin" according to those who have several, and it is not gold at all but a tawny caramel with white contrast stitching that invokes candy and makes your mouth water. There are dozens of other colors, each so vivid and unexpected that they all make even the uninitiated pine. (*"What color is that?!"* a friend who is an artist demanded of the startled owner of a fuchsia ostrich Birkin on a gray winter day. "I have never seen a pink like that before, ever!") The starting cost for a basic model—made of calf's leather rather than crocodile or ostrich skin, with gold or platinum-colored palladium hardware versus a diamond-encrusted placket and lock— is $8,000. There is a dizzying array of leathers to choose from: Togo is calf's leather, Clémence (the heaviest) is from a baby bull (*taurillon clémence*). There are Birkins made from lambskin and goatskin, too. An exotic skin—lizard or crocodile or ostrich—or custom model can set you back $150,000 or more. The waiting list, supplicants are often told, is two to three years long. In Hong Kong and Singapore, where Birkinmania has reached an all-time fever pitch owing to the sizzling economy, upscale black-market vendors do a brisk business selling brand-new, certified authentic Birkins recently purchased from Hermès. For the privilege of circumventing those four-year wait lists, there is sometimes a markup of 50 to 100 percent. "HERMÈS PARIS MADE IN FRANCE" is stamped in three perfectly spaced lines of silver or gold above the lock of every Birkin.

Men could have their sports cars, their affairs, their fifteen-thousand-bottle wine cellars, or whatever else their midlife Binkies and blankies and psychic boo-boo fixers might be. But the Birkin—the leather and the hardware and the contrast stitching and the myriad details that make it a Birkin and make it desirable, including and perhaps especially the virtual impossibility of getting it—would be mine. For all that I had lost and stood to lose still (we lose these things more slowly in Manhattan, committed as we are to looking like we're in our twenties or thirties until we're in our fifties, but we do still lose them)—taut

thighs, unwrinkled skin, fertility, the ability to experience excitement about the latest issue of *Vogue*—I would have that boxy,
structured, expensive, playful, sexy, functional bag. I was done,
I decided, with bridge-line tote bags and compromise formation
bags like the Marc by Marc Jacobs numbers that I had noticed of
late that the twentysomethings and even teen girls on the Upper
East Side toted around. I was getting on, and I wanted the real
thing, and I felt that I was finally, somehow, entitled to it. I was
middle-aged, it was true, a reality that made me choke whenever
it occurred to me. But I was still young enough, still beautiful
enough and blond enough and thin enough that a Birkin and I
could shine together. I was also old enough to afford it, and perhaps connected enough, after this much time in Manhattan, to
get it. This age, my age, was obviously the sweet spot of Birkin
acquisition, and the Birkin was now somehow both my consola-
tion prize and my right.

But of course there could be no fantasy of having a Birkin
without confronting the question of actually getting it. *How?* As
is the case with so many Manhattan "gets," asking and being re-
buffed were part of the Birkin game, as was waiting, being put on
the wait list, and being told the wait list was closed—this I knew
from friends who worked in the fashion industry and friends who
were simply fashion-obsessed. Sometimes, if you knew someone
at Hermès, I had heard, you could get a Birkin more quickly—
perhaps in six months or a year rather than three years.

The mother of my girlfriend JJ had once told us both, over
cocktails, about being in Hermès one afternoon when a nice-
enough, well-dressed-enough woman about the same age as JJ
and me walked in and announced, "I'd like a Birkin." She was
quickly informed that, in fact, there were no Birkins and that,

in fact, the wait list was currently closed. "You didn't hear me; *I would like a thirty-five-centimeter black Birkin with gold hardware*," she insisted, her voice rising, and when her request was refused again and yet again, she threw her hands up in exasperation and huffed, "Fine! I didn't want to do this, but I'm bringing my husband in here!" Seconds later she reentered with her mega-celebrity comedian husband, and was promptly ushered into the back room where Birkinbusiness is conducted. A triumph.

Far more common are the anecdotes about humiliation and rejection at the hands of the ferocious and notoriously *froid* guardians of le Birkin. Like the one about the friend of a friend who actually cried, right there in the store, when she was icily informed that the wait list was closed. She had gone in every week for *months*, she told her girlfriends, buying a belt or scarf she didn't need each time—that was a lot of scarves and belts, they murmured sympathetically—in the hopes of building up the amount of goodwill needed to prove to the salespeople that she was Birkinworthy. Or the woman who made her husband, who was traveling on business, take a side trip to a certain Asian capital city to get her a Birkin (his business trip was to *Germany*). There's the woman who was offered Kelly bags in every shape, size, and color by the Hermès staff but turned them all down in her single-minded fervor for a Birkin, only to learn later through a fashion editor friend who knew someone on the staff that she had been pegged as "difficult" and would now probably never get a Birkin.

Of course, it was humiliating and stupid to be told that a wait list was closed, like some kind of nightclub you weren't impor-tant or fabulous enough to get into. It was absurd to have to wait at a velvet rope of sorts for the privilege of plunking down at least $10,000 for a bag. I knew all that. But these hurdles were not merely an obstacle. The difficulty of this particular get, its near-impossibility, was part of the thing-in-itself, as intrinsic to the Birkin as the story of its origins and its date stamp.

Somehow, it would be worth it. I knew this the same way I knew that the Birkin came in a big orange box, festooned with brown ribbons, and that inside there was tissue paper of a very specific thickness folded just so into, I kid you not, a special little pillow for the purse to rest on. I had been in Manhattan for twenty-odd years, and I knew something else as well: that I was setting out on the kind of quest—clichéd, easy to ridicule, the apex of frivolity, really—that was likely to make me hate my town more than I ever had. It was another version of trying to get school applications or fighting for a better table at a restaurant ("Please just give me a nice table first, so we can skip the step of me complaining and you moving me. Please," I began saying to hostesses and maître d's as sweetly as I could manage toward the end of my second pregnancy, when my patience with everything, including my town's sadistic rituals concerning who sits where, had worn threadbare). I knew that my Birkin quest threatened to leave me wrung out and resentful. And maybe even disappointed, should I have the luck and fortitude to actually get what I wanted so badly after jumping through all the requisite hoops.

Even as I decided for a fact that I must have a Birkin, I felt tired and defeated just considering it. I also felt fired up and ready for the kill. Manhattan has a funny way of turning your desires inside out so that you can see their seams, what they are really made of. Here on the Upper East Side, I was learning, we organize our wants and our identities, in part, around specific rarefied gets or rather, "impossible-to-gets." A Birkin signifies many things, and one of them is the utter plaintiveness of not-having, even (especially) in a world of excess. Sure, the Birkin is something you want, but it is also the essence of the experience of wanting, with deferral and disappointment and waiting and hope sewn into its every stitch.

When you ask yourself *why* everyone in Manhattan, including you, wants a Birkin, and why there is such a fervor for the thing itself, it is easy to fall into circular logic. The answer is so self-evident: *Because I just do.* There are more-nuanced theories, of course. In a town that values its signifiers of privilege and success—obsesses over them, really—the Birkin is a megastatus symbol, perhaps the ultimate one, for women. And, not coincidentally, also for the men who can get them for us. "A wife with a Birkin is an *excellent* narcissistic extension for a successful man," Manhattan clinical psychologist Stephanie Newman mused when I asked for her thoughts. "He gets to prove how powerful and special he is—he got her this expensive, rare thing." For the one in every million women who insists that No, no, no, she doesn't want a Birkin, I can only say, give her one and see if she doesn't use it. The cachet, the social turbocharge it provides, would be too much to resist, sort of like her choosing the Hyundai over the Porsche when both sets of keys are proffered. I don't think so. You want it because it is somehow, vaguely, within reach—a stretch, but not utterly impossible. And because it is beautiful. And, it's true, because you would command a very particular, twisted form of Manhattan respect, also known as envy, from others—other women in the know, other women whose opinions you value and whose admiration you covet—with a Birkin.

It is a game among a certain set to incite the envy of other women, I was realizing as I logged my days on the Upper East Side. Much has been written about the male gaze—how it objectifies, redraws the hierarchy between men and women, renders one a looker and one the to-be-looked-at. But to live on the Upper East Side, it was dawning on me, is to see and feel the "looks" exchanged between women, or imposed upon us by one another—a gaze that is not infrequently ravenous, competitive, laser-like in its precision and intent. The gaze draws you into the game, even if you don't want to play. It is a way of defending yourself, sometimes, of propping yourself up. *Don't you give me that look*, you say with your look; *that's not nice!* Other times women use it to build themselves up by tearing another down: *Where is the flaw?* women ask with this gaze, assessing other women. Where is the imperfection in what you have—your belt, your shoes, your outfit, your hair—that will reassure me, make me feel it is not so good after all, that you are no better than I am? Birkins, lusted after and "scarce," bring out the girl-on-girl hostility, the female fascination latent in so many interactions and gazes between women in Manhattan, gazes that crisscross the sidewalk and the street and the restaurant of the moment and the charity event—at the Pierre or Cipriani—as we check out one another's shoes and other accessories, gazes laden with significance, with sumptuous, shiny, covetous, delicious *meaning* that our husbands and children are blind to. There are the covert and not-so-covert gazes as we wait for elevators in school hallways, gazes that take in an entire wardrobe in an instant, women swallowing other women whole like boa constrictors, in order to digest them and pick apart the details later: *Who is she? Why does she have one? Who's she married to? What does she do? Why her and not me?* Relations among women on the

Upper East Side are charged as they are perhaps nowhere else in the country or the world, and handbags, like cars, just might serve a lot of different functions all at once. A communication about where one stands in the inevitable hierarchy of Manhattan, a barometer of your wealth and connectedness and clout in a city where money and connections and clout are everything. A fashion statement. A security blanket, a way of self-soothing in a uniquely stressful town.

My request wouldn't surprise my husband, I knew, because I had been talking about Birkins for years. Not in the same unironic way as Other Women, I hoped, but still. "There's one!" I would tell him, pointing and squinting, as excited as a naturalist spotting a rare South American bird in Central Park in winter. If I was lucky, I would have an opportunity to size up the bag and the owner, convinced that this juxtaposition would let me know whether it was a fake. The bag, I mean.

My obsession with the Birkin faded and waned and returned over the course of two decades, periodically reactivated by stress (such as a Birkin sighting) like a dormant virus. Even now, twenty years after my first sighting, at a different, more financially comfortable point in my life, a point when I could almost justify such a crazy expenditure, getting one would require some doing. And some calling in of favors. And, horror of horrors for an antisocial writer, perhaps even some ingratiating. But first, some obsessing. That I could handle. No problem. Upper East Side mommies are experts at obsessing, after all. Whether it's terrorism, finding a summer camp, researching a child's impetigo or graphomotor issues, or downsizing from a classic nine so we can get a place in Aspen without selling the one in the Hamptons, I was learning, we obsess and obsess, spending long hours locating and then devouring the websites that abet and nourish our fixations. On our laptops and iPads, we follow our daydreams of the perfect summer vacation or stalk the shoe that will transform our wardrobes and improve our lives. My friend Candace has bookmarked seventeen real estate sites in her quest, one she readily admits she will never really pursue, to move to Bronxville. "It makes me feel better," she says with a shrug.

My obsessive quest led me inevitably to websites such as bagsnobs.com and iwantabirkin.com. I spent night after night on eBay after my son was in bed, researching Birkins—the prices, the hardware, the details that separated the Real from the fake. One night, after I had been cooped up there literally for hours, my husband came into my "office"—the former maid's room, off our kitchen—and I quickly, shamefacedly logged off a site. "What was that?" he wanted to know as my computer screen swallowed an image of a Blue Jean 35-cm Birkin. "What were you looking at?" I answered him honestly: "Sorry. It's porn." This piqued his interest, until he realized I meant *handbag* pornography.

"Well, why not?" Lily asked me as our kids played in the park one sunny day. "They're made like tanks, those Birkins. They're really one of the few truly well-made handbags left." From her perch in the fashion world, she made the whole idea of getting a Birkin sound *sensible*.

Over lunch, I spoke to Candace and we agreed, shaking our heads, running the numbers, that the Birkin cost as much as a quarter of a year's tuition at a private school, as much as a winter warm-weather vacation. It was two or even three months of maintenance. Twice as much as a table at the *Nutcracker* benefit. "Well, when you put it that way," Candace said, pushing her chopped salad around on her plate slowly, thoughtful now, her expression changing, "it's not *really* that bad . . . if you keep it forever, which you will. And you use it all the time. And you stop buying other bags. When you monetize that . . ."

My friend JJ's mother, who told us the anecdote about the celebrity's wife, had five Birkins and at least as many Kellys (or were they Kellies?) and JJ suggested she might introduce me to her salesperson at Hermès. "Just get it," she said. Even though we don't get paid much for what we do; even though you need one like you need a pair of sequined boots in the rain forest; even though it is insanely, stupidly impractical. Don't just stand there, wanting, Lily and Candace and JJ were saying. *Do* something. This might have been my strangest and most self-indulgent call to action ever.

My husband just sort of groaned when I told him. It was unlike me, really, to make a request for something expensive. It has always given me a certain sick feeling when women act as if their finances and financial well-being have nothing to do with their husbands', as if these baubles don't cost the couple as a unit. My husband knew that I was basically stand-up in this regard—when he asked what I wanted for the requisite push present when our older son was born, I requested that he put some money in my IRA, to the horror of one of my girlfriends, who'd asked for diamonds—and that counted for a lot. "I just think that I should have a Birkin bag," I explained. "I just really, really want one." Okay, my husband agreed. What color? He would get it tomorrow. I laughed—a loud, braying, mirthless, ungenerous laugh

that seemed to alarm him. Then I sighed. He *couldn't*, I explained.
I handed him a list of contacts I had written out, starting with JJ's
mother's name and cell number. "What's this?" he asked, his eyes
narrowed, squinting. "This is your dealer," I said. "Or your fence.
Or whatever. Please be nice to her. I really want this bag."

My husband would have to call JJ's mother—we'll call her
Myra—who would in turn call her Hermès salesperson—let's
call her Deirdre—who would in turn assist my husband when
he came in. But first, Myra, bless her heart, had a heart-to-heart
with Deirdre. JJ called me and reported gleefully that her mother
had told Deirdre that I was a well-known author ("Yes, I've heard
of her," Deirdre had said—here JJ and I shrieked with laughter at
the idea of someone being so polite that she would fudge having heard of a nobody like me) and that I would be a very good
customer, and that I deserved a Birkin, and that I wanted black
leather, 35 centimeters, with gold hardware. Even though Myra
thought this was a really big mistake; I should get palladium,
which, she explained, was seasonless.

This conversation completed and the groundwork laid, my
husband was notified by Myra that he could go in to meet Deirdre, which he did, and Deirdre very sweetly informed him that
she was going to do her best, she was calling Paris, and she was
trying very hard to make it happen; it just might not be by my
birthday, which was, after all, right around the corner and she
was, after all, bypassing the wait list, which was, depending on
whom you spoke with, either three years long, a bunch of BS, or
closed. The night my husband conveyed all this to me, I lay awake
in bed at 2:00 a.m., having just started out of my sleep with the
realization that I didn't even know how much this bag would
cost, exactly. "I mean, I get mine in Paris and Rome, and with the

exchange rate, I don't even know. I don't know how much they are in New York," Myra had told me when I haltingly, fumblingly asked about exact price in one of our phone conversations. "I only bought my Kellys here."

My friend Jeff Nunokawa is a professor of English literature. His specialty is the Victorian novel, and he often writes and lectures about the peculiar way Dickens, Eliot, and other Victorian novelists figure women not only as enthusiastic consumers of luxury commodities but also as luxury commodities themselves. I wondered what he would have to say about more contemporary luxury consumption by women, as exemplified by Birkingate, and about hostility and competition among women on the post-Baudelairean sidewalk. First, however, I had to explain the terms. Jeff is not one of the many friends with whom I have bonded over a love of fashion, and initially he thought I was talking about Birkenstocks. "I'm sure it really *is* a nice purse," he began gamely, once I had explained that we were talking about bags, not sandals, and explained what a Birkin bag was, and what Hermès was, and gave him a quick overview of the madness of the Birkinquest in Manhattan circa the 2010s. Then he added, diplomatically, "And I *do* get that people care about these things." He paused for a moment and then, gathering the various threads together, he asked, in a tone at once authoritative and playful, "But why women?"

Liking "nice" things, coveting them, lining up for them, getting on a wait list for them, subjecting oneself to various humiliations in order to procure them, wanting them even more because they are allegedly out of reach, scarce—we are generally quick to dismiss this as feminine folly and false consciousness, as being suckered in and "duped by fashion," Nunokawa summarized neatly. But, he suggested, we are wrong. Sure, it's crazy, and sure, when we live in New York, we sort of lose our sense of the craziness of such a quest, and it comes to seem normal. As in: women just want Birkin bags. And this ridiculous process of ingratiating oneself with a salesperson in order to get one, of obsessing and pulling strings, of hoping and waiting ("Let's call them cake lines, shall we?" Nunokawa suggested gleefully) which seems like the dumbest and most pointless thing to do—well, Why? And why women? Here Nunokawa turned to the example of a fictional character from another era, Edith Wharton's Lily Bart, deeming her "as real as it is possible to be in one sense—in her relationship to beautiful, expensive things." As Lily's quest to marry becomes increasingly urgent, propelling the narrative forward and playing with our own hopes, we realize that Lily does not just want things, Nunokawa reminded me, she wants them spectacularly and desperately because she, too, wants—she needs—to be a wanted thing.

So, too, with women in Manhattan and our Birkinquests, Nunokawa suggested. "It's not just that women—women of a certain class or social set, contemporary Lily Barts—love the fashionable commodity," he explained to me. "It's that they *are* the commodity form." These Birkin pursuers are not just deluded or dumb, he continued. They are up to something, something more than just elbowing one another out of the cake line for a bag. By chasing Birkins we're not just making ourselves into chasers of Birkin bags. "These women are reminding men, society, and themselves that they inhabit a privileged, identificatory relationship to those bags." Going after and procuring something precious and scarce, we are also trying to rejuvenate our own scarcity, to reinvigorate the sense of everyone in our society of our own value. Our proximity to a sumptuous luxury item like a Birkin is selfish, frivolous—and efficacious, Nunokawa concluded.

Whatever it was, I was going to bump this cake line.

In the end, it went down like this: my husband went on a trip to Asia, and Deirdre suggested he might more easily snatch up a Birkin there; she would make a few calls. But in Hong Kong, he got the song and dance about a three-year wait list. And in Beijing, he was told the same thing (this is how I knew, before the world economists knew it, that China had surpassed Japan to become the second-largest economy in the world). And then on the last leg of his trip, he called me late at night, and I happened to pick up, and he said, "Do you like the gold ones?" He had browbeaten a salesperson at one of the Hermès shops in Tokyo into presenting him with not one but three Birkins to choose from. I chose the gold with palladium hardware, knowing Myra would be pleased.

It was done. But that night I tossed and turned in bed. I fixated and I obsessed that Myra would feel I had somehow insulted her or compromised her standing with Deirdre by not following up and buying it in New York. Over and over I conjured a vivid and terrifying vision: JJ infuriated with me for mishandling things and creating a situation in which she would be in the middle should her *mother* feel I had broken some unspoken but important rules about the etiquette of Birkin acquisition. Or something. The next day I woke up exhausted from my ruminations, which I replayed in my head all day long and which blotted out all my other thoughts. That evening my husband returned home from his trip with jet lag, dirty laundry, and an enormous orange box. "DON'T TOUCH THAT," I barked at my son when he approached it with fascination. Under the ribbons, inside the box, under the tissue paper, on top of its pillow, inside the beige dust cover, was the bag. The placket was covered with off-white felt, lest the hardware scratch or be scratched. I peeled it away carefully, like a surgeon, to reveal the gleaming silver buckles and lock placket. And inside the fetish object there were more fetish objects: the puffy, accordion-like plastic that held the bag's shape. The little lock and keys in their leather sheath. And the rain guard. Yes, the Birkin bag comes with its own raincoat. It was lighter than I imagined. It was beautiful and simple, with masterful contrast stitching. It was 35 centimeters, and it was a sonnet. My husband laughed when he saw me get a flashlight to inspect the Birkin's interior and seams. Then I ran to the phone and ordered flowers, and a flowery thank-you note, for Myra. For all her help, and all her trouble.

You'd think I would have simply been happy to attain this Holy Grail of bags. But instead I eventually transferred my anxiety over whether I had offended Myra and JJ and Deirdre by *how* I had gotten the bag to the bag itself. For days I fretted that my Birkin, though purchased from an Hermès store, might be a fake. I researched the placement of the artisan's stamp, the stitching, and every aspect of its construction. *What if it wasn't real?* Oh, for the love of God, it's real! JJ—who hadn't been angry at all, and whose mother hadn't been angry at all, just thrilled for me, as someone's mother who was obsessed with Birkins would be— shouted at me over the phone. "You just can't accept that the search is over. You're afraid you'll feel empty now that you have what you wanted! And you feel like maybe *you're* a fraud. Maybe you don't deserve it. You do!"

If you are going to live on the Upper East Side, I was realizing, it helps to have a friend who is a psychoanalyst.

I carried my Birkin everywhere, except in the rain. Then I had to leave it home, for fear of, well, of harming it. One day, with a little time to kill before picking my son up from school, I went into a clothing store across the street. It was a rare moment of shopping for myself rather than my offspring, of shopping rather than working or fretting about work, and it felt indulgent and luxurious. The young saleswoman welcomed me and, a few minutes later, offered to put the things I had chosen in a dressing room for me. "You can leave your bag on that bench. I'll watch it for you." She smiled. "And I promise not to take it, even though I really want one." We laughed, and as she continued to eye the bag, I handed it to her and told her to try it out. She did, regarding herself from every possible angle in the store's many mirrors. It was awkward, having something she wanted, and not a little uncomfortable. To take the edge of discomfort off a bit, I responded, when she asked me if I loved my Birkin bag, that yes I did, it was a workhorse, and it was nice, but it was, after all, just a bag. And that all the hoopla around it struck me as so much hype. She smiled and cocked her head to the side as we made eye contact in the mirror. "A few days ago someone came in with a two-tone *crocodile* Birkin," she said sweetly, "and it was the chicest thing I have *ever* seen." She paused for a moment, then continued: "After seeing that, it's hard to get excited about one like yours." She extended her arm, offering me my bag back.

   A good thing, too, I thought to myself, *because you'd have to sell a LOT of cashmere sweaters to pay for one, even one like mine. If you could get anyone at Hermès to sell you one. Which I doubt.* But I didn't say any such thing. I only considered it as I paid for the clothes that I could afford and she couldn't, and contemplated how, on the Upper East Side, there are many, many ways to run a woman off the sidewalk.

CHAPTER FOUR

Manhattan Geisha

Fieldnotes

Males of many species fight, display, vocalize, and otherwise compete for the opportunity to mate with available females. This is explained by Bateman's principle, which states that the sex investing the most time and energy in producing, provisioning, and protecting offspring becomes a limiting resource over which the opposite sex will compete. In most animal populations, sex ratios are roughly equal. However, as a portion of females are perpetually removed from the pool of potential mates due to reproduction and intensive care of offspring (and pregnancy and lactation, in the case of mammals), females of many species most often become the "limiting sex."

Census data shows that among the higher-order primates of the Upper East Side, however, there are dramatic imbalances in sex ratios. Due primarily to migration from outlying regions (transfers from natal troops), reproductive females outnumber males two to one. This unique ecological circumstance has changed relations between the sexes, and relations among females, in unique and notable ways.

Males on the Upper East Side, it seems, have become what females are in other settings: choosy and coy observers of displays for their benefit. Meanwhile, extremes of ornamentation and elaborate "beautification practices"—not infrequently involving the physical mutilation and reassembling of their bodies and faces into a more "pleasing" arrangement by various "body and face shamans"—are central to the lives of the reproductive and even postreproductive females under consideration.

So are daily, highly competitive, precisely choreographed, and grueling group endurance rites. These are believed to not only purify and enhance the appeal of the female body but also magically ward off the physical effects of time and even defer mortality. Females perform these rites in their native habitat, but take them to extremes in their summer migratory setting, approximately one hundred miles to the east.

W E HAD another baby, a boy, not long after my older son started nursery school. And this time around I was more aware than ever that the standards for pregnant women and new mothers in Manhattan—particularly on the Upper East Side— were mind-boggling. Both uptown and downtown pregnancy were high-stakes, nine-month-long competitive marathons, to be sure. But there was no question that the women of the Upper East Side deserved trophies for their all-out, extreme-sport-caliber exertions when it came to gestation. All around me, women in their third trimesters teetered on stiletto heels and went to dinner parties and restaurants-of-the-moment and charity events until midnight. They wore fantastically formfitting designer maternity clothing and were assiduously, astonishingly groomed and main- tained. Just as they continued to dress and socialize as if nothing had happened, they persisted in sprinting around the reservoir and working on their abs in fitness classes. Pregnancy on the Upper East Side, it seemed, was about having the best, buffest, sleekest pregnancy possible, which meant a pregnancy in which you acted as if you weren't pregnant at all. The expectations regarding one's appearance—to be glamorous and gorgeous— were unyielding, exacting, eternal.

Compared with my gravid peers, I was a shameful slacker. I just couldn't keep up. I was gassy and itchy. I had acne. I was exhausted before I even got out of bed. In the self-care arena, I was off-roading, totally veering from the social script of uptown pregnancy. Whereas the first time around I took prenatal yoga and prenatal Pilates and prenatal everything, with this pregnancy I didn't do a lick of exercise beyond venturing out to "run" errands (waddle was more like it) or walk to my office share, where I intended to write but promptly fell asleep. I didn't think about food much at all, beyond strategizing how to keep down the Ensure my OB had insisted I drink, since I was actually losing weight from severe morning sickness. My eyes were constantly red—the blood vessels there burst from the violence of my many-times-daily vomiting. I looked like a stick who had swallowed a basketball, my husband observed. And this, I slowly realized, made me something of a lightning rod for the women around me, a projective test for their attitudes toward *their* bodies and diets. "You bitch," said one. "*I* want terrible morning sickness next time!" "Oh my God, you look *fantastic*," another enthused, entirely ignoring my gray, blemished skin and focusing on my scarecrow-like arms and legs.

My preschool-aged son, too, was something of a Rorschach for the women I spent my days with now. "Wow, he's so trim and has *such* long legs," they observed over and over as we hung out together at the edge of the playground watching our kids. Something about their tone suggested that they viewed his physiology as an achievement on my part, or his. I had never before seen adult women focus on children's bodies so intently, or extract so much meaning from them. I frankly missed my son's chubby arms and cheeks, those markers of toddlerhood that had made him so adorable. But I could swear that some of these other mothers envied me for having a skinny kid.

I found a lot of their beliefs and cultural codes strange, but in other ways, I was a lot like the UES mothers I knew. Their preoccupations and standards, like the desire for a Birkin, were rubbing off on me. My more or less unconscious adjustment process is called habituation, the simplest form of learning, in which an animal, after a period of exposure to a stimulus, stops responding and starts accommodating it. Hypervigilant, skittish prairie dogs living near humans eventually don't even bother to give alarm calls when we walk by; we start to seem like white noise to them. Deer get used to how utterly rank we smell (in Michigan I learned that sometimes before you see a deer, you can hear it give a tremendous snort, a harrumph of disgust at your vile stench, if you are upwind) and come in close to eat from our gardens. And so, surrounded by people dressed in ways I would have found confoundingly foreign just months before, I now outfitted myself a little more conservatively, a little more expensively, a little more carefully. It felt like the last surrender, a giving up of my former self. But once I gave in to it, this process of habituation, it was not unpleasant. It made my life easier, in a way, to be like a prairie dog that has stopped noticing so much, or a deer that has decided the alarming smell isn't really so alarming after all. That previous part of me, a way of responding and being, the young downtown mom with a choppy haircut and big plans, was gone. Yes, I found myself wanting smooth blond blond blonder hair, and a Birkin, and a Barbour jacket, and whimsical emerald-green velvet Charlotte Olympia flats with kitten faces on them. And I surrendered. And so it was that, as soon as I went into labor on a brilliant fall day, I decided to venture forth and get a blowout.

First I called Lily, who had just had a baby herself, a beautiful little girl named Flora, who stopped fussing whenever she lay on my husband's chest. Lily and I considered whether my latest round of contractions was some kind of false-alarm false labor, as so often happens before the big day and had been happening to me for about a week. Lily guessed it wasn't. But, as a mother of four, she was her usual calm self about timing. "It's not the *third* baby or anything. We know you always have those into your pant leg, or in the taxi. But this is the second one. Maybe go for a walk and see what happens."

I walked right to the salon, where they washed and dried my hair. I figured I could squeeze in a manicure and pedicure. After these, I considered tending to things below the belt, but my contractions were now a minute apart, so I called my husband instead.

"*What?!* We have to go!" he cried. As we cruised down the East Side to the hospital, the driver of the oversized, overpriced SUV my husband had arranged to take us there intoned, "Please miss, you are not having baby in this car! Wait!" Minutes later, with my feet up in the stirrups, I apologized to my OB for the unkempt state of things down there. He observed, while my son's head crowned, that many of his patients had Brazilian bikini waxes right before delivering, something he just couldn't understand. He mentioned that requests for elective C-sections "so things don't get stretched out down there" had skyrocketed. And that many of his patients had plastic surgeons on call so they could get tummy tucks immediately after delivering their babies. That's nuts, I thought as I gave a final push. But even as they put my newborn on my chest—he was so blond, and so big! He was so beautiful!—I wished my thighs had been hairless as I delivered him. And in spite of almost giving birth in an Escalade, I am not above admitting that, when I look at the pictures of me holding my son immediately postbirth, I am glad I got the blowout.

Nearly without exception, affluent new mothers in the West sub-ject themselves to the physical and emotional rigors of "getting their prebaby bodies back." The phrase, so vernacular and upbeat, is also disingenuous and cruel, suggesting that such a fantasy is even technically possible. Primaparas and multiparas (those who have had one or more kids) are not nulliparas (those who haven't), after all. You don't get your prebaby body back, ever, because you cannot go back to being a person who hasn't had a baby. *Because you had a baby.* The corollary to the compulsion to conduct your-self as if pregnancy doesn't slow you down one bit is the wish, afterward, to pretend that it—the whole messy matter of your abdomen and vagina and breasts and ribs having been strained to extremes you don't even want to consider— never happened. No saggy breasts or tummy rolls for us. As if this weren't unrealistic enough, we are expected, and expect to be able, to "get back to normal" within an absurdly accelerated time frame.

After the birth of each of my kids, I thought with longing of a Chinese custom that keeps a woman in bed for an entire month after she gives birth, and out of the fields or the workforce for another several months thereafter. She is attended by female rela-tives, and forbidden to exert herself in any way, so that she can focus entirely on nursing and recovery. Here, in contrast, hospitals can eject us twenty-four to forty-eight *hours* after we give birth (my mother's generation got a week). To parents in the nonindus-trialized, non-Western world, this custom seems utterly barbaric.

True to our social script, I was quickly home with a new baby. Unlike some of my conspecifics, who opted for formula because, they told me, they didn't want droopy breasts and mashed nip-ples, I committed to breast-feeding, as I had with my first son, and quickly got into a routine with our newborn. I was lucky that nursing was easy for me, as well as for my sons. I knew it conferred long-lasting benefits to the baby, but like most Manhattan moms, I was keen on breast-feeding because I had heard it helped you "get back your prepregnancy body" more quickly. It burned something like six or seven hundred calories a day, my girlfriends told me. In the end, my morning sickness had relented a bit and I managed to pack on the recommended number of pounds. So now I stuck with nursing not only for my son's sake, but also for my waistline. And then, when the baby was around five months old, I decided it was time to get back to working out.

For although my OB wisely counseled that childbirth and recovery were "nine months up and nine months down," like most of my peers, I did not feel I *had* nine months. I was in a hurry, impatient to be the old, taut me, apprehensive and preoccupied beyond reason that it would never happen. Mothers all across the country feel a version of this fear; women's magazines such as *Fit Pregnancy* and *New Mommy Workout* and stringent postpregnancy exercise DVDs and online classes attest to our collective terror. But here on the Upper East Side, the anxieties and pressures are greater. Whereas women in Nebraska and Michigan might hop on the treadmill in the basement when they can, and skip Dunkin' Donuts, and take their time with the last ten pounds, perhaps resigning themselves to all or a portion of it remaining, my tribe of mommies was another matter. Just as we had to excel at being beautifully pregnant, so, too, we had to be the most gorgeous mothers of infants, babies, toddlers, and young children that it was possible to be.

As this was the Upper East Side, the first order of business, once I had decided to exercise, was to shop. Lululemon was the brand of choice; it had eclipsed Athleta and was an intrinsic and ubiquitous part of the Upper East Side mommy uniform by the time I was ready to rumble. Skintight yet thicker than regular spandex, shockingly comfortable, with whimsical details (fun prints abounded) and smart concessions to women's actual lives, needs, and desires (pockets in places that didn't create bulk, for one), lululemon was an inescapable part of life in my neighborhood. It telegraphed, "I have time to exercise, and here's the payoff." Part of lululemon's appeal, I realized the first time I tried on their pants and a fitted jacket, was that these items weren't merely unforgivingly tight and formfitting. And they weren't merely clothing—they also functioned as a kind of girdle or exoskeleton, smoothing out bumps, holding everything up and in while they appeared to bare all. For the first year or two after lululemon hit the streets, women wore their lulu pants with longer lulu tops or jackets to cover the derriere and loin areas. Or tied long-sleeved lulu shirts around their waists. And then came a moment when women collectively declared, "I have a crotch. And a bottom. Deal with it." Habituation was swift. What had at first looked outrageously exhibitionistic—exposing the ventral and dorsal sides of a female *Homo sapiens* between her waist and pubis—quickly became no big deal. What choice did men have but to become desensitized by the barrage of lululemon-clad nether regions, the nearly constant, inescapable exposure?

And so I came to own lots and lots of lululemon. I bought fitted lulu jackets and fitted lulu pants. I bought fitted cap-sleeved tops with plunging necklines and vibrant-hued, fitted tanks. I bought snug lululemon bras specially designed to fit under the tops and tanks. There were even special lululemon thongs and underwear designed of microfibers to be "invisible"—with edges that faded into nothing, so you wouldn't have VPL. There was a fitter at lululemon, who put you up on a box in front of a three-way mirror like a regular tailor does, and talked to you seriously about which shoes you would be wearing and how long the pants should be and how large the hem should be, as if they were real trousers and you were a businessman at Brooks Brothers. Well, it *was* a business, I would soon learn, this "working" out, and a serious one at that.

Thoroughly outfitted, I looked into fitness options, and quickly learned that there had been a sea change not only in exercise togs but also in exercise *practices* since the births of my two children. As I cluelessly did Pilates and yoga and sprinted in the park when I could, all around me, members of the tribe I studied had been splintering into subtribes, each pledging its allegiance to one of two tremendously popular cults: a ballet-barre class called Physique 57, or a spin class called SoulCycle. *How ridiculous*, I thought when my friend Amy sent me a Youtube video of women at SoulCycle sitting on their stationary bikes, their lower halves whipping round and round at lightning speed while their upper halves did various yoga poses. I imagined how perplexed archeologists of the future would be by such an artifact ("They move, yet they make no progress"). *Give me a break*, I sighed internally when another friend described her Physique 57 ballet-barre class as we sat at a café, earnestly intoning that it had changed her body in a mere six 57-minute sessions. She sounded like an infomercial. Then she lifted her shirt to show me her abs, and I nearly spat out my green tea. She was *cut*. After less than six hours. I was suddenly game.

Reviewing the company's website, I learned about their state-of-the-art studios, mirrored affairs in upscale locales tricked out with special props—ballet barres of different heights, balls for squeezing and toning, rubber strips for stretching and ab work, mats and pillows, carpeting that cushioned during floor work. I read the Physique 57 "story": it was founded by two former Lotte Berk disciples after that wildly popular, ballet-style workout guru threw in the towel at her Hamptons studio. I watched the video testimonials by those who worshipped at the Physique 57 temple—women who ran the gamut from absolutely torn to zaftig/fit. Many became tearful describing their transformation. The promise was that I would see changes in my body within eight sessions, each of which was less than an hour, thus saving me 180 seconds every time I went.

Attired in lululemon, I arrived at a studio not far from home one spring morning. The space was airy and clean, with high ceilings and white walls and wood floors in some rooms, blue carpeting in others. The pretty young woman at the front desk who checked me in noted it was my first class, and gave me a release to sign. Then she chirped, "Do you have your *socks*?" Huh? She meant grippy socks, I learned, black or gray anklets with a small 57 embroidered at the back, the bottom sprinkled with light blue rubberized dots intended to prevent me from slipping on the carpet. I bought a pair immediately and, pulling them on, thought of the cult members who had committed suicide in the 1990s while wearing identical Nike sneakers. "You'll probably want a bottle of water," the receptionist observed helpfully, handing it over and telling me she'd put the charge on my bill. As at a private club, I had a chit.

I was relieved to see my friend Monica, an überfit, harddriving hedge-fund manager and mother of three, stretching by a mirror. "I didn't know you did Physique!" she enthused as we kissed each other hello. "Give me that." She dropped my water bottle at a three-foot-wide "spot" at the ballet barre in front of the mirrored wall. Then she grabbed two five-pound weights for me, setting them next to hers on the carpeted floor. "You've got to stake out your real estate before everybody gets here," she explained. Great; I had a guide. The room filled up all around us as we chatted, the women packed in tightly, all strangely serious and silent, stretching and staring into the mirror in front of them. Without exception, they wore black lululemon pants, either full or capri length, and racerback lulu tanks and black Physique 57 grippy socks. Most looked incredibly fit, with lean triceps and flat stomachs and tight bottoms that seemed to defy gravity. There were no men in the class, with the exception of a tall, dark vision, muscled and sleek, wearing a headset. "Good morning, ladies," he purred. "Let's get those heart rates *up!*" His voice blared through the strategically placed speakers in the corners of the room, and we snapped to attention.

A Beyoncé track pounded forth, and we were exorted to step high, step high, lift opposite knee to opposite arm, twist, twist. Thus began a workout so rigorous, so difficult, so comprehensive, and so painful that at several points I feared I might vomit. We worked every imaginable muscle in our arms with our weights while simultaneously doing squats and lunges and dips with our legs. We did push-up after push-up. "When you get to that point of fatigue, I want you to *overcome,*" the instructor intoned, as if this were our own civil rights movement. That was just the ten-minute *warm-up.* We now returned our weights to their wire baskets on the shelves in the corner of the room. I was taken aback at the aggression with which the women, most in their thirties and forties, flung them, and the speed with which they then raced over to their spots at the barre. Somehow everyone knew which identical bottle of water and small white towel was hers. *How*? "Over here," Monica whispered, and I took the spot next to her.

To my bewilderment, the instructor requested that we "take a small upright V position at the barre and begin with a simple pulse." I copied my friend, thinking I understood—we were doing mini pliés, ballet-style. No problem; I had done these my entire ballet-practicing girlhood. But after a hundred of them, I thought my legs would fall off. And we were just beginning. We lifted one leg off the floor, and then the other, in a precise sequence that worked every single leg muscle to the point of utter exhaustion and indescribable, burning pain. I looked around at the other women, trying to catch the eye of someone else, as one does in such dire but ultimately funny circumstances, when others typically raise an eyebrow or smile to communicate, "You're not alone!"

Nothing. Not a smile in the room. Not a word. The women averted their gazes, inhabiting their own split-off, atomized private zones of achievement and torment. What was this, the *subway*? I had never experienced a workout so grueling in a room so devoid of jokey, friendly camaraderie. Or one so silent. There were no whoops or groans or *Oh my Gods* or vocalizations of any kind. It was a lot like the halls of my son's nursery school—you could be forgiven for suspecting you didn't even exist, such was the unfriendly unrelatedness and sense of disconnection that prevailed in the tightly packed room. Occasionally the instructor would make a funny remark about one of us to break the ice, or say an encouraging word, or offer a correction. He communicated for everyone, it seemed, and had the only personality in the room.

While I had to stop repeatedly, my friend went on and on, not missing a single beat or plié or squat. This was an overachiever's workout. She was as focused on it, I realized, watching her out of the corner of my eye, as she was on her deals at work or the process of getting her kids into a good school. Like a machine, she was careful, precise, and steady. Meanwhile, everyone around us, dressed in identical uniforms, did all the identical moves in perfectly synchronized, identical harmony. Arms raised. Arms down. Punch. Pull. Then came stranger commands, in a language everyone around me understood.

"Hover! You're wearing kitten heels," the teacher barked. Then: "Put on your highest stilettos!" and "Wear a pencil skirt and sit at your desk in a swivel chair"—meaning bend at the knees, pivot, and face the barre at an angle. Next came "water-ski," a command that apparently meant "Get close to the barre, lean back with your entire weight while holding on with your spent, aching arms, and thrust your pelvis up to the ceiling." We did this over and over, until our legs shook and we forgot that the movement couldn't be more sexual, or more painful. Now that thigh work and seat work were over—They were? Thank *God*, because my ass had never burned like this before—it was time for abdominal work. This might have more aptly been called vaginal display. We sat with our backs to the wall, hefted our legs up above our heads, pushed our hands up into the barre above us, and pulled our legs, held in a diamond shape, into the barre again and again. I was glad there were no men in the class as I tried not to stare at the dozens of pudenda straining against lululemon spandex all around me. I figured everyone else must find this as odd as I did, but once again, there were no smiles, no eye contact, no interaction of any sort. We worked every conceivable muscle in our abdomens, slicing to the side, pulling to the sky, bicycling our knees to the opposite elbows, until I wanted to howl with pain.

Afterward, we lay on our backs on our mats, panting, and thrust our pelvises upward to the strains of Mavin Gaye's "Let's Get It On." I thought I might faint—from the physical agony and the indescribable strangeness of this disconnected group-sex experience. When it was over, I gasped good-bye to my friend and hobbled home. I took a hot bath with Epsom salts, nursed the baby, and fell asleep with him in bed. For three days, I could not walk up and down stairs, or even walk, without considerable pain. But when I recovered, I went straight back to the class. I felt driven and compelled—to master the movements, to chase the perfect body for 57 minutes, to put everything else out of my mind, to block out the world. I was hooked. I would follow.

For a while I went every other day. Then I bumped it up to every day, at which point I noticed that there were women who asked each other, "Are you staying for the next class?" They were doing this *twice* a day, some of them. The grueling pursuit of the perfect body was, it occurred to me, an endurance rite. Every class was a mini-initiation ceremony, a shortened, everyday version of the once-in-a-lifetime Sunrise Dance that Apache girls undertake to mark their transition to womanhood. For four entire days, nonstop, the menstruating girl dances a specific and meticulous choreography. She wears special garments and pigments to mark the sacredness and specificity of this moment in time. In so doing she demonstrates her commitment to her people, her tribe, and her gender. At the end she is exhausted—and initiated. She is utterly changed after the dance, a confirmed member of Apache womanhood. And the women of Physique? They proved, class after punishing class, that they had the strength, time, resources, and energy to commit to their transformations.

And they were, in fact, a recognizable tribe. Most had an unmistakably hardened body type, an easily recognizable (to an insider) dancer-like posture, and a deliberate, precise gait and physical aspect that reminded me of ballerinas I had known. Indeed, in an "only in Manhattan" development, I often found myself standing next to ABT or New York City Ballet ballerinas and Rockettes during my Physique 57 workouts. They were tall and stunningly supple and sometimes, without even realizing it, I strove to do just as they did—to kick as high, to reach as far, to turn out as beautifully. The bar was so punishingly high at the barre. We expected ourselves to perform as well as professionals because our physical selves, like our motherhood, had become professionalized. Beyond an identity, it was a calling, a vocation, something to excel at.

My body did, in fact, change quite quickly and remarkably. Sure, I still peed when I coughed. But from the outside, I was altered and, by Manhattan standards, "improved." My arms were sinewy and defined—a gay male friend remarked at lunch, when I wore a sleeveless blouse, "Nice guns!" My tummy was not just flatter—it was taut, with muscular shadows and indentations. For once in my life, I wasn't self-conscious about my thighs. And my bottom was, if I did say so myself, newly pert.

My husband was surprised and pleased. I had always been relatively thin and blessed with a good metabolism, so I didn't have to worry about my figure a lot. But now I had more energy during the day, and slept better at night. As a result I was in a better mood, and much better company than I had been in the immediate postbaby haze. Given all this, I became a proselytizer, trying to convert as many friends as I could, which was not hard to do when they saw and heard about all the benefits I had reaped. With a few smiling, happy girlfriends in the classroom with me to blot out all the unfriendly self-absorption, this exercise routine was, for my thirty-five dollars per session, perfect.

We decided to rent a house out of the city for the summer, in the Hamptons. I would go out for the whole summer to be with the kids and write, courtesy of a sitter who would come daily to lend a hand, and my husband would spend weekends with us there, working during the week in the city. "The Hamptons" is a beachy area at the far eastern tip of Long Island—but it is a mythical place, too, and for many, a dream. While plenty of perfectly ordinary people live there year round or visit, there is enough superaffluence on the East End that the standards of wealth are utterly skewed. Twenty-million-dollar (and up) waterfront mansions with private screening rooms, five-thousand-bottle wine cellars, helipads, six-car garages, private Pilates studios, and even private synagogues are not so unusual. Not a few of my older son's school chums' families had such "weekend/summer" places. Our Hamptons rental was, in comparison, bare-bones modest: a three-bedroom affair with a pool and a shady backyard in a leafy suburban enclave with a community bay beach. I couldn't have been happier that first day as my older son rode his bike along the quiet street while I followed behind with the baby, who craned his neck from his stroller, mouth agape. He was hearing birds for the first time. Adding to the idyllic aspect of this summer that unspooled before us, for me, was the knowledge that there was a Physique 57 studio within striking distance. Driving rather than walking to class would be a fun excursion every other day or so, I figured.

The next morning I headed off to class—and an unexpected shock. I showed up a good fifteen minutes early, but the parking lot was already jammed. As I rolled along looking for a space on the gravelly hill leading up to the studio, a woman peeled around the corner in a black Maserati, swinging into my half of the road and nearly broadsiding me. We both slammed on the brakes and then she flipped me off, revved her engine, and roared by. A blonde in a black Range Rover behind me took umbrage at my shocked, split-second pause and leaned on her horn, yelling, "Come on. *Move already!*" A woman wearing a vivid purple tank top in a red Porsche 911 convertible raised her hands in exasperation, shaking them near her face, which was twisted into a rictus of rage, as I pulled into a spot—who knew what *her* beef was.

Rattled and hustling to make my way into the studio, I found a space on the floor and was quickly surrounded—by the woman from the black Maserati, the woman from the black Range Rover, and the woman from the red Porsche. What on earth, I wondered, made them feel they could be so hostile toward the very people they knew were likely to exercise *right next to them* for an hour? Maybe, I hypothesized, it was the fact that once they arrived, they were so self-absorbed, so focused on perfecting their bodies, that others *literally did not exist*. Now, while we huffed and puffed and pretended no one else was there, I noticed that I was also surrounded by big, enhanced breasts. And supersculpted cheekbones. And big, round faces, taut with filler. The Hamptons, it seems, was ground zero for a hyperambitious, hypercompetitive culture of body display and forever-young faces. While women on the Upper East Side wanted to look buff, those who flocked to the Hamptons wanted to look buff *in bikinis* while sur-rounded by the twentysomething models and fitness instructors who came here every summer to party and find rich boyfriends. Now the bar was so high, I could no longer see it, let alone hope to reach it. But my peers were not giving up so easily. Aging, like a bad birthday, was unfortunate, a lousy break—and something to be overcome with effort, commitment, and zeal.

Another thing that piqued my interest at the Hamptons Physique 57 outpost was that it shared physical space with SoulCycle. Both outfits had their studios in a converted barn on Butter Lane in Bridgehampton. Now that I was fighting them for park-ing spots, I began to pay closer attention to this other subtribe. From what I could tell, they were just like us in their intensity, commitment, and strong identification with their clan. And, sure, we all wore the same tight exercise pants, sometimes with lines crisscrossing the derriere, drawing attention to our bottoms in a way that put me in mind of the bright pink estrus displays of nonhuman female primates. "Look at me! I'm in heat!" our spandex-encased, highlighted bottoms seemed to scream. But the similarities ended there. For one thing, the SoulCyclers were clubbier, if that was possible, because they were chummier—with *one another*. But not with anyone else. I learned this the hard way when I said hello to a group of SoulCycle moms I thought I recognized from home—and was roundly ignored.

Their tribal allegiance also extended to their uniforms, which bonded them together while setting them apart from us. While we were wannabe ballerinas, they were wannabe biker chicks, rich mommies who, improbably and astonishingly enough, dressed like gangsters. The first time I saw a woman sporting a red handkerchief folded and tied LA-gangland-style around her head and a pair of tight exercise pants that said POSSE down the leg, I wanted to sidle up to her and whisper, "I saw you at Margie Levine's daughter's bat mitzvah at Temple Emanu-El last month. You are so *not* a Blood or a Crip!"

It wasn't just what they wore or how they acted that set the SoulCyclers apart from us Physiquers. It was what they did. They bought bikes in the studio or studios of their choice, at up to $8,000 per year for one in the front row. In class, they yelled and groaned and shouted with abandon as they spun to deafening, pounding music. They sweated. They swore. For all I knew, they farted. They let it all go, getting in touch with their ecstatic inner fabulous gangster stationary bike rider. One woman who did both classes explained to me that while SoulCycle was a sweaty nightclub/hot-yoga-class mash-up (they turned the lights out in the room and spun by the light of a candle), Physique 57 was an uptight girls' school.

The sense that they are wilder and more fun and cooler, the Birkin to our Kelly, is clear in one of the most widely told stories about SoulCycle. Legend has it that a mother at my son's exclusive nursery school, married to a billionaire financier and notorious womanizer, discovered her true self at SoulCycle. Miserable in her marriage, it was said, she took up the spin, fell for her female instructor, left her husband, and lived with and cycled next to her Soul Mate at the front of the class at the East Side studio happily ever after. That story says it all. They were wild and brash and experimental, and we were straitlaced and risk averse. They took chances, and let their freak flags fly, while we took careful sips from our BPA-free water bottles. They were lesbians and we were straight. Or, they were butches on stationary Harleys, and we were femmes in kitten heels.

I won't lie—I thought the SoulCyclers were a little too *too*. The Queen of the Queen Bees was a SoulCycler, and that alone would have clinched it for me. But, having lived downtown for years, I must admit I also snickered internally at my sense (which could have been entirely wrong) that many of the SoulCycle mommies seemed to believe exercise could make them not just fitter but also *cooler* and *edgier*. Give me a break, I thought when they hooted like wannabe subversive rappers and called one another "thug." They reminded me of teenaged suburban girls piling on the black leather and taking Metro-North or the Long Island Rail Road or the PATH into the city for the evening, in a bid to be tougher and more countercultural than they were. *I'd rather be mistaken for a prissy matron,* I thought when I saw them fist-bumping outside class, *than try too hard. So go ahead and misunderstand and underestimate me.* It's true: in my Physique 57 loyalty, I had kind of gone around the bend.

But however you look at Physique 57 and SoulCycle—two very different versions of exercise and "female-ness" available to the tribe I studied—both are a lot of work. And both confer an *identity*, a fantasy that being there doesn't just elevate your heart rate and make you fitter but actually changes who you are. I could not stop thinking, that summer, of the girls who apprenticed as geishas in pre-WWII Japan. Isolated, rigidly hierarchical, and punitively demanding, the *okiya* where they were trained by older geishas was an entirely separate world, one with its own rules, beliefs, and codes of beauty and conduct. It took years of hard work and assiduous, dedicated study to master the effortless-seeming, highly choreographed rites and rituals of geisha-dom, to learn to be beautiful in "the geisha way." But after this process, each girl was transformed from an ordinary person into a "flower." She was the most desirable of all things to men, a flawless hostess and ideal companion, an incarnation of the most lauded cultural ideal of womanhood. And so she earned the admiration of an entire society.

All this working out, all this zealous, dedicated striving to be a particular kind of fabulous, fit, and chic Manhattan Geisha with children, all this identity and ambition tied up in your exercise practice, would have been unfathomable to my mother and her generation. She and her peers dieted. After having babies, they survived on black coffee and Special K with skim milk, cantaloupe, melba toast, and low-fat cottage cheese for a period of weeks or months. Later in life they did fast walking, or perhaps they tried jogging. But mostly, they watched their weight by watching what they ate. For them, it was hard to be hip over age thirty. They were given, and gave themselves, permission to let themselves go a little bit at a certain point. Sure, they went out and had fun. But they were tired, and they usually didn't have full-time or even part-time nannies, owing to economics and ideology, and many of them looked like it. By the time they were in their midthirties, they might even have let their hair go gray.

Nothing could be more foreign to the tribe I studied and lived among. Not for them the giving up. Ever. Not for them the languid, passive not-eating of the past. Theirs was an active and engaged quest for thinness, one predicated on always *doing*. Like geishas learning the arduous tea ceremony or the rules of sophisticated conversation, the women all around me were willing to practically kill themselves in their quests to look as though they had the effortlessly perfect, graceful bodies of twentysomething nulliparas. As for food, fat free and low cal was pathetically passé. It had to be organic, biodynamic, detoxifying, and antioxidant-rich. It had to work as hard for them as they worked on their bodies, or they would just skip it. No one knows repeated rejection more intimately than a server proffering canapés at an Upper East Side or East End cocktail party. His life *is No. No thank you. Not for me. No. No thanks. Nope.*

Why? What was the point of all this effort, this endless fighting and trying and depriving and especially all this working on and working at our selves? After all, the men on the Upper East Side and in the East End didn't really bother to flirt, or hold doors open, or look at you the way men did in Rome or Paris or anywhere else in the world. In fact, the extremely successful men of the Upper East Side and the Hamptons always seemed a little distracted and bored, because they were—by the endless smorgasbord of stunning women all around them, all the time, preening and primping for their benefit. More than one European girlfriend remarked to me that men here seemed always to be looking beyond you, to see if there was a woman who was better or prettier or more important than you at the party or in the room. That was part of the reason we tried so hard, I suspected. The mixed-up numbers, the glut of beautiful young and young-looking-for-their-age women everywhere you looked, had changed everything about how men and women related in my world. Ratcheting up the display of their bodies, recourting their husbands and attracting the glances of other men was, conceivably, an attempt to cut through all the noise and make an impression on men who were utterly habituated to physical beauty.

And yet, this explanation failed to account for one of the most remarkable social realities of summer life on the East End. Like the Physique 57 and SoulCycle classes themselves, the whole place was astonishingly and comprehensively sex-segregated.

Women came out in June, the second school let out, to set up house with the kids and the nannies. Husbands went back and forth on the weekends, but wives ran the show during the week. Everywhere you looked in the Hamptons, as far as the eye could see, there were women, women, women. Even when the men were there, the women of the tribe I studied often eschewed their company in favor of a girls' night out or an all-women's evening trunk show or a nighttime charity purse auction to benefit a school or battered-women's shelter. At dinner parties I went to, it was not unusual for men and women to sit at separate tables, even tables *in different rooms*. In spite of all the hot bodies artfully displayed, there was not a lot of sexiness in the air. In fact, there was a remarkable absence of it. "Somebody had *better* flirt with me," I used to say to my husband before we headed out for the night in Manhattan or the Hamptons. I was stunned by the lack of playful interactions between men and women. What, I wondered, was the point of life and having a body you worked on like crazy, if you didn't have fun flirting? Utterly unlike geishas, the women I studied gave the impression that they were somehow above things like flirting. Like geishas, however, they were above sex. Sure, they had babies, so we knew they had *had* sex. But their bodies, put through such rigorous paces, tended to so meticulously, turned out so carefully, were purified and not for earthly pursuits.

In fact, the exercise and careful attention to dress seemed to take the place of sex in fundamental ways. Women were too tired, too stressed, too irritated for sex in Manhattan, they all seemed to agree when we talked about it over dinner or drinks. And once out here, removed from the stressors of the city, buffered by the beach and lovely weather, their kids in camp all day or even at sleepaway camp for weeks, rested and relatively happy, they were removed from men. The whole place put me in mind of a menstrual hut, and in fact we women all spent so much time together all summer long that our periods frequently synchronized. My identification with the tribe deepened with every exercise class and trip to the juice bar after, with every ladies' luncheon and evening "event." Compared with our girlfriends, our husbands were unfamiliar to us at summer's end.

This, I learned, was their code. They strove equally to be beautiful for the men who were not there and for the women who *were*. They did it to bond with their fellow tribe members, but also to measure up to, and to take the measure of, others, day by day, evening by evening, event by event, class by class. They were like stunning red male cardinals, or breathtaking male peacocks, feathers spread, ready, always, to be seen. A beautiful, fat-free body and a forever-young face were prestigious "gets," to be sure. But they were also requisite uniforms, a corporeal version of the grippy socks or handkerchief headbands women wore to class or the paddleboards they carted in the back of their Range Rovers. My body wasn't exactly my own, it seemed to me at summer's end. It belonged to the tribe, too. It was for working on and working at and improving, tirelessly, ceaselessly, endlessly, as hard as I could, for as long as I could stand it.

CHAPTER FIVE

A Girls' Night In

Fieldnotes

The natives seem to have accepted me. After many months of my observing their tribal ways, countless attempts to mimic and participate in their rites and rituals, and numerous overtures of friendship on my part, the hazing process may have ended. I have been invited to a gathering of high-ranking females at the dwelling hut of a wealthy and powerful chieftain and his wife.

Most tribal events are comprehensively sex-segregated. Events inside and outside one's personal dwelling appear to be opportunities for females to bond; build coalitions via social inclusion, social exclusion, and gossip; and reaffirm their places and the places of others within the dominance hierarchy. In these contexts, self-presentation—including adornment of the body with particular textiles and of the face with specific pigments and enhancements—is of utmost importance.

T HE INVITATION came by email. "I don't know if you got my voice mail on your cell," the mom from my son's class wrote, "but I haven't heard from you. I'd love to have you join for dinner next Thursday night at my place. Some fun girlfriends. LMK, Rebecca."

Oops. No, I hadn't heard her message; all my friends knew I rarely used my cell for anything but texting and email. But I still felt anxious and remiss, like a bad guest already, as I puzzled over what "LMK" might mean ("Let me know!" a friend explained later, surprised I didn't already K) and dialed Rebecca's number. After leaving a message apologizing for not responding sooner and saying I'd love to attend, I sent her an email, too. How should I sign off? I wondered. "Xx"? No, Rebecca hadn't, so I wouldn't presume to.

It wasn't the first time I'd sent an email to Rebecca, a beautiful, dark-haired mother of four whose husband was one of the most successful financiers in the city. But it was the first time I'd received one. Previously, my email correspondence with her had been notably one-sided; obliging my little son's requests, I sent friendly suggestions that our sons might play and had never gotten a response. Sometimes I was able to flag her down in the hallway to set something up for our kids, particularly after she saw me chatting with Alpha Dad, who had lifted my status and my son's with his attentions. And, as I ran into Rebecca around the city at exercise class and at Michael's—a midtown restaurant I thought of as the campfire of the tribe I studied—and in other

131

clubby contexts that suggested we might have something in common (both of us shopping for clutches at Bergdorf Goodman for
the same event one day; encounters at a few fund-raisers), she
became friendlier.

When word of my book project got out ("I'm studying what
it's like to be a mother on the Upper East Side," I explained to
anyone who asked), Rebecca and a number of other mothers had
become decidedly more open and interested in saying hello and
chatting. Some even suggested we have lunch or coffee to discuss their take on how one lived and mothered here and what
it all meant. They weren't all warm or friendly—perhaps some
didn't trust me, in spite of my assurances that I wasn't writing a
tell-all or a satire but a memoir of my own experience, inflected
by sociology and anthropology and a sense of humor, too—but
many were. They wanted to talk about more than what we usually chatted about in the hallways—what we were wearing and
where we were going on vacation. Some of them told me stories about rough patches in their marriages, or about growing up
poor, or about feeling on the outside ("I'm from San Francisco.
To a lot of these people, that's sort of like I'm from Mars. They'll
never really accept me"). I had more in common with them than
I expected. Away from the school hallways and the luncheons and
the galas, they were approachable and comfortable. As one told
me, "I think the issue is that a lot of these high-achieving, harddriving, highly competitive mommies and daddies can be perfectly nice one-on-one. But something about the group dynamic
makes some of them awful."

It was nice to see a new friendly face or two at drop-off; in
spite of the bump in rank Alpha Dad had given me and my son,
those school hallways, jammed with steely-eyed alpha mom-

mies in heels, could still feel daunting. My downtown life and connections continued to ebb as I poured more energy into caring for our children and my work, so having friendly relationships with the women at my older son's school and my younger son's playgroup, a social life that paralleled my children's, felt at once efficient and utterly necessary. Moreover, in the status- and hierarchy-obsessed tribe I was studying, having Rebecca invite me to her apartment was something like an endorsement, a grown-up version of being asked to sit at the lunch table with the cool kids. Part of me knew it was ridiculous to care, but another part of me—the one that had worked hard to understand this group of women, get some playdates for my little boys, and make a friend or two myself—was gratified to be invited in by a gatekeeper as influential as Rebecca. And if these women wanted to explain their world to me, as I was hoping they might at Rebecca's, all the better. I just prayed the Queen of the Queen Bees would not be there. I had my limits.

"What are you going to wear?" Candace asked me over lunch a few days later. She was a fluent interpreter of our town's cultural codes. "I have a doctor's appointment on the East Side later; that's why I bumped it up," she had explained as we sat down and she noticed me noticing her Chanel jacket and bouncy blowout.

"No idea," I admitted, explaining that I couldn't ask any moms at school or playgroup, since I didn't know who was invited to Rebecca's and who wasn't. Candace agreed, nodding as she sipped her iced tea, taking in the scope and delicate nature of the task at hand. "Dress to fit in, not to stand out," she suggested. "You want to let the hostess shine, right? Like at a wedding."

"Actually, it's sort of a moms' night *in*," I mused. "No husbands. So it will probably be a little more casual."

Candace looked dubious. She had listened dutifully and sympathetically for months now to my stories about the incredible over-the-topness of my new tribe's outfits and attitudes. Something of a socialite herself—"but in quotation marks," as she always said—she knew these women and their ways firsthand, too, from nights out at charity events and restaurants, and from luncheons for causes. Having grown up in California and married a native New Yorker whose parents were fixtures on the social circuit a generation earlier, Candace viewed the world I studied with irony and humor, and was an outsider/insider after my own heart, a natural anthropologist. "It's *not* going to be casual," she pronounced flatly.

She was right, I realized, about "low-key" being a foreign concept in this world. The perfect bodies honed from hours at Physique 57 or Soul Cycle would be complemented by high-caliber wardrobes and airbrushed-looking faces and perfect but never fussy hair, whether men were present or not. Everyone, it seemed, was forever ready for the close-up, prepared for the photo op, with never a wrinkle or a wisp out of place. This "always beautiful"-ness wasn't the same as natural beauty—it was natural, effortless beauty's polar opposite. The Upper East Side women I knew worked as hard at looking perfect on the playground as they did at the Playground Partners Luncheon, and made no secret of it. This commitment, this unwavering determination to leave nothing to chance when it came to their faces and wardrobes, this *studied-ness*, was as much a part of their daily uniforms as were their expensive flats and cross-body bags. Indeed, they were so prepped and primed that some days I expected there to be a "step and repeat"—an area where one stood, like an actual celebrity, to be photographed—outside the playgroups, the schools, the coffee shops around them, the $5,000 birthday parties for five-year-olds, and anywhere else the tribe gathered.

Looking perpetually photo ready cost them significant time and not a little bit of anxiety—this I knew from getting myself together most mornings, having realized early on that I was the only person showing up for drop-off with a scrunchie in my hair and lines from the sheets still pressed into my face. I started to get a weekly blowout, upped my sunblock to tinted moisturizer, and added pinkish lip balm to the mix. Even jogging clothes should look nice and flattering and yes, fashion forward, it seemed. On days I couldn't jump into my running togs because of a meeting after drop-off, I found myself mulling over the right look, snapping at my husband that I didn't have *time* to get our son ready for school—I had to get *myself* ready. I knew how absurd this was as the words came out of my mouth, yet I was swept along by the cultural tide of high expectations, the hot and cold running Prada, the flawless faces, and the dazzling daily displays all around me. All before 9:00 a.m.

That these women basically had several "uniforms" made the daily task of getting dressed a little easier. Other than lululemon for drop-off and playgroup, the Upper East Side clothing lexicon was remarkably consistent, with minimal and very subtle variation, if any. For starters, there was the bag. Favorite brands and styles were Céline (Luggage Bag, Nano Luggage Bag, or Trapeze Bag); Chanel (large Boy Bag); and Hermès (Evelyn, small Jypsière, or Kelly worn cross body; Garden Party Tote in spring and early fall; holy-grail Birkin 30- or 35-cm in black, Blue Jean, or gold). The Valentino rockstud bag is beautiful and fashion forward, but no one in the tribe I studied and hung out with had one. It was not comme il faut; it was not done.

Ballet flats were popular in months of little or no precipitation—Lanvin and Chanel and Chloé were favored, especially by tall women. Lanvin wedges and Isabel Marant wedge sneakers were popular choices for "low-key" drop-off days, when moms didn't have something to rush off to immediately, because these women were always, as far as I could tell, looking for a height advantage, a literal leg up on everyone else. Sky-high platforms and stilettos with bright-red lacquered soles said, "I'm going somewhere—and I'm not taking the subway." There were boots in fall and winter and into spring, of course—high, teetering black boots of softest leather and suede by Manolo Blahnik and Christian Louboutin and Jimmy Choo, some of them open-toed, and fur-lined biker boots by Brunello Cucinelli. Skinny jeans and leather leggings were popular on casual days. On rainy days these were topped with classic trench coats (always with some update that kept one perpetually shopping, such as leather arms or a laser-cut lace hem), and accessorized with wildly colorful Pucci rain boots and whimsical Chanel ones with signature camellia flowers affixed. In winter, the mommies donned licorice-black, shiny Moncler down puffers. Fur vests were so popular with haute moms that a friend jokingly suggested there should be a photo essay about them in all Upper East Side school newsletters. And on the coldest days, there were more furs—sumptuous beaver and glossy black sable and indescribably soft (I knew from brushing against it with my ungloved hand in the jammed elevator) chinchilla coats. Lustrous and astonishing to behold, they cost more than my first book advance, I was sure, but were worn with the kind of casual aplomb usually associated with a jean jacket.

And on days when there was a charity or cause breakfast of some type after drop-off or Mommy & Me, it was all-out, full-throttle, dressed-up mayhem. There were simple but stunning long-sleeved leather dresses by The Row, and fun, bright, young Chanel jackets with fringe and fringed Chanel dresses underneath, and floral Givenchy ensembles accessorized with intricate lace-up heels, and "fit-and-flare" Alexander McQueen numbers that showed off toned legs and flat tummies. There were snakeskin leggings and paper-thin leather jackets and delicious, cream-colored, demure silk blouses to counterbalance their edginess. There was encrusted, embellished everything. Stunned by the bright-fuchsia, bejeweled jacket a tall blond mother of three wore as she swept through the halls for drop-off one morning, I googled it in my office later—and learned that its price tag was over $7,000.

But it wasn't just about being able to pay. There was a premium placed, among a certain rarefied set of moms within the already rarefied Upper East Side setting, on being first. I learned this when a fashion-forward mother of two showed up one February morning in a white cotton dress with what looked like gold leaf on the front, and studded, neon-green slingbacks. She was shivering, but she had crossed the finish line before anyone else. And now the rest of us, if we should wear this particular dress, would be merely imitating *her*. This happened in early fall, too—women decked out in their autumnal finery, light wools and new boots and the latest Chanel jacket in spite of the warmth that still hung in the air. Plenty of women in Manhattan love fashion. But this was something else again, this showing up everybody else by wearing it first, this joyless-seeming race to have it before others did, and display it best.

Intrasexual competition—competing with other species members of your own sex—is a widespread evolutionary selection pressure. For many years, primatologists and biologists focused almost exclusively on *male* intrasexual competition, probably because it was so conspicuous. Adaptations such as larger body size, weaponry, ritualized displays used in aggressive contests, and dramatic ornamentation and behavior in courtship displays are all plain to see and pretty easy to interpret. They give the guy of the species an advantage in procuring and keeping access to a breeding female, or several of them, the evolutionary endgame for males of every stripe, feather, and shoe size.

More recently, however, biologists and primatologists have shifted their focus to the subtler aspects of *female* intrasexual competition. Mostly, female mammals—be they mice or chimps or *Homo sapiens*—are competing, when they need to, for breeding opportunities and to attract preferred mates, just as males do. But for females, the expression of aggression is context specific. If a female house mouse (*Mus musculus domesticus*) is living without a lot of other female house mice nearby, and there are plenty of males in the mix, her body won't bother to secrete the special proteins (MUPs) that give her urine a strong scent that clearly communicates "Stay away!" to other female house mice. Surrounded by other female mice, however, her urine changes dramatically so she can get her message across: "This is *my* turf, ladies!" Such plasticity has evolved because competitive signaling, as biologists call it, is *costly*. It takes energy and time to secrete those proteins, energy and time that could otherwise be expended by females on maintaining good nutrition, optimizing fertility, seeking nesting materials, being pregnant, lactating, and caring for one's young.

Because aggression is potentially dangerous and competitive signaling is costly, it is now believed, female mammals, including primates, have learned over the eons to compete "under the radar." That is, they inflict social rather than physical violence through coalitions, subtle signals, and nonphysical aggression. When female chimps exclude and ignore and harass a new female transfer to the troop, they are making their point—"You're a rung below us"—without ever putting themselves or their offspring at physical risk the way an actual bodily assault could. Among human females, refusal to cooperate with someone, destruction of her reputation (so that others will refuse to cooperate with her), gossip, and social exclusion are all effective ways to devastate a potential competitor. And, because punishments are often delivered circuitously and simultaneously by several group members, there is no "defending" oneself. The nasty looks and holier-than-thou attitudes of the Queen of the Queen Bees and her acolytes in the school halls and playgroups went unconfronted because they were subtle, compared with a punch to the solar plexus. But they were similar in their effectiveness.

Acutely aware of males' taste for novelty, scientists have observed, female primates in established groups may be intensely vigilant about and hostile toward female newcomers, particularly when sex ratios are skewed in males' favor, as they are so dramatically on the Upper East Side, where there are two reproductive females for every male. Escalated aggression between females, scientists who study it tell us, is reserved for just such intensely competitive situations, which yield high reproductive reward, or the defense (or perceived defense) of one's mate status or one's offspring. And the aggression is, as we saw with mice, "plastic," that is, tailored to the specific environment, ecological conditions, and resources. That is why one mom, at soccer practice, refused to turn around or acknowledge me at all when I told her, three times, sitting just behind her, that my son would like to join the summer playgroup she was organizing. That is why, when another mom intervened and said, "Wednesday's son, too," the high-ranking mom said, back still turned to me, "*Fine*. Caroline, Nancy, Sarah, Pamela, Daniela, Julia, and *her*." That is why, looking at the same white cotton embellished dress the fashion-forward mom had worn to drop-off in February as it hung in my own closet, I felt that she had soaked it with her pee.

Even if this covert competition and aggression was less costly in the biological sense, it must be really *expensive*, I figured. What, I wondered aloud to Candace as our Cobb salads materialized before us, did one *do* in order to be a beautiful-enough woman with children in this world? And how much did it cost in actual dollars and cents? Candace's hazel eyes, free of crow's-feet thanks to good genes, good diet, and some good, strategic recent Botox, lit up. "Let's figure it out!" she suggested. Why hadn't we thought of this before? Our salads were soon forgotten—this was more fun than eating. When we were done, our notes about what we guessed a Manhattan Geisha of the Upper East Side tribe I was studying did for and spent on her upkeep—based on conversations, observations, and a heavily padded version of what we did for ourselves—looked like this:

Head-to-toe analysis of annual cost of self-maintenance for high-mid- to high-ranking UES woman with kids in private school

Hair and scalp

Haircut & color (5x/year @ $500) $2.5K and blowout (weekly @ $70 per, incl. tip) $3.5K = $6K

Hair & makeup stylist for events (10x/year @ $150) = $1.5K

Consult and follow-up w/specialist who does not accept insurance, regarding hair loss due to color, stress, hormones, and/or autoimmune issues caused by stress and hormones = $2K

Face

Quarterly Botox, Restylane, and fillers ($1,000 x 4) = $4K

Monthly peel ($300 x 12) = $3.6K

Monthly facial ($250 x 12) = $3K

Monthly brows: waxing, tweezing, sugaring, or stringing ($50 x 12) = $600

Laser (for sun damage, collagen stimulation, etc.) = $2.5K

Facial skin-care products (cleaner, moisturizer, serum, sunblock, eye cream) = $1.5K

Facial makeup = $1K

Body

Exercise classes = $3.5K

Personal trainer = $7.5K

Nutritionist = $1.5K

Juice cleanses = $3.5K if weekly

Mani/pedi = $2K

Massage = $9K if weekly; $4.5K if biweekly

Spray tan = $500

Spa getaway/s = $8K if biannually

Plastic surgery incl. breast augmentation, lipo = wild-card
   items

Wardrobe

   Clothing
   Seasonal F/W = $3K–20K
   Seasonal SP/SU = $3K–20K
   Events = $5K–20K
   Resort/vacation
      Hamptons = $5K
      Palm Beach = $5K
      Aspen (ski jacket, pants, hat/s, gloves) = $2.5K
   Other
   Shoes/boots = $5–8K
   Bags = $5–10K

"Stupefying," Candace pronounced as we tallied the numbers
and put our credit cards on the table. Something like $95,000, on
the low end, just to be beautiful enough and well-enough dressed
and well-enough shod and sufficiently well tended to be in the
game. "We are *not* telling our husbands," she intoned seriously
as we kissed good-bye and parted on the street. Although maybe
that would have been a good idea, since we were cheap dates
compared with others we knew. "Hey!" she shouted seconds later
from the window of the cab she had just hopped into: "We didn't
even count drivers and Ubers to get to and from the stores and

appointments!" She was right. But I didn't have the appetite to revisit our figures. I felt dizzy. In spite of this fact, I had an outfit to plan, and some shopping to do.

And so I came to find myself puzzling over what to wear to a girls' night in. I knew that many of the women I now spent time with hired hair and makeup artists, sometimes even to prep them for lunch at Rotisserie Georgette with girlfriends, and personal stylists to curate their wardrobes—for parties and events but also, astonishingly, for school pickup and drop-off. Manhattan retail is a byzantine, two-tier system, one to be worked and massaged by a knowledgeable insider if you want to get the only size 0 in the city. Anyone can walk into Prada. And that is why, in addition to a stylist, you "need" a dedicated salesperson at your store or stores of choice. She texts you photos of new arrivals you might like, and when you show up, puts you in the biggest dressing room and brings you water and champagne while you try the clothes on. Don't have time to come in? She can send things to your home via messenger "on approval." Many women wear them and re- turn them after. Later in the season, your salesperson calls and whispers, "When can I *presale* you?" Translation: "When can you come in so I can let you have first crack at stuff that will be on sale in a month, that I can give you at sale price *now*?" The women of the tribe demanded special perks and plenty of privacy in their retail experiences, that's for sure. Often there were charity events at exclusive boutiques after hours, where you could browse with friends at your side and a drink in your hand, and a portion of every dollar you spent was donated to a good cause: the Guggen-

heim, Children's Aid, the Children's Museum of the East End—
you name it, it had a charity shopping night at Chanel, Lanvin,
Dolce&Gabbana, or Dior.

Thanks to some "shopping-for-a-cause events," I was now
able, rummaging through my tees and pants and riffling through
my closet, to settle on a pair of bright-pink snakeskin-patterned
skinny trousers of stretchy denim, a simple, boxy white T-shirt
with an embroidered red-and-black flower front and center, and
a bright green Chanel knock-off jacket with fringe at the wrists
and along the front placket. I knew that, incredibly, nothing about
this getup would seem over-the-top to the women at Rebecca's.

Now I just needed to figure out what to wear on my feet. Most
of the homes I went to were by now "shoes off," parents all over
Manhattan having embraced the custom of not bringing street
ick into the home via one's soles. But I strongly suspected that,
at this girls' night in, we would be allowed to wear our shoes. It
would make these women feel too vulnerable, I figured, to forfeit
the reassuring sensation of being a little taller and a little skinnier.
Being barefoot would make them feel undone and exposed. Rebecca would know that. Pulling out one of the slingback booties
I always wore "out," I saw that its heel was cracked. There wasn't
time to get it fixed at Leather Spa, and I didn't have a lot of other
options in my closet. And so I found myself at one of the tribe's
two fashion altars: Barneys. The one on Madison, of course.

"All shoes are six hundred dollars," the salesman observed with a
shake of his head as I tried on the ravishing beauties in every heel
height and configuration he had chosen when I told him about
the evening in my near future—D'Orsay pumps, stilettos, stacked

heels—and gasped at the numbers. "And all boots," he added as I anxiously flipped over a supple navy suede boot I liked to check the price affixed to its sole, "are twelve hundred." Now he peeled back the tissue paper from a Christian Louboutin open-toed, platform slingback mule of black suede with red and pink stripes and observed sagely, "These are *sick*."

This last shoe was indeed a winner, like a piece of candy for the feet, yet sturdy enough that I didn't wobble on it. And it was on sale. Still, I fretted that, given its height and the way it pinched my left big toe, it wasn't precisely a wise investment. "You could always just wear them for short periods," the salesman mused. "And if you have a longer evening ahead of you, you could get one of those *injections*."

Come again?

Hadn't I heard, he laughed, of the shots to numb your feet, or part of them, so you could do a whole night in killer heels? Apparently there were podiatrists who acted as enablers of women with high-heel fixations here and in Hollywood, and they could fix me up—or rather, shoot me up—for a price. I raised my eyebrows in disbelief, figuring the salesman was having me on. "For *realsies*." He smiled as I surrendered my Amex, making the universal sign for "crazy" with his finger next to his ear.

Beauty isn't cheap. And mostly, it is women who bear the brunt of its many costs—the not infrequently harrowing requirements of time, energy, and sheer physical fortitude that prompted our grandmothers to observe, "Beauty hurts." This truism holds across countries and cultures—in China, where the practice of foot binding crippled generations of aristocratic women; in Thailand, where women of the Kayan tribe wear metal necklaces to give the impression of an elongated neck (they are actually pushing their cervical and shoulder bones down); and in the African and Amazonian tribes where plates stretch the lips until, in some cases, they are the size and shape of a CD. Among the tribe of women I studied on the Upper East Side, "beauty" might mean an augmentation that left your breasts rigid and plastic-seeming in appearance and numb to the touch, making literal the idea that women are objects who supply sensation for others, rather than subjects who enjoy feeling it themselves. Or it might mean injections to make your face stiller, "fuller," tauter, and more strategically plumped (to convey youthfulness and prevent wrinkles), but at a price.

Studies suggest that being unable to move your face empathically as you listen to someone speak reduces feelings of connection. In essence, numbing your face very likely numbs your emotions: Botoxed subjects show less brain-scan activity in key emotional regions than do the un-Botoxed. All in the quest for a youthful face for others to gaze upon. And then what? Confronted with a motionless face, one that expresses nothing as we speak to its owner, we humans feel confounded, disconnected, and distressed. I certainly did, the day I ran into a friend who stared at me blankly throughout our five-minute chat on the street, issuing insincere-seeming laughs as I shared a funny anecdote about my kids. Was she angry? Had I offended her last time I'd seen her? I didn't think so. Then I recalled that, at our last encounter, she had been on the way to her dermatologist.

Other unanticipated aspects of paralyzing your facial muscles are aesthetic. "Why does that cute mom look so strange? What *happened* to her?" my husband asked me on a day he had done playgroup with our younger son. He figured she was getting a divorce or had lost a parent—her face seemed to have aged that dramatically, years within weeks. I knew exactly who he meant. Several of the moms had been talking about it over coffee after "class." She got Botox too soon, they agreed, and now this beautiful, previously fresh-looking woman in her early thirties, she of the sparkling eyes and easy smile, had the Face, which we initially associated with youth (unlined) but now associated with age and Botox—Sphinx-like and unexpressive. Unhappy. Old.

I often thought of the symmetrical, still-faced women around me, many of whom had had rhinoplasties before their weddings, as pretty, picture-perfect zombies. They looked beautiful, but they seemed to feel nothing, their eyes, Botoxed all around to prevent crow's-feet, dead in their faces even as they laughed or smiled. Sometimes I imagined them chasing me down the hallways of the school or down Madison Avenue into Sant Ambroeus, their arms outstretched, cornering me in the elevator or on a cozy banquette, where they proceeded to eat my brain. I was partial to acupuncture facials, having developed a huge bruise around my eye from my inaugural Botox experience. In spite of this fact, joining them—zombified, injected, quelled—seemed inevitable. Then came the fillers. I knew women with faces as big as basketballs from the endless tweakings with Restylane and Juvéderm. Their moon-pie visages atop their starved bodies seemed perfect for a photo essay in *National Geographic*: "Bizarre Beauty Practices among the Exotic 10021 Tribe of Kroywen."

Wanting to get a different kind of purchase on women's willingness to do so much and go so far in pursuit of beauty, I turned to Richard Prum, professor of ornithology, ecology, and evolutionary biology at Yale University. A specialist on the topics of mate choice, sexual selection, and aesthetic evolution among birds, Prum has a keen interest in human evolution as well. He suggested, as we chatted in his office that seemed to have mush-roomed massive piles of books and tins of green tea over the years, that beauty insanity holds sway across species. "A lot of the beauty of birds, and humans, is about the issue of *sexual* beauty, all the observable features that make a particular mate attractive and desirable," he explained. For birds, this could involve choos-ing a guy who not only looks good but also *sounds* good. Brown and white with black wings, appearing to wear a little red beret, male club-winged manakins (*Machaeropterus deliciosus*) of An-dean northwestern Ecuador don't look so different from their other songbird brethren. It's their sound, and how they make it, that sets them apart.

In his courtship displays, the male club-winged manakin ac-tually plays his wings like a violin. He emits a clicking, buzzing sound more often associated with crickets, who produce music the same way. "It's a *ridiculous* way for a bird to communicate!" Prum enthused to me, noting, "These guys are capable of just fine vocal communications. So the question becomes why? Why this fiddling?" The answer: to get the girl. Female club-winged manakins *liked* the song. They found it beautiful. It attracted them and they chose males who could play the tune. And this preference had, over the course of generations, pressured and ultimately changed male club-winged manakin behavior. What was more shocking to Prum and his then graduate assistant Kim Bostwick was their discovery that this female preference had a profound impact on not only male manakin behavior (song) but also male manakin *morphology* (body structure). Every other bird on the planet has an ulna that is hollow. But in the male club-winged manakin, the ulna is thickened, twisted, planar—and solid bone. This female preference for "winging" versus singing has had an unexpected effect—and strange consequences. The male's amped-up ulna makes it easier to make beautiful-to-female-manakins music—but harder to fly and escape predators. Meaning . . . male club-winged manakins are dying for beauty. "It's an aesthetic trait that evolved in spite of dragging down the male's reproductive fitness," Prum marveled.

The view in evolutionary biology and evolutionary psychology has long been that "beauty" is about utility and fitness. Beauty, Prum summarized neatly as we chatted, "is presumed to be bristling with information. It supposedly communicates, I'm healthy! You want *me!*" This is a functional take on beauty, beauty as a barometer of health, faces and bodies as a shorthand of sorts, the outward manifestation of "healthy" genes. In this model, straight teeth and symmetrical features "mean" that a potential mate doesn't have parasites, or heart disease. But, based in part on the fact of the irrational, exuberant, and decadent male club-winged manakin's song, a song that gets him the girl but little else, Prum doesn't buy the popular belief that beauty is just information; he believes it is more likely "stuff happening"—stuff that helps individual birds attract others. Evolving a beak that can crack a nut is pretty straightforward. "But seducing a mind," Prum observed with wonder, opening his eyes wide, "is an infinity problem." Natural selection alone, he says, cannot account for aesthetic preferences like the one for the crazy violin solo of the manakin, a song that may get him a mate, sex, and offspring but also imperils him in basic ways, so that he may get none of those things. In the world of the manakin, as well as the rarefied world of the female primates

I studied, Prum suggested, beauty is often decadent, irrational, and out-of-bounds. It can be exuberant and stunning, ruinous and potentially deadly. It is often a system unto itself, untethered from practicality and functionality, a world apart.

Rebecca lived in a massive triplex in a "great building" on Sutton Place. This location aligned her with a slightly older, more genteel lower Upper East Side, before it had stretched itself out, Manifest Destiny–like, to reach all the way to the low Nineties. It was said that Rebecca's husband had first bought the apartment from Rebecca's parents, and then decided to buy the entire building. He wasn't a developer; he was a hedge-fund guy, and presumably, buying a building—the one he lived in—was something to do. The elevator opened directly into Rebecca's home. There I handed my coat to a staff member, taking in the unreal views of the river—I had never seen it from this height or distance, right across the street, at the penthouse level, a perspective that gave it and the rest of the neighborhood the aspect of a diorama or stage set. Another elevator then swept me up to the third floor of the apartment, the very top floor of the building and, apparently, Rebecca's private aerie. There were light-colored flowers everywhere, and beige furniture, and a beautiful long beige marble table facing tall windows. Staff members dressed in beige offered clear drinks (vodka, tequila, and white wine) and simple, light canapés. There was a Hockney—it looked like a portrait of Rebecca—and a massive Cecily Brown and a Tauba Auerbach. I had heard talk of couples with "art budgets" of up to $200 million, and it wasn't hard to imagine as I took in what hung on Rebecca's walls. To the side was an off-white Eames table piled with hostess gifts in bags from Tiffany and Ladurée and Diptyque. My hostess gift—cookies I had baked with my son—had been eagerly and gratefully accepted by the hostess's adorable twin sons at the door. There was something else on the table, too, I noticed—a jumble of what looked like gems. Drawing closer, I saw that the women had all brought little bags and dropped them here—tiny Hermès Kelly bags in jewel tones (one looked to be bright-red crocodile) and quilted, graffitied, and lacquered Chanel bags and diminutive Dior bags with Ds and heart-shaped medallions hanging from them. I placed my own bag—a relatively humble black clutch with a red rose—with the others. And took a deep breath. This was definitely not a bunch of moms ordering pizza and hanging out.

Rebecca, looking radiant, floated over and steered me toward the middle of the room, introducing me to the women I didn't know. Many were the wives of billionaires who owned TV networks and Fortune 500 companies and ran real estate empires and hedge funds. Some were moms from the school, and some were not. There was a former fashion editor who was now a fashion plate and full-time mother of three, with another on the way. There was a former news anchor who had recently quit her job to spend more time with her three kids. She was pregnant with twins. There were, inevitably, a couple of stunningly beautiful and extremely smart "art consultants," a niche profession that expanded and contracted with the fortunes of the One Percent. No one was fat. No one was ugly. No one was poor. Everyone was drinking. And everyone seemed comfortable and friendly in a way they didn't at school or on the street or at events. The usual wariness was gone. It dawned on me that the women were *relaxed*. I relaxed a bit, too, as I noticed that the Queen of the

Queen Bees was not in attendance and my uniform was in sync with what the others were wearing—on the money, so to speak, albeit steeply discounted.

The talk went beyond the usual chat about kids and vacations. There was talk about politics and of a friend not there that evening because she and her husband had recently separated, and of another friend of many of the women in the group who was on her umpteenth round of IVF, supposedly in the hopes that another baby would keep her traveling husband interested and closer to home. Something tugged at me when there was very quiet talk, and lowered eyes, and obvious sadness and compassion about this woman's previous miscarriages, and another friend's devastating amnio results. I was ashamed by the realization that I had assumed, stupidly, that the lives of the women around me were charmed in every way. They weren't. And then the talk shifted again and it was, as always, of what everyone was wearing.

The magnificent, extravagant setting and impeccably dressed and made-up group couldn't have been further from the Efe and Aka people of the Ituri Rain Forest in the Democratic Republic of Congo, or the !Kung San of the Kalahari desert. These hunter-gatherers are radical egalitarians, meaning they live in groups without hierarchy or socioeconomic stratification, as humans did for nearly all of our evolutionary prehistory. Among these tribes, no one owns anything and no one's status is any higher or lower than anyone else's. The notion of property is unknown. This state of affairs is reinforced by several mechanisms. One is object demands. It is common for one woman to walk up to another and demand her beads, for example, or for a child to approach an unrelated adult and demand a portion of his or her food, or for one man to demand and receive another's spear tips for hunt-ing. Saying no is unheard of. These gift demands reinforce the notion that nobody owns anything. Self-effacement and down-playing one's own achievements and those of others is another way to ensure no sense of hierarchy develops. "We're not sure who killed the duiker we found under the acacia tree," someone announces after a successful hunt, knowing full well who did. "Maybe it was someone from another group. We will get it, *all* of us, and we will distribute it to *everyone*." The man supplying coveted meat cannot take or receive credit. Everyone and no one killed the duiker, and so everyone is and remains equal.

Of course, the fastidiously turned out women at Rebecca's—elegant, refined, polite, and rich—would have fainted if I walked up to any one of them and demanded, "Jane, give me your three Pomellato stacking rings and Lanvin Happy bag NOW!" But there was a strict etiquette regarding compliments that struck me in this setting as it never had before, bringing to mind these Afri-can hunter-gatherers. At all costs and by all means, praise about oneself, in this and other women-only settings, was to be aggres-sively deflected. All evening, "Is that blouse Chloé? It's such a beautiful color on you!" was met with, "This thing is four years old. And I look like I haven't slept in a decade!" When told "Your skin looks amazing!" the proper response was "It breaks out all the time. If it looks good, it's just the makeup, believe me!" "Did you lose weight? You look incredible" was met with a flat denial and a diversionary parry along the lines of "No, these pants hold me in like a girdle. But I heard you're working out with Tracy [Anderson] every day, and it shows!"

At first I figured that these deflections and denials and returns served to ward off envy. If someone liked what you had, you had to discount its value so she wouldn't resent you and ultimately harm you with resentful intent (in the Mediterranean and Middle East this is referred to as "warding off the evil eye"). But I was wrong. Actually, through this kind of discursive volleying, this back-and-forth of praise and self-abnegation in response to it, the hierarchy among women of endless means, a system that could quite easily be in constant flux given the ease with which one could get and have whatever one wanted, was kept stable. The compliment was a test: Will you affirm that you are one of us, and answer as we answer? Do you know your place? Or are you going to try to shine and rise above? Only Rebecca, I noted, was allowed to simply accept a compliment. When told she looked fantastic (she really did), she smiled and said, "You are so sweet!" Like the wealthy and socially influential toddler-playgroup mom who merely nodded condescendingly and gave a tight smile whenever someone told her she looked gorgeous (the same one who had performatively exiled me and my son from the summer playgroup), Rebecca was in charge here, and everyone was acknowledging it. Everyone might look beautiful, but no one was admitting it. That was the pact.

Over a delicious dinner—gluten-free and organic and healthy, placed discreetly in front of us by the staff—the talk turned to a West Coast interloper on the New York social scene. A wealthy couple from LA, specifically the wife, had recently upstaged a titan of industry, a longtime fixture on the charity scene, at a gala in his honor. At the moment it was announced that he was donating a million dollars to the cause in question, the brash brunette had jumped up and shouted, "We'll donate two!" The room went silent at her gaffe, and her gall. She was promptly taken to task by the arbiters of the New York charity circuit—by word of mouth, in print, and by social exclusion. The jury was out about her in the room where we now sat. "She's very LA. Very direct," one of the women tactfully observed. "When I was first introduced to her, she asked who did my breasts. She said, 'There's no way those are real.' They are!" The others laughed and nodded, agreeing that it was mostly just an issue of the LA couple's not yet knowing the rules, the Manhattan-specific social laws and codes they themselves had long ago internalized.

The peculiar, seasonal social dance in Manhattan is at least a century old. During "gala season," from April through June, and then out in the Hamptons all summer long, and then back in the city from September until November, there are dinners for an honoree who has paid heavily for the privilege, charity and cause breakfasts, and an endless line of luncheons. The cause may be research into a disease, or conservation, or an issue such as literacy, or supporting a cultural institution. All except the dinners, when husbands materialize, are intensely sex-segregated, women-only affairs. The rules are clear. You may buy a ticket, or be asked to be a guest at someone's table, or buy a table yourself if it is your cause, a board you sit on, or a committee to which you have lent your name and/or your time. A table for yourself and nine of your closest friends might run you $3,500 to $7,500 for a luncheon, and $10,000 and up for a dinner. Many of these events also have silent auctions, long tables of luxury goods you can bid for anonymously on a chit, raising even more money for the cause. Whenever I went to such an all-women breakfast or luncheon, it reminded me of grooming behaviors among non-human primates—capuchins and howler monkeys and baboons tending to "friends'" fur, sometimes for hours, beefing up the sense of connection among them through proximity and affectionate touch, paving the way to alliances that could literally be lifesaving at some point. We weren't picking bugs off one another, but we may as well have been. In talking to one another and eating and drinking together, asking about outfits and kids and work, gathering for a cause, we were also reassuring, connecting with, and touching one another. And a phenomenon primatologists call *reciprocal altruism*—"You groom me, I'll groom you"—is in full effect all gala season long: "I'll go/give to your charity thing if you go/give to my charity thing!" This is one of the ways relationships are built and maintained among the privileged in Manhattan. It is also a way to give to a cause, while *showing* that you can give to a cause. Like all primates, humans are affiliative and prosocial. And, like so many humans living in the shadow of agriculture, we tend toward hierarchy and stratification. This breakfast-lunch-dinner social circuit of causes and charities proves it.

The evening events, with the husbands in attendance, are more likely to have *live* auctions, where paddles are raised in the quest to show one can overpay for a trip to Anguilla, a fractional jet share, a suite at a Yankees game, or floor tickets at Madison Square Garden for a Knicks game. At one school gala's live auction, it was said, the cookie jar made by the 4s went for $60,000. A class's group finger painting went for $20,000. Conspicuous consumption never felt so virtuous (or, in the case of the kids' art, so humble). Spending money is part of the equation. But who you know at an event, whom you talk to, where you sit, whose guest you are, or who your guests are—all are factors that also help establish your rank. Those who depart from the script—the woman from LA and Felix Rohatyn before her, who had grumbled publicly that it would be far more efficient to simply write checks to the charities one chose rather than attend round after round of excessive "Cancer Dances," was promptly ostracized, and eventually wrote an explanation of his views that was part mea culpa in the *New York Times*—quickly learn how entrenched and inflexible these hallowed tribal ways are.

"Social climbing" is real in Manhattan, and when I hear the phrase, I see before me stilettoed women—the Queen of the Queen Bees and her friends at the top, the rest coming up close behind—in Chanel dresses and Yves Saint Laurent tuxedo jumpsuits, glittering minaudières in hand or hanging from their slender shoulders, skillfully making their way in the dusk up a tree, negotiating the branches, finding an ideal spot at an optimal height that gives them a perfect view of the forest floor below or the savanna before them. This perspective makes them, like primates of all species, including our own *Homo sapiens* ancestors, feel safe. And rich.

As the evening wound down, women parted with thank-yous to Rebecca and kisses for one another. And tonight, as always, in departing, they said, "Will I see you at the thing on Thursday? Are you going to the school meeting tomorrow?" Like the demurral from a compliment, the confirmation of the next meet-up affirmed that they were one.

Women of the tribe I was studying paid the price for beauty, looking frozen, feeling disconnected, starving and exercising their bodies into submission. They did the never-ending work of forging and maintaining social connections and social status for themselves, their children, and the couple. But it was men who picked up the tab. It was easy to believe, that night at Rebecca's apartment, that all these women, wealthy, competent, and beautiful, were powerful as well. But there was the nagging fact, for me, always, of the apartness, the undeniable cloistering from men. "It's more fun this way!" the women would say whenever I asked. "Are you kidding? We prefer it!" the men told me at one especially lovely and friendly dinner party—where men and women sat at separate tables in separate rooms. Like "staying at home" with the kids, sex segregation struck me as a state of affairs quite possibly giving clue to some deeper, meaningful reality but masquerading, like a Save Venice ball reveler, as a simple preference. Like a designer frock hanging in a walk-in closet, one among many, sex segregation, I was told, was a "choice."

Worldwide, the ethnographic data tells another story: the more stratified and hierarchical the society, and the more sex segregated, the lower the status of women. One had to consider the initially unlikely seeming possibility that here was no exception. What were the men doing, while the women of my tribe hung together in the various retail and social zenanas around the city— the women's committees of the boards, the upscale breakfast spots next to the toddler music classes, luxe exercise studios and spas—discussing the children and the Parents Association? Usually, they were off with other men, at work, in the public world of still-mostly-men and of commerce. Sometimes they were at the Dads' Poker Night, a private-school fund-raising fixture across the city where no wife dares show up and no questions are asked. And sometimes, the women around me fretted and confided, they suspected the powerful, wealthy men they were married to were enjoying flirtations and dalliances and extramarital affairs— which field biologists refer to, when they happen among animals, as "extra-pair copulations."

Through the lens of anthropology and primatology, this is mostly an issue not so much of moral failing but of circumstance. Of course, many men of the tribe I was studying chose monogamy. But several factors conspire to allow high-ranking, wealthy men the world over to engage in extra-pair copulations at will, with no consequence, in the hypothetical and in reality. Following the typical pattern among all the great apes, it is female *Homo sapiens* who tend to disperse at sexual maturity, losing crucial social support from their families and rendering alliances among (unrelated) females predictably fragile. (Female bonobos, alone among the great apes, have come up with a strategy to improve this situation and build bonds: frequent homosexual encounters with their female troop mates.) It is easy to see how dispersal and relatively weak social bonds make it harder to contemplate up and leaving with your kids than if you lived in a compound (or on a savanna) with your own family of origin, surrounded by welcoming relatives who have your back. "I can't move back to Long Island with my parents and uproot my kids," one woman told a mutual friend, explaining what compelled her to stay with her philandering husband until their young kids were off at boarding school.

Female dispersal is not the only thing that gives males more power than their mates. Female *Homo sapiens* face a fundamental hardship, one unprecedented in the world of nonhuman primates: they are uniquely dependent. We are the only primates that practice intensive food and resource sharing, the only species in which females, in many societies, depend on males for shelter and sustenance. Female birds, Efe mothers, and chimps with offspring never stop searching out and finding food of their own. Indeed, among the !Kung San, even women with very young children bring in upward of 85 percent of the group's daily calories. Agta women of the Philippines hunt while pregnant. Their status as "breadwinners" empowers them—to leave partnerships when they want, to take lovers, to come or go, to have an active and influential voice in their communities. As in the Kalahari Desert and the southeastern Asian rain forest, resources are the bottom line on the Upper East Side, and in Upper East Side marriages. If you don't bring home tubers and sha roots, if you don't earn money, your power is diminished in your marriage. And in the world. Period.

The men I was observing and socializing with (often awkwardly—everybody seemed a little out of practice) had more than circumstances in their favor. Like male primates everywhere, the highest-ranking among them have a repertoire of strategies for compelling their females to stay, no matter what. Male hamadryas baboons use eye-flip threats and neck bites to control the females in their harem-like groups and discourage them from mating with others or even straying too far away. Rhesus macaques in Puerto Rico chase and sometimes wound females who attempt to copulate with low-ranking males. And many a nonhuman primate male practices infanticide, killing the youngest offspring sired by other males in order to bring a female back into estrus, that she may bear *his*.

Male primates of Park Avenue are more subtle, certainly, in their tactics. They subjugate their dependent females, ensuring continued unique access to them, regardless of how they themselves are behaving, by controlling female access to resources. Disbursing and withholding luxurious gifts, lavish vacations, allowances for seasonal wardrobe upgrades and "work" on faces and bodies, allowances that pay for women's charitable work, their ticket to the public world—all are common practices among a certain set. So, several women let me know, arc "year-end bonuses" for wives, which may be outlined in a prenup, or may just be given out of "largesse"—or withheld for any reason. It's an open secret uttered among those who already know, at board meetings or a girls' night out: "I'm not sure what I can give this year because I don't know what my charity allowance will be." "My yearly bonus hasn't been set [by my husband] so I don't know whether I'll take a table at the patron's or benefactor's level." These are the coercive tactics, disguised as cushy and generous enticements, that many high-ranking men use to reinforce their considerable power within their society and their ultimate power within their marriages.

The more I looked, the more I saw the asymmetries of power played out, not just interpersonally between women, but institutionally, socially, and culturally. Financially successful men in Manhattan sit on major boards—of hospitals, universities, and high-profile disease foundations—boards with yearly give/gets (the combined amount you agree to donate and procure from others) of $150,000 and more. Their wives are frequently on lesser boards, women's committees, and museums in the outer boroughs with annual give/gets of $5,000 to $20,000. Wealthy and powerful husbands are trustees of prestigious private schools; their wives are "class moms," tasked with being an official and unremunerated social and communications hub for all the other mothers. While their husbands make millions, privileged women with kids capitulate, with little choice ("I need to be a good volunteer so my kid gets into a good school," these moms were always saying), to the "Mommynomics" of the Upper East Side. They give away the skills they honed in college and in graduate school and in their vaunted professions to their children's schools for free—organizing the galas, editing the newsletters, running the libraries, staging bake sales. Schools would go under without this caste of privileged-mommy volunteers, who provide hundreds of thousands of dollars of free work per year. In a way, a woman's participation in Mommynomics is a way to feel and be busy and useful. It is also an act of extravagance, a brag—"I used to work, I *can*, but I don't need to." But compare it with what some of their husbands have done and aspire to do—amass enough money not merely to quit work but also to take the "Giving Pledge," a public avowal billionaires make to give away half their wealth.

Wives lunch with other women with children at Freds and Bergdorf Goodman while their silverback husbands move with ease among *their* watering holes. A few years ago, at the 21 Club, one could see Henry Kissinger, Roger Ailes, and William Safire all seated within feet of one another, table-hopping and reinforcing their world dominance. The Grill Room might as well be a men's club, my husband observed one day when the ratio of women to men there was one-to-four (other men told me the ratio was usually one-to-two). These are places business is done, and among the tribe I studied, business is mostly done by men.

As I stood in front of Rebecca's building that night hailing a cab, I recalled the view from her massive windows twenty-six stories above. In the most elite sector of the world's most elite economy, in a tiny corner of a specific neighborhood, a proliferation of women have left work or have never had to work. From an anthropological perspective, these wealthy women who seem and are so fortunate are also marooned in their sex-segregated world, on their lesser boards, at their charity breakfasts and luncheons, and in their playgroups and Hamptons homes all summer long.

With sex ratios in their favor, with resources under their control, with wives who are dependent on them caring for their even more dependent offspring, privileged men of the Upper East Side can do as they please. Men may speak the language of partnership in the absence of true economic parity in a marriage, and they may act like true partners. But this arrangement is fragile and contingent and women are still dependent, in this instance, on their men—a husband may simply ignore his commitment at any time. Access to your husband's money might feel good. But the comparative study of human society and our primate relatives shows that such access can't buy you the power you get by being the one who earns it. And knowing this, or even having an inkling of it, just sensing the disequilibrium, the abyss that separates your version of power from your man's, could keep a thinking woman up at night.

CHAPTER SIX

A Xanax and a Bloody Mary:
Manhattan Moms on the Verge of
a Nervous Breakdown

I am wearing an army-green vest with ample pockets and a practical rubber-soled shoe, stealthily making my way across the second floor of Bergdorf Goodman. Laden with lavender shopping bags for camouflage, I am on the hunt for The One amid the Prada and Lanvin. No luck. Adjusting my blowgun, the type biologists use in the field, I ascend the elevator to the jungle of "young and fun!" designers on 5. It is hard to choose from the specimens around me, since so many fit the criteria: remarkably thin, highly stressed, sleep-deprived, economically privileged reproductive Upper East Side females in midlife. But they tend to travel in packs, and are partial to leather leggings and jeans, so my task is complicated, all about finding not just the right animal, but also the right moment. I can wait. This is important. Thus far, I have mostly studied the troop's group behaviors. Now I need to understand them individually, from the inside out. A blood sample could reveal so much about their physiology and emotions.

And then, on the edge of the floor, one strays from her peers to look at a rack of Balenciaga. Even better, she is wearing lightweight trousers. I

*get her in my sights and, with a puff to my blowgun, quickly dart her in
the buttock. She wanders, dazed, toward the fitting rooms, falling to the
soft pile carpet in fewer than twenty seconds. As I drag her through the
heavy curtain into the largest of the mirrored rooms, Robert Sapolsky,
a neuroendocrinologist and primatologist, who has made a career of
studying the lives and blood work of olive baboons in Kenya's Maasai
Mara reserve, ushers me in and concedes, "You're getting pretty good at
this."*

*We take her vital signs and draw her blood quickly, efficiently, know-
ing there is not much time. Our petite, well-dressed great ape will come
to on the plush carpeting, see the half glass of champagne we have left
on the table in the fitting room, and, blaming herself, be too ashamed to
tell anyone what has happened. Meanwhile, we hit the street and head
to Quest Diagnostics—the one on East Fifty-Seventh between Park and
Lex. There is a skip in my step and I have the urge to whistle. I am eager
to hear the story that her blood, still warm in its vials in my pockets,
will tell us.*

As I wrote this book, I had this daydream over and over, while
riding the M86 bus across the park or jammed into the plastic depression that counts as a seat on the subway or sitting on a bench
on the edge of the playground, chatting with other moms and
half keeping track of my kids. But the morphology of many of
the Upper East Side mothers I knew from my older son's school
and my younger one's playgroups—their bodies and faces—told
a story of its own. Their gaunt visages and taut torsos and limbs
that seemed always ready to spring put me in mind, as I passed
them in the school hallways and ladies' luncheons and galas we
all went to, of animals primed for fight or flight. Their fingers and

thumbs flew across their iPhones and BlackBerries. Their jaws were clenched. Their brows were furrowed, unless they had had Botox injections there, in which case the story found expression in their mouths, which were frequently pursed or arranged in tight smiles, the kind that did *not* telegraph pleasure or happiness or relaxation but rather the very opposite: "Hi, I see you, but I'm in a rush." Mostly, though, the tale was in their eyes—wide, alert, hypervigilant eyes that took in everything, like a gazelle endlessly scanning its surroundings, as if its life depended on it.

By now, I knew about the rites of passage and initiation ceremonies a privileged Upper East Side mommy went through. I knew her identity was forged, in part, through certain rituals that were all but explicitly agreed upon: making what narrators of eighteenth-century English novels called "an advantageous match"; passing a co-op board interview and undertaking an apartment renovation; applying to prestigious private schools for her children; attending grueling exercise classes daily; and participating in "Mommynomics," the circle of charity luncheons and social and school events that allowed her to work on strategic alliances, solidifying or raising her social rank. But I often wondered what it *felt* like to be the wife of an alpha (or close-second beta) and the mother of young children on the Upper East Side. In spite of my having gone native, I would always be a late transfer to the troop, with less money than many of the women around me. I was low-ranking, and still a relative newcomer. So I couldn't be sure that my own feelings of stress and unease when I was at drop-off or a school event or a playgroup were an accurate indicator of *theirs*. Over coffee, and after school meetings, some forthcoming Upper East Side mommies put words to what their faces were saying.

They said: "When the radiator bangs, I jump out of my skin."

And: "Our daughter's teacher told us she was having a hard time finding a group of kids to play with at recess and I burst into tears."

And: "My husband tapped me on the shoulder to ask me something and it startled me so badly I screamed and fell off my chair. *In my own home.*"

"I know *exactly* what you should be writing about," Candace told me breathlessly over lunch one day. She quickly retrieved something from her purse and popped it into her mouth. She had arrived late—"Brutal traffic," she apologized—having learned just twenty-four hours before that her son had a concussion from a soccer game. Her husband was looking for a new job. Candace hadn't slept well, I gathered; there were dark circles under her eyes. She had lost weight, too, and looked so thin that she might break. I wanted to comfort her, but I also wanted to hear what she had to say, because Candace really understood the über-competitive, ultrasuccessful men and women whose lives I studied. She was married to one, after all, and as a high-end event planner, she had organized the baby showers and over-the-top kiddie birthday parties and charity soirees of some of Manhattan's richest and most powerful players for years. She had seen them all at their worst, and with their guard down.

"*Anxiety,*" Candace whispered urgently across the table now. "Your tribe of mommies and anxiety."

"Right," I said. I nodded, thinking. Then I ventured, "Um, what was that pill, Candace?"

"Ativan," she replied matter-of-factly. She exhaled with a smile and fell back into the leather chair, her shoulders and face finally relaxed. She looked beautiful and radiant, just like herself again, and she said, "Shall we order some wine?"

Anxiety and stress are diseases of the West, afflictions of the WEIRD—anthropologist Jared Diamond's acronym for Western, educated, industrialized, rich, democratic peoples. A look at the cross-cultural data regarding one reliable measure of out-of-whack anxiety, social anxiety disorder, makes the case nicely. While rates of social anxiety disorder in China, Korea, Nigeria, and Taiwan are all well under 1 percent, the US rate is nearly ten times greater. One in four Americans will experience severe and sustained anxiety at some point in his or her life.

And city people are especially, extraordinarily stressed and anxious, researchers tell us. Packed streets and buses and costly clothing and food and shelter and the din of jackhammers, it seems, produce feelings of threat and diminish our sense of control, leading to high anxiety, high stress, and escalating rates of stress-related disease. Indeed, such city-niche-specific conditions have changed the human brain, altering our cingulate cortexes and amygdalae so they are, in a vicious circle if ever there was one, less able to deal with stress than those of our country cousins.

Stanford biologist and neuroscientist Robert Sapolsky, my partner in crime in the Bergdorf daydream, has mapped out how stress, once an indispensable adaptation, got twisted around, creating the uniquely contemporary conundrum of chronic stress and its affective handmaiden, chronic anxiety. "For the average mammal," he explains, "stress is three minutes of terror on the savanna, after which the stress is over—or you are." Stress evolved as a useful, extremely short-term, lifesaving physiological state: your heart races to pump oxygen; your lungs work harder; and your body turns off anything nonessential in the interest of immediate survival (being chased by a lion is no time to ovulate, grow, or put energy into tissue repair—that's for later). With these brief bursts of terror come surges in stress hormones such as adrenaline and cortisol. Once the lion has been outwitted or escaped, the blood levels of these stress hormones go down.

Today, though, "we turn on our stress response for purely psychological states, and that's not what it evolved for," Sapolsky observes. Our blood pressure surges to 180/120 not in order to save our lives, but as we sit in traffic or worry about terrorism. And we can't find the Off button. So, momentarily, adaptive stress becomes chronic stress and perpetual anxiety. These days, "the hormones that we used to secrete to save our lives are being secreted . . . continually, when we worry about the ozone layer or have to speak in public." One of Sapolsky's most important discoveries was that among hierarchical mammals, like baboons or humans on the Upper East Side, social rank can cause massive stress, changing one's blood, mind, and body, especially where rankings are unstable and individuals are jockeying for position. Now we were getting somewhere.

There is so much we could learn from a drop of blood, which looks like a drop of wine, I thought as we sat at the table in the Upper East Side home of my brother-in-law and his wife on Passover. My older son loved this holiday, with all its ritualized food and hand washing and prayers. My little one adored the doting attentions of his older cousins and the songs, if not the sitting still. I had come to this tradition, and to Judaism, as I had to Upper East Side motherhood: through marriage. So, while my nieces and

nephews and in-laws and husband went through the motions, it
was all newish and fascinating to me, as it was to my children. At
the point in the Haggadah when we list the ten plagues of Egypt,
the punishments God rained down upon Pharaoh for refusing to
release the Israelites from slavery, we dipped our fingers into our
glasses, leaving drops of wine on the edges of our plates, one for
each plague. Blood. Frogs. Lice. Flies. Diseased livestock. Boils.
Hail. Locusts. Darkness. Death of firstborn. As I listened, I listed
in my mind another version of the plagues, the afflictions of the
tribe of women I now knew so well. Head lice. School applications. Capital campaigns. Traveling husbands. Intrasexual competition. SEC investigations. Divorce. I knew there were more.
Lots more.

Thank God for a drop of wine.

As I got closer to many of the Upper East Side mommies around
me, and others continued to keep their distance, I became more
and more preoccupied with what "belonging" might mean—to
me, and to the women who were now my friends, and to the ones
who were not. Part of me wanted to fit in and be embraced by
everyone in my adopted troop. Primates are, after all, deeply affiliative and highly prosocial, characteristics that set us apart from
other species: as with chimps and baboons and macaques, connections with others mean more to us than just about anything
else, even if we are slightly cynical moms from downtown. I was
still shaken by having been, all those months before, a playdate
pariah. I knew that such "hazing" was not uncommon among
primates of the human and nonhuman variety, and I doubted
that the exclusions and performative back-turnings had ever been

precisely personal. But I still harbored, in the most primitive parts of my brain, the fear that I might be excluded again. All women want to fit in—whether they are hippies in Berkeley, PTA moms in Omaha, or TriBeCa transfers, those who depart the Upper East Side to move downtown. Part of me was now hell-bent on toeing the line: dressing to fit in, helping with school committees, going to luncheons. Meanwhile, my front brain puzzled over what would happen if I *didn't*, or couldn't. How did you fall out, and what happened then?

Divorce and diminution of income—the DD plagues, as I came to think of them—seemed to be two events that could precipitate getting drummed out of the group. Once a woman is divorced, she likely won't have the money to play at the same level—to buy the tickets for the events, join the flyaway parties to St. Barths and Paris and Miami. There will be fewer invites for this reason—and another one, too. Women who are divorced often ignite fear among peers that "it can happen to me, too." And that "she's on the make and may try to steal someone's husband." As one divorced member of the tribe told me, "It's bye-bye for me. Third wheels are scary." A divorced tribe member may keep a friend or two, but find she has a significantly circumscribed social life.

It was no doubt frightening to think that your life as you knew it could fall away because your marriage fell apart. But the story I really couldn't shake was about a woman I'll call Lena. After the crash in 2008, the story goes, she and her husband lost almost everything. The oceanfront Hamptons home. The classic eight–classic seven combination on Park. They pulled their kids out of prestigious private schools, where they had once been big donors and board members with a measure of influence over whose kids could get in, which in turn gave them massive cultural capital. Gone. They moved to 110th street. Without telling anyone, Lena took a job at an upscale department store in an upscale mall in an upscale Manhattan suburb. Seen one way, this was an act of simple necessity. But seen another, it was brave, because it was a step down. Several women she knew showed up at the store one day, and were shocked to discover that Lena was "on the other side" now, bringing them shoes to try on. Other friends might have rallied around Lena and organized a shopping excursion en masse to the tony store where she worked, to give her a day of great commissions. They might have reached out and buoyed her up. I like to think that I would have. Instead, Lena's no-longer-peers simply avoided her. This didn't surprise me, somehow. But it angered me. It served to remind me of the foreignness of some of the women around me, the divide between what they felt and how they acted, and how I did. It was as if they lived in a caste system, and Lena was now forever tainted, ritually impure. She and her plight were terrifying—and she became a taboo object. Perhaps these women believed that Lena would find it humiliating to be around them, but I doubted it. And was that any reason to abandon a friend?

"It's almost like the attitude in this world, when your girlfriend is down, is 'Sink or swim,'" a woman who was newly divorced from her wealthy and powerful husband explained to me over coffee. The Queen of the Queen Bees would no longer speak to her, she explained, and I suggested she might be better off for it. But I knew how her ostracism, the being dropped, must feel, and I felt sorry for her, as I did for Lena.

Eventually, the story goes, Lena and her husband left town. I was interested and relieved to hear that she had become a Bud-

dhist, and was happy. But to a certain set of women, she no longer existed. "I think she moved to some hippie place? And joined
a cult or something?" is how a woman I asked about Lena's story
described it. She was dead.

The Upper East Side culture they lived in was itself a major plague
on my tribe of mommies, it seemed to me. The pressure to con-
form, the drive for perfection, and the emphasis on appearances
and keeping up appearances on the Upper East Side are extraordinary and unrelenting. My realization, early on in my life there,
that I had to get dressed up to run to the corner for milk, was just
the tip of the iceberg. You would have to be socially tone-deaf
not to sense the pressure to be perfectly turned out, perfectly
groomed, perfectly coiffed, and always at the right event with
the right person at the right time. But there is something deeper
going on, too. Lena's story taught me that like the social worlds
of the Bedouin and the Roma, the world of the Upper East Side
is an honor/shame culture. Shame and the fear of not fitting in
or of falling out or of being ostracized, rather than the fear of
going to hell or prison, are the main means of social control. And
on the Upper East Side, as in China or among certain tribes of
Native Americans, one can lose one's honor or one's "face"—not
the physical thing that you talk and eat with and put makeup on,
but your prestige, reputation, indeed your very *self*. Marcel Mauss
wrote of the Pacific Northwest Indians that

> Kwakiutl . . . noblemen have the same notion of "face"
> as the Chinese. . . . It is said of one of the great mythical
> chiefs who gave no feast that he had a "rotten face" . . .

To lose one's face is to lose one's spirit, which is truly the "face," the dancing mask, the right to incarnate a spirit and wear an emblem or totem. It is the veritable *persona* which is at stake, and it can be lost in the potlatch just as it can be lost in the game of gift-giving, in war, or through some error in ritual.

Or, Mauss might add today of the women I studied, it can be lost by losing your money. Or having bedbugs.

While bedbugs and head lice are an inconvenient and stressful fact of life for people all over New York City, for a privileged Upper East Side mom like my friend Gina, they are something else. Gina sobbed for days—not just because getting rid of them is so expensive and time-consuming and exhausting. And not only because she was covered in itchy bites and could find no relaxation, only stress, in her bed at night. And not just or even primarily because the family might not be able to sell the apartment for several years after, owing to new laws requiring sellers to disclose that their largest assets have had pest problems. No. Gina was mostly very, very afraid that her friends would find out. Her identity hinged on hosting playdates and having a perfect home, among other things. Bedbugs suggested the frightening possibility of being ostracized from the group. "Nobody will come here anymore!" she told me. If her kids didn't have a social life, neither did she. And we know what happens to the socially unaffiliated in an affiliative, hierarchical world: social death (and even physical death, if you're a baboon).

Many of the mothers I knew shared Gina's heightened sense of social shame and humiliation—about not only catastrophic life events such as divorce or going broke but also that extra five pounds or having a kid who needs occupational therapy or being unable to afford two weeks in Aspen. In an honor/shame culture, a world where you are expected to have not one dimple of cellulite or one stray hair, a world where your entire being hinges on what you give away at a potlatch, or how you keep your home, or having kids without problems, losing face is easy. There is no sin, and probably no god—the tribe was monotheistic by tradition but largely postreligious—but there is shame. As foreign as you might find it, once you enter into the cultural logic of losing face, it's clear how the very possibility of such public humiliation could stress you in real ways. Their exhausted, gaunt faces. Another drop of wine.

Candace was almost always right about the tribe, and, following her lead, I did indeed discover that there was an anxiety gender gap of sorts. Women in developed countries (but not those in undeveloped ones) are, remarkably, *twice* as likely to suffer from anxiety disorders as are men. But I had thought my tribe would be an exception. After all, I knew from firsthand experience that being a relatively privileged Manhattan mommy conferred a crucial advantage: the ability to buffer oneself not only from catastrophes such as being sick with no insurance or not having the money to feed your children but also from the assaults of everyday big-city life, by means of a massage or a weekend in the country. I figured with their exponentially greater wealth and private planes, their three-week Caribbean/Aspen (or Turks and Caicos/Vail) vacations and weeklong girls' getaways to Canyon Ranch, the places on Further Lane to get them farther from the madding city crowds, the über-wealthy mommies from my sons'

school and playgroups should be exponentially calmer. Wouldn't having your children in the very best school, or having the best possible nanny—one procured through an agency that charged a very hefty fee to partner parents with the crème de la crème of caregivers—give you a degree of calm and confidence about their well-being? I presumed all this should be enough to quell anyone's worries. And that any other stress and anxiety was something the women I knew created themselves, by fretting about the wrong things and failing to be in the moment and enjoy all they had.

I was wrong.

As it turns out, the old adage is true—once you control for factors such as poverty, illness, and hunger, money does not buy you happiness. And it certainly does not buy you a reprieve from anxiety. Precisely the opposite seems to be the case, with a whole host of specific-to-their-ecological-niche factors above and beyond the everyday stressors of city life making rich Upper East Side mommies the ultimate nerve-racked nellies. Mothering in a state of ecological release and an honor/shame culture, I was learning, was in many ways a perfect storm for anxiety. Their perfect lives were in fundamental ways the worst thing for these mommies' minds.

The cult of "intensive mothering," peculiar to the West and specific to the wealthy, was certainly a plague upon the mommies I studied. Sociologist Sharon Hays, who coined the term, defines intensive mothering as "a gendered model that [compels] mothers to expend a tremendous amount of time, energy and money in raising their children." Constant emotional availability, constantly monitoring your kids' psychological states, endlessly providing activities, and "fostering" your children's "intellectual development" are all expected of women of means, Hays observes, and failing to nurture them comprehensively, or just letting them be, borders on neglect. My tribe of mommies, unlike my mom, were forever on duty, doing baking projects to teach their kids fractions and making educational museum visits and being "involved" at school. In this paradigm, motherhood is an anxious, 24/7, depleting, high-stakes duty. There is virtually no sense, on the Upper East Side, that letting a child fail and feel frustrated could build her resilience and make her a happier, stronger person. No, if your child failed—to score 99.9 percent on her ERB, to do a great drawing in art class, to do well on an obstacle course or race—it was less a teachable moment, it seemed, and more evidence of your own failure as a parent.

But if you mother intensively, go all out, you also run the risk of being called a "helicopter mom" and chided for ruining your kids. No wonder a study of 181 mothers with young kids found that those who embraced intensive motherhood had high levels of anxiety and depression. Meanwhile, opting out and reading *Star* magazine while the kids watch TV makes you a Bad Mom. It's hard to imagine anything further off the evolutionary script of mothering—kids hanging out in multiage groups all day, the younger ones learning skills from the older ones so they can lend a hand at home, while moms spend time with their sisters and cousins, parenting together—than the plague of intensive motherhood. Another drop of wine on the side of the plate.

It eventually dawned on me that having choices and the money to make them was another plague upon my mommy tribe. This surprised me at first: we often say that rich people have options that poor ones do not, and having choices is a privilege. We're right. The option of sending your child to a private school with small classes rather than a public school with crowding issues is a distinct advantage. So is the option of choosing between the two safest cars, because you can afford either, rather than having to purchase the cheapest car with a horrible accident rating. In these and other instances, choice and the economic privilege which enables it (which Volvo, cancer specialist, or Norland nanny?) not only improve one's life quality but also protect one's life. But from observing and mothering with the mommies around me, I learned what the research shows: having too many choices is stressful. Facing more than three or four options increases negative effects such as regret, heightened expectations, and disappointment. As the choice set grows larger, those negative effects escalate, leading to *anxiety*. Only one factor mitigates this effect: *if participants are not held accountable for their choices*. Privileged, intensive motherhood presents just the opposite situation. You are utterly responsible for the potentially life-altering choice of the best and safest car seat, stroller, and organic carrots. "I have no idea whom to pick," a mom exclaimed to me in the nursery school's café one day, a pile of nanny résumés in front of her. She was about to return to work full-time. "And it's not like it doesn't matter who I choose. These are my *kids*."

Call it a "first-world problem," but only if you understand that it is literally that: in much of the world, child care is not an issue, because "it takes a village" is a way of life, not just a bumper sticker. This allows women to work, feel fulfilled, and have lives apart from mothering without guilt. Or anxiety. Another drop of wine.

Nannies and housekeepers and mannies and cleaners and house managers are a privileged mommy's most important allies. And frequently, as I learned firsthand and from other mothers, they can be her greatest adversaries. And a major source of anxiety. Before I had children and moved uptown, I always figured it was simple to have good relationships with the people who work for you in your home. If I was "nice" and respectful, our nanny would be "happy" and do a good job. End of story. Women who had problems with their nannies and housekeepers, I figured, were wielding their power against disempowered people unfairly, and paying the price. But to actually live this relationship, I quickly discovered, is to learn just how much more interesting, complex, and anxiety inducing it is than *The Nanny Diaries* suggests. First, there is the matter of money. Many of the nannies I knew made $100,000 per year or more and traveled the world by private jet. They had paid vacation, half or all of their healthcare coverage paid for, and generous holiday bonuses. So we're not talking about the salt mine here. This is why it always struck me as shocking when such nannies and their female bosses—yes, female, for it is very, very rare for a father of the tribe I study to take an active role in household administration—got into power struggles. "She thought I needed her more than she needed me," one woman told me glumly about what I realized was a fairly typical downward spiral in the nanny/housekeeper/boss relationship. "Once she realized how essential she was, she kept demanding more. It got to the point where we felt really exploited."

The truth is that, while mommies have most of the money, nannies do have power—the power to make our lives easier, or to upend our schedules and lives unintentionally or intentionally, and the tremendous power of caring for the most vulnerable members of our families. There are plenty of wonderful, loving nannies out there. One friend's nanny attended child-care seminars at the local JCC—not because she was asked to but because she wanted to. My friend discovered she had taken this initiative only when she found the nanny's notes, transcribed in broken, phonetic English and then painstakingly translated into Spanish, folded on the counter near her purse. Unbidden and uncompensated, this woman had gone to hours of trouble out of devotion not just to her charge and her bosses but also to the idea of making herself a better nanny. Another nanny risked her life when the scaffolding outside a grocery store on the Upper West Side collapsed to find her charge, a baby. Breaking away from first responders who told her it was too dangerous, she dove into the wreckage and found and recovered the baby (who was unharmed, but might not have remained so if not for her caretaker's bravery and devotion).

There are also nannies who are resentful, or have no background or interest in child care and are doing it "until I figure out what I really want to do" (the twentysomething, college-educated variety) or because they are unqualified to do anything else. Some are undermining. Some act out. Some have bad judgment and terrible attitudes. On a day that became so windy so suddenly that police urged people to stay off the street, a friend called her nanny to tell her to come home with the children. Her seven-year-old later reported that the nanny had hung up the phone and said to him, "Your mother is so freaking ridiculous." The truth is there are nannies who passive-aggressively call in sick when mothers have important events on the family calendar. Or leave the house in disarray to make a point. Nannies and mothers get into power struggles. They have arguments. Often they simmer under the same roof, needing and resenting one another. They confront and negotiate the intricacies of socioeconomic and cultural difference (in the case of nannies from other countries) or developmental gulfs (in the case of twentysomethings) and of envy ("My kid sees her more than she sees me!" a mother may fume; "Why should she have so much and I have less?" a nanny may seethe), all within the walls of a home. It can be helpful or maddening to have a nanny, or to be a nanny and have a mother as your boss. But I have never heard anyone describe it as easy.

The chemistry with a nanny, with whom a relationship can be every bit as complex as a marriage, is a wild card, and one of if not *the* most important determining factor in an Upper East Side mommy's anxiety levels and quality of life. At one point I might have scoffed, "But you have the power to fire them!" Having lived it, I now wonder, And *then* what? In a culture where, as Anne-Marie Slaughter has observed, we have no infrastructure of care, no government standards, oversight, or monitoring of caregivers, mothers and nannies are too interdependent and options are too few for it to be quite so simple. Another drop of wine.

And then there is the Gordian knot, the triple-threat plague on my people: the interplay of calorie restriction, plummeting estrogen, and insomnia that dogs just about every one of the women with young children I spoke to. There is no overestimating, I realized at a certain point in my career as a mother on the Upper East Side, how anxious and miserable it can make a person to be sleep deprived, hormonal, and hungry. Women who delay marriage and childbearing may have a sense of perspective and more thoroughly myelinated brains than twentysomethings, and more social and financial stability. But we are less energetic than our younger mommy counterparts. And it's harder for us to recharge by getting the rest we so badly need. As estrogen levels ebb and in some cases plunge from the midthirties onward, sleep becomes elusive. Lower levels of estrogen do more than keep you awake. Researchers are now realizing that women's vulnerability to anxiety and mood disorders may be explained in large part by declining estrogen levels. Estrogen calms the fear response in healthy women and female rats: the higher the estrogen was in the blood of women who were trained on a fear-extinction task by researchers, the less likely they were to startle. In short, when estrogen is on the wane, so is your sense of calm.

Now add to this mix the plague of one of the most bizarre imperatives of the UES: to be as fit, fat-free, and sylphlike as possible. On a business trip to Abuja, Nigeria, my husband visited a market in search of a gift for me. A plump woman in vibrant traditional dress, helping him sort through the brightly colored clothing in her stall, asked, "Is your wife fat?" When he answered, in confusion, "What? No, she's skinny!" the woman looked down in embarrassment. She had meant, "Is your wife healthy and beautiful? And are you a rich man?" She did not make eye contact, he reported, even as he paid and thanked her for her help. His wife was thin, and he had *admitted* it. He might as well have been covered in boils. But here on the Upper East Side, nothing sells faster than a size 00. Women are thin, thinner, thinnest. It is our very own marker of beauty and wealth, and the standard is exacting. "Aside from Hollywood and the modeling world, I don't know of any place where there is more pressure to be thin," Manhattan psychoanalyst Stephanie Newman observed in her private practice on the Upper East Side, where she has treated many patients for eating disorders. And the skinnier you are, endocrinologists tell us, the less estrogen you have. Fat is not necessarily healthy, but fat cells are estrogenic, and estrogen helps blunt anxiety. Nervous and thin go together, it turns out, like Dolce&Gabbana.

Being skinny and being hungry and substituting kale juice for a proper meal, all ways of life in the tribe I studied, affect more than estrogen levels. The conditions of a famous starvation study of thirty-six male WWII conscientious objectors nearly replicate the daily practices of many women on the UES and the standard US recommendations for weight loss today: a five hundred to six hundred calorie deficit daily for a goal of losing one to two pounds per week (the men in the starvation study had sixteen hundred calories a day, and walked twenty-two miles per week, with a weight loss goal of two and a half pounds per week). In that study, the men quickly began to experience lethargy, irritability, and significant anxiety, as well as dizziness, cold intolerance, hair loss, ringing in the ears, inability to concentrate, and loss of sex drive. They became obsessed with food and developed elaborate rituals when they sat down to eat, much as anorexics develop rituals around food preparation and food consumption.

In short, the whole experiment was a lot like a weekday lunch at Sant Ambroeus. And it's worth noting that such dietary restrictions sent a full 6 percent of the motivated and healthy participants in the WWII study to a psychiatric hospital: one man became suicidal; another chopped off three of his fingers. No wonder the women around me, women for whom "juicing" and fasting and "detoxing" and rigorous exercise for hours are a way of life, were so on edge. It was a miracle, apparently, that they were merely giving one another pointed, envious once-overs in school elevators rather than taking meat cleavers to themselves and others.

Indeed, the drops in estrogen seen in skinny women in midlife, a description that fits my tribe to a tee, make them more aggressive. In one study, researchers administered a point-subtraction aggression paradigm game to women who met the criteria for high anxiety and women who didn't. They noted a higher ratio of attack by highly anxious women, and observed, with some surprise, that the attack option of the game had no instrumental advantage in terms of gaining points, and "so constitutes a pure case of spiteful, reactive aggression." Aha, I thought as I read it, flashing back to the sidewalk charges that were a daily affair where I had set up base camp.

And for every plague, a drop of wine. Or a glass. Or a few.

Wealthy husbands on the Upper East Side collect red wine. The wine cellars in their Hamptons homes are a form of cultural capital, suggesting that they aren't just rich consumers; they are refined and erudite connoisseurs. They open a bottle of red for enjoyment, for sharing, but also for power. Like the right contemporary art, the right '94 Pomerol telegraphs not just what you have but also that you *know*. It is the husband, sometimes in consultation with the other husband at the table, who orders the bottles with the three-digit price tags when couples go out to a restaurant in Manhattan.

Meanwhile, their wives drink, usually white (red, they say, keeps them awake) to get by. To be an Upper East Side woman with young children is to drink wine. Nationwide, women are the growth engine for wine sales—and everyone in zip codes 10021 and 10075 and 10028 knows it. The New York City Department of Health and Mental Hygiene found that Upper East Siders are healthier than all other New Yorkers on nearly every measure. But they bombed one: they are 35 percent more likely to binge drink than anyone else in our town. One in five adults in the tribe I studied, in other words, has engaged in binge drinking in the past month. How many of those binge drinkers are women? There are no stats, but based on my fieldwork, and a fair amount of participating versus just participant-observation, my quasi-scientific answer is: a lot. It is nothing, nothing at all, for revelers at a moms' night out to quaff four glasses of wine each. At arts-and-crafts studios where mommies take their kids for birthday parties and rainy days, wine is served as early as 11:00 a.m. The mommies I knew drank—white wine, vodka, tequila, and, for those bent on male approval or setting themselves apart, scotch or some other "guy" whiskey—every night. Except Monday. That was a day for penance—a juice fast to make up for the weekend of drinking and eating. Tuesday through Friday, drinking was on.

"And all bets are off on the weekend," a friend explained when I asked her the rules. Meaning, start in the morning if you want, and have wine for lunch and a cocktail before dinner and more wine with dinner. For many of the women with kids I knew in Manhattan—women who wore sunglasses in the school hallways on Wednesday and Thursday and Friday mornings—drinking was a way to self-soothe and self-medicate, a solution of sorts, some-thing to bring on sleep, a reward for surviving the cab ride, the crosstown schlep, the argument with the nanny. Seeing someone underfed but overserved at a gala or dinner out, seeing someone who needs to be poured into her car by her driver, was noth-ing unusual. People might whisper about it the next day if you went *really* crazy, but there's a basic understanding and unspoken agreement, and it is this: "We drink. No big deal." There's a spec-trum, of course, from teetotaling to being an alcoholic. But what struck me as I drank with the women around me was that, be it psychological, social, or emotional, the drinking was mainly, to my eye, tribal. It is virtually comme il faut because it is part of the culture and it is part of the culture in large part because it works on the worry. "They need a bar in the pediatric ER!" Candace told me emphatically after her trip there with her son.

And it's not just alcohol. On the Upper East Side, benzodiazepines are a girl's best friend. Plenty of the Manhattan mommies I knew relied on prescription drugs, daily. Ativan. Xanax. Valium. Klonopin. Ambien. They had them all, and weren't afraid to take them. Frequently, they mixed them with wine, as was the regular practice of a glam fashion designer and mommy of two whose head was frequently in her plate at an Upper East Side restaurant of the moment—at lunch. The women I knew took antianxiety meds to fall asleep. They took them in the middle of the night, when they woke up with their hearts pounding, panicking about schools or money or whether their husbands were faithful. They took them to calm their nerves before drop-off or a luncheon where they expected to encounter more frenemies than friends (the mere idea of seeing the Queen of Queen Bees at an event, with her sneering and snideness, made me want to reach for a flask). And they took them again when they wore off. I wasn't judging, really. I used benzos myself to medicate for my phobia of flying, and one day in the school elevator, overhearing another mother, a perfect stranger, tell her friend that she hated flying and Xanax didn't help, I turned to her and suggested, with great authority and no self-consciousness, *That's because you have to take it with a Bloody Mary!*" We had never seen each other before, let alone spoken.

Some women will give up their wine and their benzos as their kids get older. For them, these are a way to smother the stress of being in charge of their children and the people in charge of their children and everything around them, all the time. When the kids are older and in school all day and the hand-to-hand-combat phase of mothering begins to fade, so does their using. But for a portion of these mothers, drinking and drugs are more than a phase. For them, motherhood doesn't just incite the urge to drink and mix; it also masks it, providing a convenient pretext and deep cover. Everybody else is doing it. So no one notices. Some of the privileged mommies will develop "a problem." At an Upper East Side AA outpost located in a church between the Prada and Ralph Lauren storefronts on Madison Avenue, exquisite, lean mommies decked out in Chanel and Céline and Valentino, all just a few blocks south, avail themselves of the program's child-care option so they can slip into a meeting. They are a secretive tribe within a tribe and they will never, ever tell. At parties, they will arrive early and carefully request something that looks like wine in a wineglass. At a moms' dinner at Serafina, they will pass off tonic with lime as a vodka tonic. They will say they're not drinking because of antibiotics, or a headache, or an early appointment the next day. They will keep up appearances and save face, because that is the rule and the way. At their AA meetings, they will settle halfway into their chairs without ever really relaxing, rustling in place like slender, nervous racehorses, their faces tense with effort and worry. Really, it could be lunch at Le Bilboquet, the unmarked restaurant and gathering place of the tribe around the corner. All that is missing are the glasses of wine.

But wine cannot blunt the biggest anxieties. One of these, I realized after the evening at Rebecca's, was *dependency*. The more I watched and listened and lunched and drank with the UES mothers around me, the more I saw that for many of them, their lives, happiness, and very identities hinged on things and people entirely outside their control.

Economic dependency on their husbands, I came to believe, kept many of the women I knew awake at night, whether they realized it or not. The knowledge that their husbands could leave them for other women, the simple realization that they could not support themselves without them, seemed to gnaw at some of the women I knew as badly as their hunger pain. Some told me, in hushed tones, that like their mothers and grandmothers, they had secret bank accounts where they stashed their allowances and other money they had access to "just in case." Several women clued me in about "year-end bonuses" husbands gave their wives—as if they were employees rather than partners. "My mother told me to get as much jewelry as possible from my husband. As insurance," a woman told me wryly as we chatted on a playground bench about a mutual acquaintance's spectacularly acrimonious and very public divorce. My interlocutress had graduated summa cum laude from an Ivy. She also had an MBA. But she had never worked.

"The very type of woman who is drawn to a master of the universe type," Manhattan clinical psychologist and author Stephanie Newman told me when I asked her about anxiety and economic dependency in her Upper East Side practice, "may well end up feeling marginalized in her own home, fearful that she cannot fend for herself and support her children." And if things do go wrong in her marriage, "divorce may be no solution, in practical and emotional terms" observes lawyer and psychoanalyst Rachel Blakeman, "for a woman whose self-concept is entirely wrapped up in having a perfect marriage." For many such women, there is no way out of this conundrum—being married to rich and powerful men—that had at first felt like The Answer.

"She shouldn't flirt with other women's husbands!" women told me pointedly about a beautiful French mother and investment banker, a mom at another school whose kids were older than mine, when I asked why so many of the mommies at our school seemed ambivalent about her. She was a transfer to the troop, having married a wealthy New York native, and she apparently found the tribe's sex-segregation practices as bewildering as I did. Like me, she could often be seen talking to men at the kids' birthday parties and concerts. Probably drumming up business, I figured, and trying to have a little fun. I found her glamorous and smart, and always searched her out. I made a point of putting my husband in her path, too. Wasn't any woman who flirted with him doing me a favor? If he was in a good mood, my life was easier. And safe fun and titillation didn't seem like much to ask in exchange for a lifetime of commitment. But for women who felt their marriages and motherhood were their entire identities, and their husbands their only lifelines, I came to realize, flirtation was anxiety inducing, even terrifying. It suggested the possibility and stood as a reminder that it could all be taken away.

Some of these women were economically dependent not only on their husbands but also on their husbands' parents. Much of the spectacular wealth on the Upper East Side is intergenerational, which can lead to strangely infantilized relationships between young adults (and not-so-young adults) and their parents or in-laws. More than one woman described to me the strange pressure of needing to please one's in-laws because they held the financial purse strings. "My husband basically stands to inherit a lot, and that gives his parents very real power over our lives," one

woman explained simply as we walked behind the group on a
school field trip. Chatting about school tuition, which she said her
in-laws paid, had led us here. She showed me her iPhone calendar,
reading off a series of appointments and luncheons to which she
would ferry and accompany her mother-in-law in the next week.
"It's not that I don't want to help out. It's that there's this unspoken script that I *owe* it, because they bought our apartment as a
wedding gift, and my husband works for his father's business."
Another woman described a typical Upper East Side situation:
she and her husband wanted a place of their own out at the beach
for themselves and their two young children. Her husband's parents nixed the idea, saying their own place was much bigger, they
had room for them there, and so their plan didn't make "sense."
Her in-laws were being generous, financially and emotionally,
but it cost the younger generation something, because they were
also being controlling. "It would be nice to feel like we were the
grown-ups," she told me flatly. "It would be nice to have our own
place and some independence." Her situation is more common
than not in the tribe I studied. Many very wealthy people in my
town are, on some level, waiting for their even wealthier elders to
die, with mixed feelings about it.

Other rich women I knew on the Upper East Side had money
of their "own"—but often this meant being financially dependent
on and emotionally beholden to their *fathers*. "I'm not complaining," one woman told me about her parents' significant wealth,
wealth she and her sister stood to inherit, wealth she benefited
from every day in the form of her bankrolled apartment and trips
to Aspen and children's educations. "But it's weird for my husband." Often, a husband works for his powerful father-in-law, or
trades on his father-in-law's cultural capital to forge his own busi-

ness, professional relationships, and deals. Rarely is this state of affairs uncomplicated, because economic dependency is almost never free. Rachel Blakeman told me, "No matter how good the deal feels financially, being beholden to someone else for your well-being and that of your kids is often emotionally costly. It can create resentment, insecurity, and all kinds of issues for a person and in a marriage."

Our female ancestors, women who gathered (and some who hunted, as Agta women still do today), had autonomy and a voice in their communities and power in their partnerships because the food they brought in, the calories they supplied, made them indispensable. Not much has changed. And so, often, the women I studied and knew and had coffee with seemed something even beyond economically dependent. In many instances their very identities seemed contingent and relational, hinging on their relationships—to their friends and in-laws and parents, but most of all to their husbands and children. If you are not in a perfect marriage—and who is?—then how can you be a powerful man's perfect wife? If you do not have perfect children—and who does?—then how can you be a perfect mother, or even a good one? And how can you save face? Divorce is not an option, and neither is trading in the imperfect children you love for perfect ones. Many of the women I knew suffered from the strange, culturally specific anxiety of being extensions and reflections of others. In this sense, even their identities, their very selves, were not precisely or entirely their own.

"Thank *God* that's over," Candace exclaimed over lunch once her husband had transitioned to his new job. I thought she meant it was stressful to be unsure where he would land, or to contemplate a period of time without income. But Candace shook her head. "No, I mean *I* can relax now. I had to look really good every second while he was out there because that's how it is here, especially if you're asking people for something. Pass me the bread." There it was—that unique stress. In this honor/shame culture, having a high-status husband made you a high-status wife. But having a great-looking wife—beautiful, with an enviable body and wardrobe and social connections to wives of other powerful men—could also reinforce and even boost a husband's own social rank and professional status. Candace's husband did, in part, owe his career to how good Candace looked in her Azzedine Alaïa dresses, to her social dexterity, her ability to charm just about everyone. Wives were their husbands' expensive baubles and bottles of wine, proof of their awesomeness, and husbands were their wives' meal tickets. Talk about anxiety. Another plague. Another drop of wine. Another glass. And another.

And then there is the final plague, the one that broke the Pharaoh's will, and broke his heart. After the lice and the boils upon his people, after the plagues of blood, frogs, flies, diseases, hail, locusts, and darkness, still the Pharaoh would not relent. And so God said, *Now I will take every firstborn son, passing over and sparing the Israelites.*

When Candace called me one day on the phone, fighting back tears, she taught me another lesson about anxious mommies, one that was, in retrospect, stunningly obvious but had entirely eluded me. She was hiding in the bathroom, she told me, so that no one could hear her. Her son had recovered nicely from the concussion that took them to the emergency room, or so it seemed. After a week of "brain rest" in a dim room, with no reading or screen time, and another week without any physical exertion, he was back up and running, as funny and smart and energetic as ever, just like his mother. But there was something else now, fourteen days after the accident. I felt my heart speed up as Candace told me this. I took a deep breath, as silently as I could, so that no matter what it was, I could be calm for her. Then she said, desperately: "His *tooth*." His tooth? I wondered. Just his *tooth*? I felt a wave of relief, but she went on urgently. "It's gray. It looks *horrible*." She began to sob. I murmured that it would be all right, and asked what the dentist had said, and played for time, listening. All in a rush now the words tumbled out: It was just an accident. A dustup. He and the other boy had collided. There had been some blood. That was all. He was fine. But now the tooth had gone gray. Killed by the impact. "It's dead in the mouth," Candace said, sounding faraway and sad.

I could hear my toddler son playing with pots and pans on the floor of the kitchen. I had set him up there so I would have time to talk. But in my mind I was seeing all the pictures on all the living-room walls in all the apartments I had viewed with Inga, all those months ago. None of those children in those portraits had a gray tooth. I considered how a single imperfection could feel catastrophic, like a massive, overpowering wave that took your entire identity as a good mother, as a person who feels safe, away from you, pulling you under. Candace cried and cried and as I cradled the phone to my ear and told her that it would be all right, everything would be fine, I instinctively reached down and cradled my belly, too. Because there was more to it, still.

It was a perfect tooth that had been killed. It was the Pharaoh's child and every child, taken by God. It was just a tooth. It was just a story. But it meant that something was wrong, and was a sign that things could go more wrong still. It meant that we could lose them. It was the ghost at the heart of so many Manhattan mother behaviors that seemed to me, until just then, incomprehensibly crazy. The need to be perfect and have a perfect life, the jousting on the sidewalk and the stressing over strollers and nontoxic mattresses and the fights to get him into the right school, the hiring of someone to teach her how to ride a bike—these are the baroque, bizarre flora and fauna that spring from a terrain of damp, fertile panic. Please, I thought, another drop of wine.

CHAPTER SEVEN

A Rainy Day

A T A moment I couldn't precisely pinpoint, I had flipped. A couple of years into life with children on the Upper East Side, I found myself less a participant-observer than a participant, less an insider/outsider and more a person for whom there really was no "outside" anymore. My connections downtown had all but faded—I saw those friends, many of whom were unmarried artists and academics, at Thanksgiving and maybe Christmas. Then they read to my children and showered them with goodies and gifts, and poked loving fun at me about my transformation, which they considered comprehensive, bizarre, and somehow endearing. They were right that I was changed. We were no billionaires, to be sure. Our home on Park Avenue was far from huge (though I did have an entire closet just for my handbags). I insisted that my children do chores. I didn't throw them huge yearly birthday parties, and when they were invited to something I considered over-the-top—a Yankees game in seats in the first row right behind home plate, a party at someone's Hamptons home complete with pony rides and tightrope walkers—I made sure they understood how lucky they were. I did not want my

children to think that all of life was one fantastic first-class experience after another. I did not want to set their expectations high,
or deprive them of the ability to find pleasure in simple places
and in simple things.

But I was an Upper East Side mommy now, because I had
come to care about the things my Upper East Side mommy conspecifics cared about: Where my kids went to school. Whether
I was doing enough for them. Whether my children's teachers
knew what they were doing. Whether my friendships were not
only gratifying and healthy for me but also useful—to me, to my
children, and to my husband's career. I wanted a comfortable, curated life. I wanted a killer body, and beautiful clothing and shoes
by Dolce&Gabbana and Prada, even if I got them on sale, and the
kind of great hair color that required the expense of tending to it
every other month. I wanted a house at the beach. Unlike many
of my Upper East Side girlfriends, I also wanted to work—to
write things I was proud of. But, like them, I wanted to be a good
wife and like them, I wanted most of all to be a good mother. Not
a good-enough mother, but one who did everything I was supposed to do, everything I possibly could, for my children.

Like an Upper East Sider, like the person living in the industrialized West that I was, I thought of motherhood in a certain
way. I subscribed to the script of intensive mothering, even as I
knew that it was peculiar to my privileged niche, and possibly
self-destructive. Motherhood, in the world I first observed, then
adopted, and finally embraced, meant giving life, and then exhausting yourself, sacrificing parts of yourself, sometimes joyfully
and at other times with irritation and aggravation and anxiety,
protecting it. I fretted and worried alongside the other privileged
mommies I knew, sure. Sometimes, I was a nervous wreck about

my children. Like Candace, I might find myself, for a few hours or a day, shattered by a gray tooth and all it suggested. But, like everyone around me, I was conditioned by years of plenty and pediatricians and preschools, desensitized to the immediacy of danger by living as I did, cosseted in a high-rise and riding around in a cushiony SUV. Because of this safety halo, aided and abetted by living in a state of ecological release and abundance and vaccines, I, like all Westerners, took risks with my offspring that our ancestors and contemporary hunter-gatherers, who live as we did for nearly our entire evolutionary prehistory, would never have dreamed of.

Valuing "independence"—theirs and ours—we place our newborns in bouncy seats on the floor while we shower, and hire nannies we don't know, or know only through word of mouth or a service, to try to get a little something done, rather than carrying our babies continuously and handing them off to close relatives for a few minutes or hours at a time. We put them on sleep schedules and feeding schedules, rather than following their lead about when they'd like to eat and nap. And, astonishingly to mothers and fathers in other cultures, we actually leave our infants alone in wooden crates far away from us, all night long. There, they sleep on their own . . . and cry. Many are the anthropologists who report describing this practice to traditional people—hunter-gatherers and foraging agriculturalists who let their babies sit and crawl next to fires and allow their toddlers to play with axes and machetes—who are appalled by what they see as our unfathomable and cruel negligence toward our infants. When they are informed that we frequently let our little ones "cry it out," they are initially disbelieving, then horrified. How, they demand, can we be so callous toward the most precious and dependent of things, a baby?

It's not just what we do but what we believe that sets us relatively privileged Western parents apart from the rest. Here we take for granted that our families of two, three, four, five, and even six children will not only survive but also thrive. They will brush off colds and flus and chicken pox, if they get them, bypassing the more awful things—the disfigurers and paralyzers and killers such as measles and whooping cough and polio—thanks to immunizations. They will go to school and then to college, our children. And medical school or business school or law school. They will marry, in time, and have children of their own. They will make us proud. They will bury us. This is our script.

And so, as I mothered day to day as one did on the Upper East Side, I didn't contemplate, in any sustained or careful or serious way, just how closely the territories of mothering and loss overlap. It's a secret, until it happens to you.

How could I possibly be pregnant? Like some protagonist in a sitcom—or Lifetime Television for Women tragedy—I stared at the two purple lines on the pee-soaked stick and then back at the instructions on the cardboard box.

No way. It was impossible. We had used birth control that failed, those couple of months ago, yes. But we *knew* it had failed, and so I immediately used emergency contraception prescribed by my doctor, following the instructions to the letter. Then I had my period. Scant, but a period. *Twice.* And so there was just no way I, the forty-three-year-old mother of a toddler and a seven-year-old, could be pregnant. What were the chances of emergency contraception failing after contraception failing? *And what were the odds of getting accidentally knocked up at forty-*

three? "How'd you manage *that?*" I could imagine my friends who had gone through round after round of IVF asking. Gripping the marble bathroom counter, I now vaguely recalled family lore about Cherokee and Scottish ancestors having babies at improbably late ages. "Change-of-life babies," my grandmother called them, the bizarre-sounding euphemism suggesting, in retrospect, that it happened often enough for there to be a term for it. It was possible, then. Barely. Maybe the test was wrong. I grabbed the second one, hopeful, hands shaking, and peed on it.

Then again, I considered as I flushed the toilet and waited, these double purple lines might explain a few things. I had been pretty sure I was going through an early and very sudden menopause in the weeks preceding this moment in the bathroom. Or losing my mind. Or dying. My head felt stuffed with cotton. I couldn't think. I snapped at my kids and my husband. Everything—Where is my phone? Why aren't the teachers helping him more? When will the renovation overhead end?—irritated me more than usual. And I was so tired that I fell asleep at my desk, and standing on line at the grocery store ("Excuse me, miss? Um?"), and at Pilates, right on the reformer, mid-stretch. I called my doctor and told him something just wasn't right. We made an appointment—for what, I didn't know; to talk about how it felt to become suddenly insane and sick with an ineffable but undeniable whatever it was?—and I waited. Coffee didn't help my foggy, tired, weak-feeling malaise; the smell of it made me sick.

Oh my God. I was *nauseated*. By coffee. And now, I realized, by other things, too. A lot. *Duh*. I glanced down. Yes, of course: another set of double purple lines. Do not pass.

Naturally, unnaturally, against all the odds, I was pregnant.

I sucked on a ginger candy in my OB's waiting room, waiting. I was here to tell him what we were going to do, he and I. I considered, as I glanced at all the magazine covers of happy, smiling pregnant women all around me, how peculiar yet entirely predictable was the situation in which I now found myself—in primatologist and evolutionary biologist Sarah Hrdy's formulation, as a bipedal, hairless, semicontinuously sexually receptive higher-order primate living in the shadow of agriculture.

Throughout our evolutionary prehistory, as remains the case among many foragers and hunter-gatherers today, women had babies spaced by three- or four- or five-year intervals. After all, a life of foraging and gathering and just-right caloric consumption of mostly plants and nuts and just a bit of meat kept you trim. Women with low body fat ovulate and menstruate less frequently—maybe four times per year. This, plus the burdens of lactation, nursing, and child rearing while foraging kept our ancestors in a very low fertility state long after their babies were born. By the time the next baby rolled around, they had a four-year-old to help out a bit with the newborn. But put women on farms, a drastically more sedentary state of affairs than gathering, and make calories more plentiful, and you quickly ratchet up body-fat levels—and fertility. This lifestyle, with its hallmark monthly menses, stuck with us when we moved out of the fields and farmhouses and into the malls and McMansions and apartment buildings, of course. And so babies spaced a couple of years apart became the norm. This is why, in every town in America, you see a mom pushing her tiny baby in a stroller while the two-year-old rides on the stroller board. Over time, the original, pre-agricultural state of affairs has come to seem strange to us. We humans are forever changing up our own game.

And so here I was. I had a young toddler and a second-grader (I just shrugged and said, "It's a Pleistocene parenting gap," whenever people asked about the age difference between the boys), and I was ten weeks pregnant, I figured. Once my doctor invited me in and closed the door, I lost all semblance of composure. I tearfully explained what my husband and I discussed after the day of double double lines—at my age, with a young toddler, and my medical history, and so on, we simply couldn't. My OB nodded and said the right things. He gave me some forms he had signed, and I left and went to the hospital and filled out more forms for the procedure. I felt numb around the edges as I wrote down the information and handed the chart to the quietly compassionate administrator who told me, with a small, sympathetic smile, to come back the next morning.

Instead of going home or to my office, I walked to Central Park and sat near the lake, in a little wooden pagoda under the trees. It was a weekday morning, sunny and cool but not cold, and there was hardly anyone else around. As I watched a few turtles swimming around in the murky, algae-covered water, I thought about motherhood. I thought about being, all at once, a loving, generous, giving, doting mommy and a flexible, dry-eyed strategic thinker, dispassionately playing the odds like David Lack's mother birds. I thought about reproductive trade-offs and retrenchments in maternal care—those moments, all those moments throughout history and evolutionary prehistory when breeding females of every species had to make hard choices. Feed both twins, or just this one? Sometimes, there is only so much, and so much of oneself, to give. Send this babe to a foundling house, where he might well die, in order to continue to work and provision the children who had made it out of the danger zone of infancy already? Or keep him at home to invest in his well-being, thus possibly damaging the chances of the others? Eject the joey while running from the predator so I have a better chance of surviving? Only if I'm a young-enough kangaroo to breed again, and willing to place a bet on just-right ecological conditions—plentiful food, good weather, few predators—the next time around. And so on.

All of motherhood, always, has been about such trade-offs and choices, as sociobiologist and scholar of motherhood Sarah Hrdy tells us. Like our female early *Homo* ancestors, and like animals everywhere, we seek to balance the well-being of our offspring with that of our future offspring, and with our own. Otherwise everyone dies. Or does less well than they might. Whether privileged or poor, Hrdy notes, "women are constantly making trade-offs between subsistence and reproduction that are similar in outline." My conundrum was ages old, nothing special. But it felt catastrophic.

I stayed in the park, next to the water, for hours. When it was nearly dark, I went home and spoke to my husband at length. I called my doctor's answering service, and he called me back himself shortly thereafter, and I told him I would not be having the procedure the next morning, after all. He asked if we should reschedule and I said no, we were going to skip it entirely. Falling into our bed a few hours later, our children tucked into their own rooms for the night, I marveled at how soft it was, and how comfortable. Sleepy and satisfied and finally peaceful, I pulled my husband's arm around me. "We're lucky," I said, and he agreed.

Being a baby or child has always been a relatively dangerous proposition. Prehistorically, historically, and even today, there is no more perilous period of human development than infancy and childhood—except being a fetus. Even in the industrialized United States, with all our prenatal care, the majority of conceptions do not make it to term. An oft-cited 1988 study found that 31 percent of clinically recognized pregnancies ended in miscarriage. When you factor in unknown pregnancies, many estimates suggest that more than half of all pregnancies "spontaneously terminate."

Once you're born, the odds are strongly in your favor in the US and many other developed countries, of course. Nearly 994 out of every 1,000 babies born in the US survive infancy. But a million babies still die worldwide every single day—mostly from complications of prematurity, disease, and malnutrition. The risks during infancy and childhood were tremendous in our not-so-distant historical past and staggering in our evolutionary prehistory, and they remain so for many traditional peoples. For example, 43 percent of children living in "untouched" hunter-gatherer groups die before age fifteen. And Sarah Hrdy estimates that an astonishing half of all !Kung San women die childless—but not because they have had no children. On average, they have 3.5. The devastating math is personified in the case of Nisa, a !Kung San woman who was interviewed extensively by anthropologist Marjorie Shostak in the 1970s: Nisa had suffered two miscarriages, given birth to four children, lost two before they became adolescents, and then lost two more before they became adults.

Where childhood is perilous, how can motherhood be anything other than terrifying in its delicate contingency? Even today,
even in a context where you can forget it is or ever was hazardous
to be a child and a crapshoot to be a mother, it began to seem
to me, as I watched my anxious mommy friends and watched
myself, picking up and dropping off and cuddling and losing our
tempers, that we could never *really* forget.

Inside us, I began to suspect, as we held our breath at playgrounds and watched warily for milestones at playgroups and
released tension at girls' nights out, informing our mothering is
this deep truth, this inescapable collective calamity: that forever,
we have lost our babies as often as we have kept them. Burying
our babies is as much a part of our fundamental, deep, inherited experience of motherhood as is holding and nursing them.
Consoling ourselves and others over our lost children is very possibly with us, in there, every time we console our children over
a scraped knee. As is the case with so many other pressures that
contribute to who we are, so many other realities that form the
shifting and variable backdrop against which we become mothers, the software of motherloss is and must be, I became convinced in my years in the ostensibly safest of places, the Upper
East Side, still in there. And on some level, the very deepest one,
mustn't it inform every single decision and choice we make about
our children? Aren't we all mulling it over all the time, even when
we don't realize we are, just like Candace?

Evolutionary psychologists who seek to understand the impact of loss on mothers and on our entire species put it this way:

> Child death has played an important role in the evolu-
> tion of humans. Of all stages of development, and at all

historical times beyond modern history, childhood has been associated with the highest levels of mortality. Compared to other evolutionary pressures such as surviving as an adult or finding a mate and having children, the odds of failure to directly contribute to one's genetic line are greatest in childhood. The enormous potential evolutionary pressure exerted by child death should have significantly influenced human psychological adaptations. Despite this potential influence, child death may be one of the least studied influences on human evolutionary psychology (Volk and Atkinson, 2008).

In a town like Manhattan, in a tribe as privileged as the one I studied, tragedy hits with a strange double force. You are knocked in the head by the fact of it, first of all, and then by another echoing pain—the knowledge that you are neither cosseted nor safe, in spite of all your attempts to have made it so. You work out. You have the pediatrician's number memorized. Your home is insured in detail and carefully ordered—you have a professional organizer, for God's sake, who charges $200 per hour to hold the chaos and uncertainty at bay. And yet. When you scratched the surface, just about every mother I knew had lost a child, or her sister or best friend had, in ways that are practically unspeakable. At two weeks pregnant, or at twelve. At thirty-nine weeks, a cord looping its way around the baby's neck, a vine killing a flower. The newborn suffocated by the baby nurse who rolls on him in the night in her sleep. The two-year-old who falls at the playground—a little fall, nothing, she didn't even seem to hit her head—and dies of a concussion a few days later. The toddler who tumbles from the window, dying in traffic, breaking every single heart in the city. The one-year-old who goes to the best hospital in town for a simple, straightforward procedure and never comes home. Three girls, swept away in a fire. The ferocity of the fire, of the loss. Here. Right here. In our world. On the Upper East Side, a place that feels safe, a place where anything is possible, until it is not.

I had been sick a lot during the pregnancy, nauseated beyond anything I had experienced before, but no one was alarmed by this. I threw up daily, but I had with the other pregnancies, too. I threw up first thing in the morning, and then when I brushed my teeth, and then when I took my son to school. I threw up midconversation with moms outside school and on the phone. I threw up in bags in taxis. I took it as a sign that the baby was doing well, since that's how most obstetricians take such things. Still, it did take a toll, being sick and exhausted every day, and I felt bad that I couldn't play with my younger son the way he'd like. "Let's pretend Mommy is a blob and you're a little boy," I'd say, lying on the floor of his room. He would pull all his toys up and play around me. Later in the pregnancy he would pat my breasts and my stomach, smiling. "Funny," he managed one day through his pacifier, patting.

I had lost some weight, but I had in the last pregnancy as well, and the baby was progressing nicely, passing all the measuring tests and genetic tests and amnio with flying colors. When we found out it was a girl we were stupefied—*We don't have girls! We have boys!* we wanted to tell whoever was in charge of these things—and that is when my husband, who had been ambivalent about doing this all over again in his fifties, came around. Sometimes he would say, excitedly, "There's going to be a baby!"

She was a burden, in a way, this baby, taxing our space and stealing the older one's crib and requiring private school and college tuition and a renovation and four or five more years of a full-time nanny. That was why I had felt, until the very last possible second, that this baby could not possibly be. But now, the more we planned for her, the more excited we were about having a her to plan for. We prepared and plotted and slept easily. I decided I wanted her to have my last name, and my husband, who had put up a terrible fight about it with the previous two, agreed without a single bit of pushback. I also decided, without telling my husband, that I wanted to name her Daphne. How could I not submit to her, this baby who so wanted to be born? How could I not give her a name?

You don't think of New York City as a place teeming with nature, but it is. There were lots of trees on our block, and a leafy entrance to Central Park not far away. In the early summer mornings the birds do not sing—they screech. I could hear them before we even stepped off the elevator to walk through the lobby of our building, on our way to my obstetrician first thing that wet day. I had called the previous afternoon to report that I might be bleeding, it's hard to tell with black underwear, and when I put a Kleenex down there it was light pink, not red, and that was okay, right? In a tight voice my doctor told me to lie down—from his tone I knew he meant *really* lie down, not some halfway, maternal kind of lying down where you keep popping up to read one of your kids a story or get dinner ready—and drink some water and call him back shortly. Then I called my husband, who said, "You bleed when you're pregnant. You always have. It's what your body does." I agreed with a sigh, mentioning that my doctor seemed to be taking this very seriously, but that it would be fine. He went to a work-related event after my sons' nanny agreed to stay late. "It's probably nothing," I told her.

When I called my OB later to check in as instructed, he said to drink more water, and hold absolutely still until I was in his office first thing the next morning.

Now the doorman swung the lobby door open, and the bird sounds were nearly overpowering, mostly blue jays making their urgent, unbird-like screams, and we stepped out, first under the awning and then into the rain toward the waiting black town car. That's when my husband, never one to be rude, asked, "No umbrella?" Our building's doormen typically walk you to your car carrying an umbrella for you when it's raining. That way you experience seamless cosseting and comfort, door-to-door. But the rain wasn't really serious—not yet—and our doorman shrugged it off with a laugh, as did I. Then I crawled into the car and lay down across the backseat with my head on my husband's lap, and my husband said, "I don't know what the hell is wrong with people." He looked out the window as we drove across the park—quiet and desolate and gray in the rain, not the hepped-up, crowded, insipid park of sunny weekend days but the park I loved, emptied out, quiet, moody—and shook his head. "He should have used a fucking umbrella. My suit is soaked."

"What do you see down there?" I asked the doctor. I didn't feel nervous. I had been told to go on bed rest before because I might well have had a miscarriage—most recently a year and a half ago or so, I mused now, my feet pressed against the Minnie Mouse washcloths, if that's what they were, that covered the stirrups, and everything had been *fine*. Lily, the calmest mother I knew, had exchanged long, reassuring emails with me about it for days and talked with me on the phone for hours as I cried. I went on bed rest, and we got a home health aide who did Sudoku and made me penne with Bolognese sauce. I watched *The Real Housewives of Orange County*. I told Lily and Candace about every episode, in great detail, and they listened and laughed and kept me afloat. Everything was *fine*, the way it had been fine with all the other things: the time I started bleeding bright red in my first pregnancy and the doctor gave me fifty-fifty odds; the time during the birth of my first son when the nurse, watching the baby's dipping, arcing vital signs during the absurdly long labor, exclaimed to the doctor, "This baby is coming and going, and I don't like it!"; the problems with my husband's ex-wife and his daughters as he and I tried to make a life together; the dramas and disasters that seemed to never end. Everything was always fine.

"You don't want to know," my OB sighed from underneath the pink sheet draped primly over my lower half. Now he pushed back in his rolling chair to where I could look at him, and when I began to hoist myself up on my elbow for this conversation, he said, very quietly, "Lie down."

Lying flat on your back is a strange way to get bad news. Unless the person looms over you or you close your eyes, you're just staring up at the ceiling and listening. And then, depending on the severity of the badness of the news, you might experience what I had previously thought to be a cliché or a dramatic device—you might find yourself looking down at your own body. A voice was saying "bulging membranes" and "incompetent cervix" and "her foot is sort of sticking out of your cervix" and I was wondering,

How did I get up here, and who is that woman down there who looks so upset? It was as if her whole face were crying—contorted, red, melting into itself. Her roots were pretty dreadful, too.

When my husband grasped my hand, I slammed back into myself. It was a painful sensation, like bumping your elbow, except your whole body is your elbow, and I felt dazed and flattened somehow as I demanded, croaky-voiced and incredulous, "What?" Now I could see my OB's face as he said, simply and with a forced calm quietness, "These things usually don't end well." He looked pale and tired. I noticed then that I was wringing my hands together, but it felt more like searching for something and trying to rub it away at the same time, and I willed myself to stop.

"So do you think I'm going to lose the baby?" Now I felt almost serene. Was that the worst thing? Okay. Was he going to tell me something worse? I doubted it. We hadn't been sure we wanted this baby and at the very last minute we decided that we did, and now we might not have her. But we would. Wouldn't we? Everything was going to be fine. He mentioned a cervical cerclage, a little stitch or two to hold the cervix shut, and I said that I knew what it was, and told him I had written a story about it for a woman's magazine once, it had prevented a woman I interviewed from going into preterm labor, and then she hung upside down for a few weeks, and everything was *fine*.

It can only have sounded like so much yammering to my doctor, who nodded and repeated that he was sending me to the hospital right now.

"Like, right now?" He nodded. For how long? my husband asked, squeezing my hand. "Well,"—my obstetrician played for time here, I have to suppose in retrospect, and then he said, slowly and precisely—"it really depends. It could be a long while. Or not." There was a doctor at the hospital who specialized in high-risk cases, he went on, mentioning this other doctor's name—oh yes, I loved him, he had done my amnio all three times, he was wonderful, I prattled and chatted—and this doctor might have some other ideas. So go. Go right now? I asked again, aware that I had asked this before but unable to remember the answer. Yes, he said, unsmiling. I got myself ready and he told me he liked my shoes. I told him that they were called skimmers, and that they were for the rain, and that girls have all the fun.

Once I was admitted, I asked a resident who came in why they hadn't elevated the foot of my bed. Why was I just lying flat? Wasn't the point to keep the baby in there? She smiled. "Do you really think it's a good idea to spend the next eighteen or twenty weeks with your feet up? Come on, now." I stared at her, smiling at me as though we were in on the same secret, like we knew the same things. I nodded in confusion, my impulse to agree apparently unaffected by the dim realization that I was agreeing, quite possibly, to a tragedy. For a moment I understood what she was saying, glanced it, and then I ducked away.

What the hell did she *think* I thought? I thought there was going to be a way to make this all better. I was waiting to talk to the high-risk OB who had done my amnio every time, the one who was so young and cute and smart that all the mothers and expectant mothers called him Doogie Howser behind his back. He could fix anything, and he would.

They were going to do an ultrasound later, hours and hours later, so my husband would go home for a bit. I made a list of things I wanted him to bring back to me when he returned that afternoon. This included makeup and toiletries, a collection of academic papers on women and aggression, and a Henry James novel I had already read four or five times. And I wanted a picture of my sons. Looking at their faces would be like reading Henry James again and again—I knew the outcome, and it was comforting, in spite of the difficulty and sometimes the pain, to trace those same familiar contours over and over with my eye and with my mind. Someone brought me some horribly vivid green Jell-O and I thanked her and asked her to take it away and, with an understanding smile, she did. Another doctor came in later and asked me how I was and what I did and when I said I was a writer and researcher she said, "Don't research this, please. You'll drive yourself crazy." I promised not to, and then I started to cry and she said something kind like they all did. Gesturing to the photo of my two young sons I had taped up next to my bed—my older son laughing while his baby brother screamed at the top of his lungs, perhaps because his big brother was pinching him off camera, or perhaps just because—I told her that I already had two kids. If I didn't I don't think I could bear this, I said. So it could be worse. She looked at me for a moment, and then she said, very quietly, tilting her head to one side, "It could be worse, but it could be better, too," and she was right.

"Here's the baby; here's the heartbeat," the ultrasound technician said, unable to meet my eyes. Then she fled, leaving her clipboard and her glasses behind. "I'm going to give it to you straight," Dr. Doogie Howser said as he walked in, looking at the ultrasound projected on the wall. My beautiful baby in silhouette, floating in her grainy gray shadow world, the mysterious not-knowing, not-

known world, the sound of her heartbeat playing loudly, sooth-
ingly, reassuringly, like something that will never stop.

"Okay," I chirped. It was going to be fine.

He started to talk, quickly, like someone wanting to be finished, and it was this quality that I noticed before I really heard
or took in the words. The upshot was that Daphne was doomed.
There was no way. Well, there were extraordinary measures, but
the chances that those would save her were heartbreakingly, sick-
eningly slim. And the risk to me was tremendous. Infection, high
blood pressure, death. Daphne was dying inside my body, and
simply too premature and too unhealthy to survive outside, even
in one of the world's best NICUs. His voice went on, quiet and
quick, urgent, firm, a voice that was reasoned even as it said un-
reasonable, insane, and impossible things. *There isn't going to be a
baby. She wasn't really waving at you in that ultrasound last week. You
didn't want her and then you changed your mind and now you can't
have her.*

I said *No*, intending just to cut him off, to say *No, wait, what
about*, to steer him to another way of understanding it, to lead
him to the part of the room or the sentence or the idea where
Daphne was fine and everything was just fine, to the place where
broken things can be salvaged and put back together. But I must
have been screaming instead of talking, because the doctor be-
side him said, "Oh my God," very softly and put her face in her
hands, and then she reached over to turn on the light and the
room was garish and antiseptic, and there was no way to hide
from anything. No more grainy, beautiful shadows, no baby Rorschach to watch, to be lulled by, to follow to another place.

Sometimes women wanted to have labor induced and then de-
liver the unviable fetus, the doctor was saying, and some wanted

"to let nature take its course" and expel the fetus . . . "Are they *crazy*?!" I demanded of no one in particular, cutting him off. But Doogie Howser seemed to think I really wanted to know, and he said, "Well, some women find that, for closure, they want to go through the process, and see the—"

I cut him off again. "How big is she?" I demanded and he said, "We don't really . . ." but I urgently needed to know this now and I practically shrieked, "How big is she? *Tell me how much she weighs!*" and so he made an estimate and I began sobbing again, but it was an easy decision, now that I knew. She was someone to me, and I could not wait and let her dwindle away into nothing; it could not be a slow, fading good-bye like that for my baby. I noticed now that my husband's eyes were closed, and he kept them that way for a long time as I stared at him. Daphne was kicking a lot now, and when I looked down I noticed how absurdly, extremely pregnant I looked for someone just into her sixth month. Because I am small, and because this was the third baby, I had popped early, and looked much farther along than I was, and it was, in that moment, unbearable to contemplate the huge nothingness that had opened up in the very spot where there had been a body that changed and grew, plans, a newly decorated room, a baby.

Letting nature take its course, the doctor was saying, could take a few days, and now I knew what people meant when they wrote or said that they felt cornered "like a wild animal." I was trapped, crouched in a spot that was getting smaller, and I used my words to try to push my way out, but it was hard to talk—the words came out like breaths and gasps, and I was angry at myself for that.

"She isn't in pain," Doogie Howser was saying now, "and you didn't do anything wrong." And when I asked him, "How do you know? How do you know it isn't my fault?" he grimaced and closed his eyes for a moment, and then he opened them and said, "Because I know. I just know it's not your fault." Something had pierced his expression, it seemed, as he said it—he was suddenly a person talking to another person, trying to coax her back into the world.

I stayed alone in the hospital the night before the surgery, insisting that my husband needed to be at home with our children. Since I was in the labor-and-delivery area of the hospital, I heard babies crying as I slept. I jerked awake again and again, realizing I was in the hospital where I had given birth to my children, thinking I had to get my baby, that it was my little girl who was wailing nearby.

Dr. Doogie Howser would do the surgery, and he came by the next day in the morning to tell me, somewhat sheepishly, that it was scheduled for 3:00 p.m. He was sorry for the delay, he said, and then he looked at what I was reading and we chatted a little about Henry James. And then I waited, first alone and then with my husband, talking and doing nothing. I couldn't eat, but I didn't want to. Daphne was kicking so hard, fluttering so much, that you could see it through the hospital gown I was wearing. The doctors explained that this had to do with the amniotic fluid seeping away. To me, that sounded a lot like she was suffocating. I kept telling her, in my head and aloud, that I was sorry, and that it wouldn't be long now. At one point I turned to my husband and said, "We've had some good times," something I always say to him when something terrible is happening, and he smiled.

I thought I was okay as they wheeled me into the OR, which

really does look dramatic in the same way it does in television shows when they do those shots from the perspective of the person being wheeled in. I was fine until we got inside, where it was hushed and very somber with bright lights, and everyone was in their green scrubs and masks and shower caps, and they started to transfer me from the gurney to the operating table—is that what it is called?—and Daphne fluttered and kicked, and in spite of or because of the fact that they had told me this was happening because nearly all the amniotic fluid was gone and she could not survive, it felt so pathetic that I said something like, *Please hurry, I can't stand it, she's kicking so much.* I noticed a nurse crying—she was wearing a pink surgical mask—and then Doogie Howser was holding my hand and talking to me. He asked me if I had anything surprising, like piercings, that he should know about, and I laughed and we talked about all the surprises he had had along these lines. He kept holding my hand for a long time, which was at once awkward and reassuring, like a date almost, but a date with someone who is about to perform a surgical procedure on your dying baby because she doesn't have a chance in hell and you can't sit around and wait to expel her. I asked the anesthesiologist what she was going to give me and she said, "Something to make you go to sleep," and Doogie Howser rolled his eyes and said, "I don't think you know what we're dealing with here. Tell her *exactly* what you're giving her and *exactly* how much." She did—it was some kind of benzodiazepine—and I remember telling her that I wanted her to give me the maximum dosage, so I would be completely out, gone, but to make sure that I didn't die from anesthesia. And I wanted clean lines, I managed to say as I was going under; I had children and I didn't need to die of some stupid, entirely preventable infection.

Afterward my OB was there, and my husband, and we chatted and then Dr. Doogie Howser came in, probably to get a sense of how I was doing. He said hello and asked, "Do you remember what we talked about after the surgery, when you were waking up?" I opened my eyes very wide, feeling alarmed, wondering, searching. I had no idea. "Was it anything we can't repeat in front of my husband?" I ventured, and everyone laughed except Doogie Howser, and then eventually he left the room and I was left wondering what the hell I had said. *What had I said?* To this day I wonder what I said; to this day my response to losing Daphne is to wonder what the hell I said to Dr. Doogie Howser in the moment I was swimming out of the blackness. The anxious, nagging worry is a black cord that connects me to him, and to her.

The doctors had all said "the pregnancy" and "the fetus" when we discussed what was happening and everything that could not be done. The fetus could not be saved. The doctors could not take any steps to prevent this stillbirth of the fetus. It could not be turned back or turned around or stopped. The fetus was unviable. Then, the social worker who came after "the surgery" called her "the baby." This sharp and sudden semantic shift was presumably intentional. Shut down the mother in your brain so you can have the procedure. Open up the mother in your brain now that she is dead and disposed of so you can mourn. The way we always have for the forever in which we've lost our babies. The social worker asked if I wanted a funeral and I said no. Doogie Howser had already asked, and told me that if we didn't, she would have a "hospital burial," explaining that basically she would be dispensed of as medical waste. "Which she isn't," he was quick to add, and

I said, "Well, I guess she is," since we hadn't been able to donate any stem cells or use her tissues in any other way. Now the social worker asked if I wanted a memorial box. It had a baby hat inside, she explained, and the death certificate, and a little hand and footprint, and I grimaced, I think, feeling that was outrageous somehow, and ridiculous. I imagined what I might do with such a box. Shove it into a dark spot high in a closet? Put it in the storage unit? What? We talked about how I felt singled out—who the hell loses the baby just into the sixth month? You feel safe after twelve weeks; who knew? And *why?*—and she pointed out that all the women in this wing of the hospital had lost their babies during the second or third trimesters. *A whole wing of us*, I thought. Something to feel good about.

Motherhood is carved out of death's territory as much as it is out of the territory of the living. No one told me that. Not the pediatricians, and not the upbeat magazines like *Fit Pregnancy* and *New Mom!*. But when I turned to anthropology, to the books already on my shelf and the ones I bought in the months after I lost Daphne, trying to understand, I saw this massive true secret, stretched out but never worn out, across what seemed like eons. Nisa's losses helped me make sense of my own. And now I learned something else, too, the obvious lesson that had never occurred to me before: when a baby or a child dies, the world stops. In a small but very real way, a way that cannot be undone or denied, the world ends. And then slowly, over the weeks and months and years, it is the job of everyone who loved that baby or child, who has ever loved *any* baby or child, to remake the world, to get it to start again. And then again, another job, more work: to somehow find a way to live in a world where something like this can happen. To live with the daily bitter taste and the unfairness, the flat, anguished sensation of having been turned inside out, of being unprotected. The crazed but logical, urgent-feeling need to hide away your littlest one, the one who is left, the obsessive fear that now he or she will be hit by a car or walk into the pool or somehow, anyhow, be extinguished. How long had it been, I wondered day after day, week after week, that women had felt this way, had known this and forgotten and remembered it? It was in us, I knew.

When Lily's three-year-old daughter died—unexpectedly, quickly, essentially from a cold—we made keening noises and fell to the floor, all of us who loved her, all of us who loved our own children, everyone who heard. The ripples went outward from Lily to us, her girlfriends, first. And from us to all our closest friends, to all their friends and then to every single woman and man with a preschooler in Manhattan. We were stunned, with pinched faces and tight voices and red eyes, as we brought our children to school and talked in the hallways and over coffee and on the phone. We cried and cried. We are still crying. Even those who only knew someone who knew someone who knew someone who knew her. *No.* How did this happen? It can't be. What happened, exactly? Why? What will her mother do?

Flora was three and three-quarters years old. Her hair was wispy and blond and her eyes were huge and blue. She was a fussy eater and she didn't like anyone to touch her head. She loved cooking and school and ballet. She was just becoming herself. One night, about a week before she collapsed, she and her big sister came to our house to play with my sons, and while I was getting dressed to go out with Lily and my husband, there was a tiny knock on my door, and there was Flora, with a gift wrapped in white tissue paper and a gold bow. *This is for you*, she said shyly, smiling, looking at the floor and then daring for a moment to look directly into my eyes. I kneeled and kissed her. "Thank you, Flora," I said. She had walked so far, all the way down the long hallway of our apartment, away from her mother and her big sister and the other kids and the warm, bright room with the television playing *The Cat in the Hat*, on her errand toward me. She helped me open the gift—a skirt that Lily had made—and then Flora headed back down the hall, all on her own. Later I told Lily this story and she made a choking noise and said, "She was getting so brave. She was doing more things like that."

She was here, and then she was gone. The mind understands it in pieces, the smallest bits. Not *She is gone* but *She will not wear that tiny sweater with yellow flowers on it again, or those pink rain boots*. Her small cubby at school, the one that held her pink backpack and whatever she made in art that week, is emptied out. I am holding her princess umbrella in my hand and she won't, she can't, do that again. How much time? How long to assemble all the pieces into a whole and take it in, the loss of her, the truth of her being gone?

Gelada baboon, chimp, and mountain gorilla mothers have all been observed carrying, grooming, and cradling the bodies of their dead infants. Often, they do this for so long that their babies' remains become mummified. In the case of the chimps and geladas, the mothers carry the corpses of their offspring in highly atypical ways—by the limbs, with one hand, or by mouth—suggesting that, even as they gently care for them, they realize their babies are no more. I felt connected to them whenever I thought of it, like an animal, dragging my deluded hope and heartbreak and instinct with me up and down the avenues, and I suspected Lily did, too. There was no comparing the loss of a toddler, a little person you had known and loved for almost four years, with losing a baby you never met. I was careful not to. But Lily would sometimes say, "I feel like you understand because something awful happened to you." To all of us. But mostly, most awfully, to Lily. To Nisa. To so many others, singled out for singular, universal, unremarkable, remarkably unbearable sadness.

It took a long time to realize, to really understand, that I was not pregnant anymore. One day I gathered up all the maternity clothes, and all the postbaby clothes—the nursing shirts and nursing bras and the soft sweaters with funny slits for breastfeeding—and put them in a grocery bag and placed them out on the service landing, the place for garbage and recycling and things to be repurposed as well, in the owner-to-doorman-to-doorman's-family-or-church cycle that happens in buildings here. *There,* I thought.

That's when a kind of fog came down, and I could never remember where my keys were and I answered emails four times, and I raged. I raged at myself for misplacing my wallet and throwing my shoes in the garbage can after taking them off, as if that were simply what one did. I raged when I realized I had put my cell phone in the refrigerator. I raged at my doctor for not understanding that I had Alzheimer's. What else could account for this inability to remember what I had said and done and where I had been and what I had promised? I felt cold all the time. My older son drew a picture that I came across in his room: two stick figures, one with a huge belly and a tiny body with Xs instead of eyes inside; the other with a box and lines coming out of it. *What's this?* I asked, and my son said, "It's when the baby died. That's the doctor and his machine." He wrote letters, one to Daphne and one to Flora. *I'm glad you're my baby sister, even though you died*, he wrote to Daphne. *I miss you, please be in touch if you can*, the one to Flora ended.

We were marooned together, our little family, it seemed, in our sadness. My husband didn't understand the depth of my anguish and my anger—how could he?—and on the worst days I felt walled off even from him, as if he were someone who just came and went against the backdrop of what I had lost. I tried to work, thinking that writing might help, but my mind was unreliable and disobedient. I couldn't remember words—some that anyone might forget, like *ephemeral*, but also words like *that* and *also*. I would call Candace or my friend Jeff, the English professor, and ask them to tell me what I meant, what I was trying to say. They tried to help me through the disorientation and bitterness, one word at a time.

Sometimes, the world outside our home seemed to be ebbing away. The things I had cared about or focused on—not just my work but also the work of finding a place for me and my sons in a world that had gone from utterly alien and alienating to familiar to almost-normal—seemed ridiculous to me now, bent and refracted through the lens of loss. What was the point? Who cared about one more book? Who cared whether my kid was invited to a birthday party, or spurned for a playdate? Why had I ever cared so much? I was vulnerable and raw, but I was clear that now I had no patience for the pettier games of Manhattan motherhood. If anyone gave me the stink eye, I thought, or said or did anything nasty to my kid, I would teach her a lesson, and take her down into the gloaming with me, and let her know a thing or two about what really mattered. I dared the Queen of the Queen Bees—who, it was said, had recently, in the school halls, grabbed and flipped down the collar on the coat of another mother who wouldn't tell her where she bought it, and then mocked it as "cheap"—to come anywhere near me. Luckily for us both, probably, she didn't.

But something else happened. Every day, without fail, I heard from some of the mothers I knew from my son's school, and my younger son's playgroup. "The amnio just kept coming back the same but we kept waiting, hoping. So I was *really* far along when . . . you know," a woman who had struck me as preposterously rich and indifferent and vain told me over coffee. Now she looked at me and said, "I know what it's like, and I'm really sorry." I had been so wrung out and tired, but she insisted that I meet her. We didn't know each other well. Now I began to weep—about Daphne and about her baby, too—and she said, "I'll help you." She would. She did. She was part of this, and she knew it. They all did. Surprisingly, unexpectedly, the mothers, many of whom I had dismissed as unfriendly, self-involved, and shallow, showed me what they were made of, showed me what motherhood is.

One by one, daily, day after day, they were in touch. They took me to lunch, and sent flowers, and invited us to their summer homes. They emailed just to say hello. They told me their own stories. "I lost twins when I was twenty-two weeks along. Well, I mean, one was stillborn, and one lived for another two weeks, but then he died. And I just wanted to tell you I understand. I do." Another woman from my son's school told me how she had lost her baby at nineteen weeks and nearly died of blood loss. She had transfusion after transfusion and dreamed of her other children. We walked up and down the bridle path in Central Park in our exercise clothes, and she listened to me and I listened to her and I wondered how many other women in the park just then, or in the buildings around it, and how many mothers in wider and wider concentric circles across the city and the country and the world, were thinking about similar losses just then, just as we rounded the corner and saw what my toddler called the "crooked tree," a perfect place for someone tiny to sit, with the arm of someone who loved him propping him up from behind.

Women told me stories of losing babies the week or the day before their due dates. A woman I had considered cold beyond comprehension, I learned, had walked into her baby girl's room and found her dead, at nearly six months, of SIDS. One woman told me of her baby who died, apparently of nothing at all, eight months after she was born. She told me this story as if in passing, as if my own loss were the *real* point, and I reached out and touched her arm. "It won't ever be okay, but it will," she said with an apologetic smile as we stood there on the sidewalk.

I was ashamed and confused and relieved in equal parts when I realized that many of the other mothers I had written off, whose reserve or downright tribal clubbiness I had been hurt by, intimidated by, I had dismissed far too quickly. A good number of the women I had found so bitchy and off-putting would now not let me put them off. They offered to host my older son for a sleepover, or take him to the movies. They sent over dinner. And when people invited us away for the weekend, we went. We ate and talked, and we swam with our children and their children in their pools. We called it the Dead Baby Tour. I thought my loss would widen the chasm between me and them, but it closed it. They had lost, too. We joked, the other mothers who had lost and I, that we should make T-shirts that said, "I threw up for six months . . . and all I got was this lousy T-shirt." I had okay days and worse days and much worse days. But the other mothers, some of them the sidewalk chargers and the Birkin wielders, the ones who had made me feel that my sons and I were playdate pariahs, did not give up on me. Some of the very ones who had hazed and harassed me came over for a glass of wine. They sat and they listened and they showed an amazing and impressive ability to just be there with my pain and rage, and to care. For weeks and months and in some cases, for years.

One of the biggest shifts in the last decade of anthropology, one of the discoveries in the field that has changed everything, is the realization that we evolved as cooperative breeders. Bringing up kids in a nuclear family is a novelty, a blip on the screen of human family life. We never did child rearing alone, isolated and shut off from others, or with just one other person, the child's father. It is arduous and anomalous and it's not the way it "should" be. Indeed, for as long as we have been, we have relied on other females—kin and the kindly disposed—to help us raise our offspring. Mostly we lived as Nisa did—in rangy, multifamily bands that looked out for one another, took care of one another, and raised one another's children. You still see it in parts of the Caribbean today, where any adult in a small town can tell any kid to toe the line, and does, and the kids listen. Or in Hawaii, where kids and parents alike depend on *hanai* relationships—aunties and uncles, indispensible honorary relations who take a real interest in an unrelated child's well-being and education. No, it wasn't fire or hunting or the heterosexual dyad that gave us a leg up, anthropologists now largely concur; it was our female *Homo* ancestors holding and handling and caring for and even nursing the babies of other females. *That* is in large part why *Homo sapiens* flourished and flourish still, while other early hominins and prehominins bit the dust. This shared history of interdependence, of tending and caring, might explain the unique capacity women have for deep friendship with other women. We have counted on one another for child care, sanity, and survival literally forever. The loss of your child weighs heavily on me in this web of connectedness, because he or she is a little bit my own.

I knew that. I had learned about cooperative breeding and communal nursing in school and in my research. I had thought about it and written about it. But now I felt it.

What had happened to me must have been terrifying for the mothers who hadn't experienced it, and a nearly unbearable reminder for those who had. But they did not stop asking me how I was, and they did not stop wanting to know. There is frequently astonishing competition and aggression among women with children in Manhattan—the sartorial showdowns and calculating once-overs in school elevators. But there is also, I learned after I lost Daphne, extraordinary cooperation and support when it comes to looking out for one another by looking out for one another's children. Just like mothers in a small town, just like mothers long ago, women with children on the Upper East Side form tight relational networks that function in part as emotional support and in part as surrogate child care. They did not give up on me, because they couldn't.

CHAPTER EIGHT

Summary Fieldnotes

After some six years of fieldwork on the Upper East Side of Manhattan, among a group of approximately 150 mothers of young children living in an area of roughly 250 acres, my immersion in and identification with the tribe I studied was comprehensive. Nothing would have suggested such an outcome. I was initially a new transfer to this particular troop of higher-order primates: I had dispersed at sexual maturity from a geographically and culturally distant group, then lived in the southern corner of the island for many years, embracing the practices and ways of being that prevailed there, before migrating to their far-northern habitat, a niche of superabundance, in search of opportunities for me and my offspring. I did not practice the religion of the tribe I studied; I undertook distinct personal adornment and costuming practices and ablutions until learning their ways, and then frequently continued to avoid conforming to those; my seasonal voluntary migration patterns were distinct from theirs; and I had diminished resources in relative terms. It was no surprise that I, like many other new female transfers to human and nonhuman primate groups the world over, had low status and was hazed, even harassed, by higher-ranking troop members—who had usually inherited their status, generally from their fathers and their husbands—for many, many months after my arrival. Sometimes I suspected it would go on forever.

But primatologist Robert Sapolsky and others have observed, based on years of fieldwork among nonhuman primates, that while low status can create stress and high status is inherited and confers all types of benefits, rank is perhaps more flexible and less static among primates than many field scientists initially believed. For example, a low-ranking baboon may, through shrewd coalition building (via grooming, forming alliances during skirmishes, food sharing, and infant care), engineer agreeable life circumstances and outcomes for him- or herself and his or her offspring. Sapolsky and others further suggest that betas may have lower stress levels than alphas in nonhuman primate groups. Life might just be better when you're not at the very top, constantly fending off the envy and coup attempts of others.

While the implications of these discoveries for humans are unclear, after months of assiduous work to find allies and build coalitions, I was ultimately content with my rank, friendships, and, most important for a primate, my offspring's prospects, after several years of living among what I eventually came to think of as my tribe. In part the improvement of my lot could be attributed to my social "work"—cultivating attachments and affiliations for me and my sons; doggedly (and, arguably, pathetically) persisting in attempts to build alliances while ignoring being ignored, and thus not losing face; and optimizing the brief attentions of an alpha male. But the precipitating event of the transformation in my status may well have been the loss of a pregnancy at an advanced stage, which elicited unexpected compassion from my conspecifics. This event likely activated deep tendencies of generosity, care, and empathy among a group of women who evolved as cooperative breeders, and whose ancestors regularly cared for the children of their kin and fellow band members. While this practice no longer prevails in utterly changed ecological and environmental conditions, it is clear that when it comes to cooperative breeding, communal care-taking, and simply caring, in the words of anthropologist Steve Josephson, "the software is still in there."

I N ANTHROPOLOGIST Bronislaw Malinowski's *Diary in the Strict Sense of the Term*, the personal underside of his official ethnography of life among the Trobriand Islanders off the coast of New Guinea called *Argonauts of the Western Pacific* (1917), we see him unravel. Having moved to a remote archipelago in the name of a burgeoning social "science" whose practitioners struggled to distinguish themselves from missionaries, traders, and colonial administrators, Malinowski frequently offers a portrait of himself as "lost." This eminent founding father of anthropology experiences rage at his informants, who sometimes walk away after he gives them tobacco, ignoring their "obligation" to offer, in turn, truths about themselves and their culture. He expresses all manner of personal and professional insecurity, and even a kind of emotional and psychological free fall, as he adjusts to bewildering surroundings—living in a hut, the sweltering sun, a foreign language, and an entirely alien way of life. He imagines, again and again, that he is deathly ill. He feels anxious, lonely, and sexually frustrated.

I often thought of Malinowski, about whom I had written in my doctoral dissertation, as I went through my days on the Upper East Side. I thought of his searing honesty about a conundrum beyond his control, yet essentially of his own making. I thought of how flawed and resentful and petty and unscientific he sometimes seemed, how shallow and biased he could come across in his personal, private writing, versus the cool, analytic, distant, professional voice of *Argonauts*. Malinowski, along with a handful of others, basically "invented" anthropology, a discipline I have always loved for its powerful blending of storytelling and insight, its uneasy but undeniable juxtaposition of one individual outsider's personal experience and the overarching narrative of a culture. I am not an academic anthropologist—I did not major in anthropology, even as I studied it and later made a career of understanding it and writing about it and teaching its history in my cultural-studies courses. Nor did I ever go anywhere remote and observe and record the behavior of chimps, apes, baboons, or monkeys as primatologists do. Anthropology and primatology were simply disciplines and ways of seeing that I studied and fell in love with, and then applied to my own experience of moving to and adjusting to life in a foreign culture, a society whose unfamiliar rites, beliefs, and rituals initially left me feeling baffled and alienated.

While I never left Manhattan and did not need to learn a new language, the experiences Malinowski wrote about in the *Diary*—of exasperation and cultural dislocation—are nevertheless utterly familiar to me. I longed to belong, and sometimes intensely resented the people around me who seemed so indifferent to, sometimes even contemptuous of, anyone who was not one of them; I felt spurned when my overtures of friendship went unreciprocated and unacknowledged; I experienced a version of culture shock from such novel, unfamiliar surroundings and cultural practices, and from being ignored and on the outside; and I sometimes fought back a petty desire to send up those I sought to understand. Not infrequently, even knowing that the hazing I experienced was not precisely personal, I felt downright hostile about it ("My feeling [about my informants is sometimes] 'Exterminate the brutes,'" Malinowski wrote in a moment of rage). I understood many of these "fieldwork feelings," every day.

But the tribe of mommies I had studied and lived among for years ended up surprising me. I cannot recall ever feeling more intensely hazed than I did in the initial months and years of my fieldwork, it is true. But nor had I ever felt more cared for and tended to, more truly befriended, than I did after I lost my unborn daughter, Daphne. The previously implacably Other-seeming other mothers who reached out to me—the ones who had seemed haughty and even heartless, the ones by whom I had felt stared down, snickered at, pointedly ignored, and turned into a playdate pariah, the ones who had, themselves, lost or had sisters or friends who had lost—did so with a sense of purpose and dedication and generosity that took me by surprise. Eventually, I think, they forgot what had brought them to me and motivated them to be tender and generous, rather than callous and indifferent and occasionally even nasty, in the first place. And then, they simply continued to be kind. "How did we become friends again? I'm so glad we did . . . I guess it was school?" a shiny-haired friend in Chanel sunglasses reminisced as we lingered on Madison in the sun after coffee one morning. I did not tell her what had brought her to me because we were friends now, and the kernel of the friendship was deep and it seemed a shame to disturb it. I let it be.

Sometimes, I still meet women with young children on the Upper East Side who are friends of a friend, or on a committee or board with someone I know—a tenuous connection—and they strike me, upon first or second or even third impression, as standoffish or unfriendly. I am no Pollyanna about my species, but now, as I take in the indifference of another mother, or her distraction or harshness, or a dismissive or competitive comment,

I have a sense, born of experience, that under dire circumstances I would likely see a better, deeper part of her, and she would see the same in me.

Primatologist Frans de Waal is at the forefront of the emerging field of animal empathy, which deals not only with primates but also with canines, elephants, and even rodents. All of these mammals, but perhaps especially primates, he explains, "are sensitive to each other's emotions and react to those in need." The claim seems modest enough, one de Waal and Jane Goodall and Robert Sapolsky have been making, based on the evidence from their fieldwork, for many years. There are literally thousands of documented cases, de Waal points out, of chimps consoling conspecifics who are upset by hugging and kissing them. Apes "will voluntarily open a door to offer a companion access to food, even if they lose part of it in the process." Capuchin monkeys will seek rewards for others, coming to prefer, when offered two different tokens, the "prosocial" one, which rewards both the capuchin itself, and its companion. Science is slow to accept anything that smacks of anthropomorphism—projecting our own human traits onto animals—because it seems soft and sentimental and inaccurate.

Yet it is impossible to ignore the preponderance of evidence suggesting that animals care for one another, often at a cost to themselves. The frozen heart of science is melting when it comes to accepting a "less blood-soaked" version of our evolutionary history (de Waal's characterization), one that emphasizes how we were shaped by cooperation and compassion as well as violent conflict and indifference. In part this hypothesis about the cooperative origins of humanness stems from watching what nonhuman primates do every day. Yes, chimps can be violently aggressive and are attuned to power in ways that would no doubt elicit the admiration of the most cutthroat Manhattan hedge-fund manager. Certain nonhuman primates are virtually Machiavellian, de Waal observes—he even studied Machiavelli early in his career to better understand the ways the chimps he has observed "schmooze and scheme" and don't bat an eyelash at killing a rival. Yet they also live in tight communities and may show remarkable care for others, as when a female named Daisy who loved wood shavings hoarded hers—in order to bestow the entire cache upon a sick male named Amos, so he could make the nest where he rested more comfortable. Extrapolating how he might feel from her *own* feelings—"Love those wood shavings, they're so comfy!"—she took a personal hit (no wood shavings for her that day or night) in order to ameliorate Amos's discomfort. This act of altruism was based not on—or not merely on—a calculation of what she stood to gain in return. It was instead motored by a deep sense of empathy. She was, de Waal observed, essentially plumping the pillows of the hospital bed of someone she cared for, knowing it would feel good.

Why care?

De Waal suggests that "for mammals, maternal care is the prototypical form of altruism, and template for all the rest." Gestating a fetus, giving your body (and, as many a human mother can attest, your mind) to something developing within you, and then

delivering it, lactating in order to nurse it (or otherwise provisioning it), and making it the center of your universe not for hours or
days or even weeks but for *years*—these everyday acts of motherhood blur in fundamental and profound ways the line between
self and other, between self-interest and literally exhaustingly
comprehensive compassion, empathy, and care for someone else.

Sarah Hrdy suggests that the origins of empathy, the deep
mutual understanding that leads us to do for others as we know
we would like others to do for us, even at tremendous cost, lie in
not only maternal care but also in cooperative breeding, the "it
takes a village" practice and philosophy, mostly just quoted by
Hillary Rodham Clinton in the industrialized West, but amply
evident still in other cultures, where, as it is said in several West
African countries and tongues, "A child has many parents."

Hrdy and anthropologist Kristen Hawkes and more recently
Katie Hinde have shown that, in de Waal's words, "the human
team spirit started with collective care for [our] young, not just
mothers but adults all around." These adults included men but
were mostly, Hawkes and Hinde showed us, other women—kin
and the kindly disposed who simply helped out when it was necessary, and who were helped out in turn when they needed it.
Science suggests that being a cooperative breeder isn't just doing
good—it also *feels* good. For de Waal, rhesus monkeys eloquently
make the case that maternal care and communal care feel good
for those who do it. Every spring, when the rhesus monkeys
have babies, juvenile females go nuts trying to lend a hand—and
get their hands on them. They stay close by, attentively and tirelessly grooming the mothers of the beguiling infants until a mom
agrees that the sitter can have a moment with her baby. These sit-

ters snatch the babies with all-consuming zeal, de Waal reports, "turning them upside down to inspect the genitals, licking their faces, grooming them from all sides, and eventually dozing off with the babies firmly clutched in their arms." This nodding off with the babies happens like clockwork and without exception, "giving the impression that the babysitters are in a trance, or perhaps ecstatic." Clutching the babies close releases oxytocin in the sitters' brains and blood, lulling them into a delicious sleep. They invariably rouse after a few minutes in order to return the babies to their mothers.

Such observations of our nonhuman primate relatives, as well as extensive neuroimaging experiments, have led anthropologist James Rilling to conclude that "we have emotional biases toward cooperation that can only be overcome with effortful cognitive control." In other words, caring is our first impulse; only our minds stand in the way of doing so every time.

Our two sons were eventually accepted at schools on the Upper West Side, and with my work and my husband's, going back and forth from the East Side every day during rush hour seemed like too much to contemplate. We moved across town. Mommies on the Upper West Side are thought to be more casual and friendly and relaxed than Upper East Side mommies, and I have generally found that to be the case. Nobody makes too big a deal about playdates; the kids just sort of tumble over to a nearby playground when school is over. I am rarely charged here; I never feel underdressed. And I live closer to Candace and Lily now.

Sometimes, though, I miss the immaculateness of the Upper East Side, the sense of safety, its burnished, formal sedateness.

When I want to see my Upper East Side girlfriends, or have an Upper East Side experience—lunch at Sant Ambroeus or a browse at Charlotte Olympia or window-shopping along Madison—it's relatively quick and easy to pop across the park. Many of my East Side girlfriends have children who attend school on the Upper West Side now, so sometimes we meet on my side of the world, too. Like so many other uptown dwellers, I cross over. But those two places—Upper East and Upper West—do feel very distinct to me still, as they do to most other New Yorkers. I can love and appreciate and embrace the difference, now that I'm no longer in the trenches on the East Side, trying to decode it all and fit in somehow.

I had to retire my Birkin. In Paris for a vacation, I consulted a doctor in the Sixth about a persistent numbness in my arm. The neurologists I consulted in New York ruled out the serious things but had no solution to offer, no root cause to suggest. I was unable to type, which was inconvenient, to say the very least, for a writer. I spent several days of our trip massaging my right forearm and fretting. The chic Parisian doctor sat behind her desk and like a chic Parisian, she took in not just my story of a writer being unable to write but also my outfit, my bag, every part of my outward appearance. Then she spoke in an emphatically French way. She blamed my heavy bag, pronouncing, "It's zee Birkahn, or zee writing. You shoooze."

Lily had twin daughters two years ago, and she named me their godmother. I see the girls almost every Thursday and have taken it as my mission to dote upon and indulge them. They are energetic and curious and beautiful, Lily's girls, and they are endlessly entertaining. Lily is more a mommy than anyone else I know, better at it and calmer about it than I ever was with only one baby at a time. Sometimes we talk about Flora, and she tells me that it does not get easier, or better, but that often she is happy, and I tell her that I think I understand.

My sons are big boys now. They can do all the things we in the West so want our children to do—read and write and do math, mostly. I urge them to make their beds, to get off their iPads, to write thank-you notes, to look grown-ups in the eye and speak politely. And then I get lazy about it and let them be. In the summer, we go out to the beach and I watch them swim in the pool and go on the tire swing. I see them come together with other groups of kids, kids they know and don't know, on the beach and in the neighborhood, as I make chitchat with the mothers and fathers I know and the ones I don't, taking in the fact that, even in a place as precious and curated and privileged as the Upper East Side and its satellite, the East End, childhood can be rambunctious and unplanned and easy, and motherhood can be relatively simple. It can feel good.

A few times a year my husband and I travel without our boys—to Europe, mostly, and other places his business takes him—and while we are there, I pine for my children. I marvel at how different childhood and motherhood are from continent to continent, town to town, place to place. And how strange and interesting and touching the practices of a tiny tribe on a tiny corner of a tiny island I once studied seem from a distance. I think of the words of Charles Darwin, not the Darwin whose work has been oversimplified and deployed to justify ruthless self-interest and to rationalize the notion of "the selfish gene," but Darwin the father, the one who lost three children and mourned them so deeply that he was nearly incapacitated, and who joyfully helped his wife raise seven more to adulthood, and who balanced the work he loved with parenthood, and who taught us so much: "The social instincts lead an animal to take pleasure in the society of its fellows, to feel a certain amount of sympathy with them, and to perform various services for them."

Yes, I was feeling upbeat and compassionate and generous and sympathetic, not to mention good about myself as a mother and a writer, when we found ourselves at a family-friendly party on the immense, immaculate lawn of someone's immense, immaculate home in the Hamptons not long ago. I had sold a book and delivered the manuscript. There was interest in Hollywood. In the small and gossipy circles I still spent time in, this was news, and people wanted to talk. Much of the talk was goodwilled and supportive, the parents of kids my sons knew, people I had come to know through motherhood, expressing the hope that things would work out, that the book would be a success, along with a lot of joking inquiries about whether I would be naming names. As we chatted about that and other things, too, such as where our kids were going to school now and how they liked it, my older son came over. He looked flushed and told me under his breath, "Mom, I don't feel so good." I turned to touch his forehead—he had a raging fever. "Take this water bottle and go sit under that shady tree where nobody else is sitting, and I'll be right there to take us home, sweetie," I told him, scanning the party for my husband and our younger son.

That's when she materialized before me—the Queen of the Queen Bees, the meanest of the Mean Girl Moms. I had done well at dodging her for many months, ducking into the stairwell whenever I saw her in the hallway at school, turning to real friends when

I saw her at an event, and generally just praying she would pass. Now I made a little gasping noise in spite of myself, hoping she was on her way somewhere else. She didn't usually bother with me—why bother with someone you don't notice? Even viewed through the gauzy lens of cooperative breeding and caring, even when I made excuses for her in my mind—she had an eating disorder; her husband apparently cheated on her; it didn't feel good to be her, even in all her this-season Chanel—she was, to me, beyond hard to take. The recent stories of her nastiness were legion. She told women, in front of their friends, that they were ugly, that they were stupid, that there was something wrong with their children. I thought her a crass bully, and even worse, an empress with no clothes, the Chanel notwithstanding. Because she was so rich and powerful, the people who rolled their eyes behind her back were too petrified to actually confront her about her nasty antics. School administrators looked the other way because she made big contributions. Everyone else took her put-downs meekly and sat at her table at events, hoping for a scrap of I didn't know what. Business? Money? A ruffle or ribbon of her haute couture?

"Hi," she said, sort of looking through me. My mind hopped and skipped. My head bobbled.

"Oh, sorry, my son is—" I began, rattled, looking wildly from side to side for an escape route. She couldn't have cared less that I was talking and broke in as if I had no right to respond to her salutation.

"I heard about your story or book or . . . whatever. What's it called?" She scanned the lawn for better prospects. I felt my older son touch my elbow.

I told her the name of the book and turned toward him to reassure him that yes, we were going, right now.

"That's a good title," she said flatly, her gaze alighting indifferently on my son for an instant.

"Oh, thanks; we have to . . ."

"I guess your publisher gave it to you." It wasn't a question. It was an assertion. You can't possibly have a good title in you, let alone a good book, etc. I straightened up and turned to face her. She smirked.

"No, it's my title," I said, no doubt stiffly, staring her in the face now. My son coughed. She said, with a sarcastic smile, "Sure it is." For one second I imagined doing what I had heard a woman who lived downtown had done when the Queen of the Queen Bees insulted her little son. She had, the story goes, put her hand on the Queen's shoulders and intoned solemnly, "Nobody. Likes. You." And then just walked away. She was like Paul Bunyan, this Woman Who Dared, whose legend lived on in song and gossip.

Now, before I could decide what to say or do, my reverie was broken by my son. As if in slow motion, obediently, after years of training, he was extending his hand toward the Queen, not knowing any better. I imagined myself, again in slow-mo, like an action hero in a movie, jumping across the distance between them, dramatically intercepting his hand and shouting "NOOOOOOOOOOOO!" To save another mother from a dreaded beginning-of-school-year cold or fever. To look after her, as those who had shown compassion toward me had done, because she obviously needed it. I saw myself lying on the ground, my dress smeared with dirt and grass stains from my kind and heroic act. The Queen of the Queen Bees looked at me with surprise and gratitude.

And then it was a normal day on a bright lawn, and I did nothing as she took my son's hand—limply, with no interest in him. I pulled him away without saying good-bye to her, and gave our

hasty thanks to our hosts as I departed, having found my husband
and younger son. And I noted with a satisfied smile, as I turned
around for one last look at the party, that the Queen, who was
also leaving, was wiping her eyes and her nose with the very hand
she had used to accept my feverishly sick son's greeting.

My son would be fine with some ibuprofen and a little rest,
I knew. The sun was sinking lower in the bright blue sky, and I
felt a strong, slow swell of happiness come over me as our family
drove home with the windows rolled down, taking in the beautiful afternoon.

SOURCES

Baumeister, Roy, and Dianne Tice. "Anxiety and Social Exclusion." *Journal of Social and Clinical Psychology* 9, no. 2 (1990): 165–95.

Beck, Taylor. "Estrogen and Female Anxiety: Study Suggests Lower Levels Can Lead to More Mood Disorders." *Harvard Gazette,* August 9, 2012.

Bell, Adrian, Katie Hinde, and Lesley Newson. "Who Was Helping?: The Scope of Female Cooperative Breeding in Early *Homo.*" *PlosOne*, December 2013 (http://www.plosone.org/article/info%3Adoi%2F10.1371%2Fjournal.pone.0083667).

Bennetts, Leslie. *The Feminine Mistake: Are We Giving Up Too Much?* New York: Voice, 2007.

Blurton-Jones, Nicholas. "The Lives of Hunter-Gatherer Children: Effect of Parental Behavior and Parental Reproductive Strategy." In Pereira, Michael E., and Lynn A. Fairbanks, eds. *Juvenile Primates: Life History, Development, and Behavior.* New York: Oxford University Press, 1993. 309–26.

Bogin, Barry. "Evolutionary Hypotheses for Human Childhood." *Yearbook of Physical Anthropology* 40 (1997): 63–89.

Campbell, A., and M. Haussman. "Effects of Oxytocin on Women's Aggression Depend on State Anxiety." *Aggressive Behavior* 39, no. 4: 316–22.

Carmon, Irin. "Strong Proof: 'Drink' and 'Her Best-Kept Secret.'" Sunday Book Review, *New York Times*, November 13, 2013. Retrieved online April 14, 2014.

Cronk, L., N. Chagnon, and W. Irons, eds. *Adaptation and Human Behavior: An Anthropological Perspective.* Hawthorne, NY: Aldine de Gruyter, 2000.

de Waal, Frans. *The Bonobo and the Athiest: In Search of Humanism Among the Primates.* New York: W. W. Norton, 2014.

Deans, Emily, MD. "Dieting Can Make You Lose Your Mind." Online edition, *Psychology Today*, retrieved March 24, 2011, at http://www.psychologytoday.com/blog/evolutionary-psychiatry/201103/dieting-can-make-you-lose-your-mind.

Donner, Nina, and Christopher Lowry. "Sex Differences in Anxiety and Emotional Behavior." *European Journal of Physiology* 465 (2013): 601–26.

"Generalized Anxiety Disorder: An In-Depth Report." *New York Times*. Retrieved online http://www.nytimes.com/health/guides/disease/generalized-anxiety-disorder/print.html.

Gesquiere, L., et al. "Life at the Top: Rank and Stress in Wild Male Baboons." *Science* 333: 357–60.

Glaser, Gabrielle. "Why She Drinks: Women and Alcohol Abuse," *Wall Street Journal*, June 13, 2013. Retrieved online April 12, 2014.

———. *Her Best-Kept Secret: Why Women Drink—and How They Can Regain Control*. New York: Simon & Schuster, 2013.

Grant, Adam M., and Barry Schwartz. "Too Much of a Good Thing: The Challenge and Opportunity of the Inverted U." *Perspectives on Psychological Science* 6 (2011): 61.

Hays, Sharon. *The Cultural Contradictions of Motherhood*. New Haven, CT: Yale University Press, 1996.

———. "The Ideology of Intensive Mothering," in *From Sociology to Cultural Studies: New Perspectives,* ed. Elizabeth Long. New York: Blackwell, 1997.

Hewlett, Barry, and Michael Lamb, eds. *Hunter Gatherer Childhoods: Developmental and Cultural Perspectives*. Piscataway, NJ: Aldine Transaction, 2005.

Hoffman, Stephan, and Anu Asnani. "Cultural Aspects in Social Anxiety and Social Anxiety Disorder." *Depression and Anxiety* 27, no. 12 (December 2012): 1117–27.

Hrdy, Sarah Blaffer. *Mothers and Others: The Evolutionary Origins of Mutual Understanding*. Cambridge, MA: Harvard University Press, 2009.

———. *Mother Nature: Maternal Instincts and How They Shaped the Human Species*. New York: Ballantine, 1999.

Konner, Melvin. *The Evolution of Childhood: Relationships, Emotion, Mind*. Cambridge, MA: Harvard University Press, 2010.

Kramer, Karen. "Variation in Children's Work among Modern Maya Subsistence Agriculturalists." Dissertation. University of New Mexico, 1998.

———. *Maya Children: Helpers at the Farm*. Cambridge, MA: Harvard University Press, 2005.

Lurey, David. *The Anthropology of Childhood: Cherubs, Chattel, Changelings*. Cambridge, UK: Cambridge University Press, 2008.

Mauss, Marcel. *The Gift*. New York: W. W. Norton, 2000.

Offer, Shira, and Barbara Schneider. "Revisiting the Gender Gap in Time-Use Patterns: Multitasking and Well-Being among Mothers and Fathers in Dual-Earner Families." *American Sociological Association* 76, no. 6 (2011): 809–33.

Sapolsky, Robert. *A Primate's Memoir: A Neuroscientist's Unconventional Life Among the Baboons*. New York: Scribner, 2002.

———. "Peace Among Primates" and "How to Relieve Stress" at http://www.beinghuman.org/mind/robert-sapolsky.

Scutti, Susan. "Binge Drinking—Rich Women Most Likely to Binge Drink." *Medical Daily*, April 24, 2013. Retrieved online April 14, 2014.

Shostak, Marjorie. *Nisa: The Life and Words of a !Kung Woman*. Cambridge, MA: Harvard University Press, 2000.

Small, Meredith. *Our Babies, Ourselves: How Biology and Culture Shape the Way We Parent*. New York: Random House, 1999.

———. *Kids: How Biology and Culture Shape the Way We Parent Young Children*. New York: Random House, 2002.

Smith, Harriet J., *Parenting for Primates*. Cambridge, MA: Harvard University Press, 2005.

Smuts, Barbara. "The Evolutionary Origins of Patriarchy." *Human Nature* 6, no. 1 (March 1995): 1–32.

Sterck, Elisabeth, et al. "The Evolution of Female Social Relationships in Nonhuman Primates." *Behavioural Ecology and Sociobiology* 41 (1997): 291–309.

Stockley, P. and A. Campbell, eds. *Female Competition and Aggression: Interdisciplinary Perspectives. Philosophical Transactions of the Royal Society/Biological Sciences*, October 2013.

"Summary of Vital Statistics 2012, The City of New York: Pregnancy Outcomes." New York City Department of Health and Mental Hygiene, 2014.

Symons, Jane. "Caveman Fasting Diet May Leave Women Diabetic." *Express* (home of UK Daily and Sunday Express), January 27, 2013. Retrieved online April 13, 2014.

"Take Care Upper East Side." *Community Profiles*. New York City Department of Health and Mental Hygiene, 2006.

Thompson, Clive. "The Ecology of Stress." *New York Magazine*, September 15, 2010. Retrieved online at http://nymag.com/nymetro/urban/features/stress/10888/.

Volk, A. A., and J. Atkinson. "Is Child Death the Crucible of Human Evolution?" *Journal of Social and Cultural Evolutionary Psychology* 2 (2008): 247–60.

Walter, Chip. "Why Are We the Last Apes Standing? How Childhood Helped Modern Humans Conquer the Planet." *Slate*, January 29, 2013. http://www.slate.com/articles/health_and_science/science/2013/01/evolution_of_childhood_prolonged_development_helped_homo_sapiens_succeed.html.

Warner, Judith. *Perfect Madness: Motherhood in the Age of Anxiety*. New York: Riverhead Press, 2005.

Weisner, Thomas, and R. Gallimore. "My Brother's Keeper: Child and Sibling Caretaking." *Current Anthropology* 18 (1977): 169–90.

ACKNOWLEDGMENTS

I am grateful to the women with young children who taught me to be an Upper East Side mother. Initially, I was as wary of them as they were of me, but they proved what all primatologists know: we are remarkably prosocial and affiliative beings whose long, intensive, and highly cooperative parenting trajectories have in large part made us who we are. The group of Upper East Side mothers who embraced me and my project were masterful and generous native guides, showing me the Way while unlocking the belief system behind it with intelligence, humor, and a great sense of fun. They shared hilarious anecdotes, and heartbreaking ones, on all the big issues for primates—power, parenting, sex, anxiety, and loss, to name a few. They took me behind the scenes, opening up their homes, sharing their insights, thoughts, feelings, and—so important to us great apes—their food. Thanks to them, I went from being an outsider to knowing the warmth of sitting at the campfire in the company of others. I am equally indebted to the friends who listened and advised and put things in context. Thank you, then, to Regan Healy-Asnes, Lindsay Blanco, Jackie Cantor, Vivien Chen, Amy Fusselman, Elizabeth Gordon, Lauren Geller, Barrie Glabman, Judith Gurewich, Marjorie Harris, Eva Heyman, Suri Kasirer, Jennifer Kingson, Kelly Klein, Ellen Kwon, Nancy Lascher, Simone Levinson, Wellington Love, Eve MacSweeney, David Margolick, Jennifer Maxwell, Jackie Mitchell, Liz Morgan Welch, Arianna Neumann, Solana Nolfo, Jeff Nunokana, Debbie Paul, Rebecca Rafael, Barbara Reich, Tina Lobel-Reichberg,

Jessica Reif-Cohen, Atoosa Rubenstein, Erica Samuels, Jen Schiamberg, Caroline Schmidt, Adam Schwartz, Carole Staab, Dana Stern, Rachel Talbot, Amy Tarr, and Amy Wilson.

Trish Todd's editing was insightful, incisive, and patient, undertaken with the sensitivity of a mother who knows exactly how protective other mothers are of their babies. She was and is a book shaman par excellence. Thank you to Richard Pine, who went beyond the call of duty, and to Sandi Mendelson, who never rests. Bethany Saltman helped immeasurably with research. I am grateful to professors Katherine MacKinnon, Richard Prum, Katie Hinde, and Dan Wharton for taking the time to enlighten an outsider whose basic misapprehensions of their worldview did nothing to deter their generosity or forbearance. Any imperfections in the book's science are entirely my own responsibility. Thanks also to experts Heidi Waldorf, MD, Dennis Gross, MD, Stephanie Newman, PhD, and Rachel Blakeman, JD/LCSW, whose insights on beauty and anxiety informed my thinking on these topics.

Without the dedication of several alloparents tending to my children, I could not have written this book. Thank you to Carlos Fragoso, Elizabeth Dahl, and Sarah Swatez. My children have also formed very real and meaningful attachments to their caring cousins, aunts and uncles, grandparents, and half sisters, to whom I am indebted. Thanks to my own mother, who somehow found the time to teach me to love anthropology, biology, Gloria Steinem, and Jane Goodall and her Gombe chimps, even as she raised three children far from her own kin, with no nannies in sight. Special thanks to my friend Lucy Barnes, who with characteristic generosity and kindness asked me almost every day, "How's the book?" and made me the godmother of her daughters, Sylvie and Willa.

My children, Eliot and Lyle, taught me to take the risk of maternal love. I love you, monkeys. Finally, my best reader, and the best choice I ever made, is my husband, Joel Moser. Thanks to him I became a mother, and learned that the pair bond, in spite of being an anomaly and a blip on the screen in evolutionary terms, can feel like home. For that I am eternally grateful.

PRIMATES
of
PARK AVENUE

WEDNESDAY MARTIN

Wednesday Martin's new memoir, *Primates of Park Avenue*, is an inside look at the unexpectedly stressful and anxious lives of Manhattan's most elite set: Upper East Side mommies.

The book follows Wednesday on her journey to join the "it" crew in Manhattan, and no detail—no matter how trivial or painful—is left out. We read about the feelings of exclusion and unhappiness Wednesday experiences as she learns to navigate the sometimes cruel streets and female "friendships" west of Lexington Avenue. We hear about her epic quest to own an Hermès Birkin bag and about the cutthroat nature of preschool applications on the Upper East Side. Through it all, Wednesday straddles the line between subjective insider desperate to find a place for herself and her son and academically detached outsider using her background in anthropology and primatology to help make sense of her world—a world she realizes might seem silly and unsympathetic from the outside. Wednesday is both participant in and observer of the rituals of motherhood in Manhattan's richest neighborhood.

DISCUSSION QUESTIONS

1. On page 2 of her introduction, author Wednesday Martin asks herself "who were they really, these glamorous, stylishly turned out women with sophisticated babies?" Answer Wednesday's question with your group. Who are the women of the Upper East Side *really*? Is there an Upper East Side in your town? Did your conception of these women change after reading *Primates of Park Avenue*? Why or why not?

2. Later in her introduction, Wednesday discusses her strong desire to fit in with the mommies of her new neighborhood, and for her son to fit in by extension. She writes that from her studies in literature and anthropology, she knows that "without a sense of belonging, and actually belonging, we great apes are lost. . . . Particularly female ones . . . do not fare well" (p. 8). Do you think that all people feel this way to some extent? What about all mothers? Is wanting to fit in and feel a sense of community particularly important for new mothers?

3. Why do you think Wednesday Martin chooses to frame the beginning of her memoir as an academic study? Does the

format add humor? Does it give greater credibility to the author? Both? Think about how you would describe your own world anthropologically. Are you part of a tribe? If so, which tribe?

4. Discuss the way gender figures into life on the Upper East Side, according to *Primates of Park Avenue*. Wednesday writes on page 24 that "in Manhattan, the woman is in charge of finding a place for the family to live." What else do the women seem "in charge" of in Manhattan? Of what are they decidedly not in charge?

5. "Women on the Upper East Side, particularly women in their thirties and women on the downhill slope of middle age, are utterly attuned to and obsessed with power" (p. 83). Consider this power obsession in connection with Wednesday Martin's obsession with acquiring a Birkin bag. What is the implicit connection between expensive handbags and power? Does owning a Birkin on the Upper East Side make one more powerful? What is your tribe's "it" bag? Is it a "fetish object"?

6. Many of the women in *Primates of Park Avenue* are described as hyper-dedicated, particularly when it comes to their bodies. Describing a workout class in the Hamptons, Wednesday Martin writes that these women, herself included, put themselves through hell "to bond with their fellow tribe members, but also to measure up to, and to take the measure of, others, day by day, evening by evening, event by event, class by class" (p. 129). Does their physical appearance symbolize something intrinsic? Something about their

worth? What is the connection between the body and the person, in the case of an Upper East Side mommy?

7. What surprised you the most about Wednesday's memoir? Which aspect of these women's lives feels most foreign to you and your life? Which aspects feel more familiar?

8. How does the loss of Wednesday's unborn daughter, Daphne, change the course of the story? Do you think losing a baby changes her perspective on life—particularly life on the Upper East Side?

9. Compare and contrast Wednesday Martin with her new circle. How are they similar? How do they differ? According to what you've read, does Wednesday retain her objective view of this "tribe," or does she become too similar to be objective?

10. "From an anthropological perspective, these wealthy women who seem and are so fortunate are also marooned in their sex-segregated world" (p. 162), writes Wednesday Martin about the marriages she sees all around her in New York City. She describes these so-called arrangements as "fragile and contingent and women are still dependent . . . on their men" (p. 163). Does sex segregation and complete dependence on one's partner seem strange in the twenty-first century, or do these marriages appear to be relatively standard? Do you agree with Wednesday that these women are perhaps in a less enviable position than one might assume? Why or why not?

11. Consider the ways in which anxiety is described in *Primates of Park Avenue*. Do you agree that "having too many choices is stressful" (p. 178), or that a luxurious lifestyle ultimately leads to more—not less—unhappiness?

12. Discuss the title of the memoir: *Primates of Park Avenue*. Do you agree, as the title suggests, that these women who live a certain kind of lifestyle on the Upper East Side are really no different than any other women anywhere? Are we all just animals, doing what we can to survive and create the safest, most favorable conditions we can for our families?

13. *Primates of Park Avenue* is ultimately a testament to the strength of all women to endure the pain that so often accompanies motherhood. In her grief, Wednesday discovers another side of the beautiful, competitive women around her: love. In her time of need, these women come forward and offer emotional support and understanding, bolstering the bond between women of the same tribe who know "just how closely the territories of mothering and loss overlap" (p. 198). Discuss this "secret," as Wednesday coined it, with your group members. Why do you think motherhood, in particular, feels so deeply connected to loss?

ENHANCE YOUR BOOK CLUB

1. In her quest to understand the women with whom she now shares a zip code and a way of life, Wednesday Martin plunges into a thoughtful, observant study of the Upper East Side mommy, the kind of woman she is fast becoming. In addition to firsthand observation, Wednesday uses her academic background to make sense of the rituals, beliefs, and desires of the classic Upper East Side woman. One source she turns to is literature; on page 100, she finds these women and their desires to be similar to the character Lily Bart and her wishes in Edith Wharton's classic *The House of Mirth*. Have a movie night with your group to watch the film adaptation of *The House of Mirth* (2000). After the movie, discuss how Wednesday and her new crew resemble Lily Bart. Do these women covet luxury items because they want "to be a wanted thing" too?

2. Many of the activities in *Primates of Park Avenue* are attended by women only, as the Upper East Side is, according to Wednesday Martin, a very sex-segregated society. In light of this, host a Girls' Night inspired by the one Wednesday attends at her friend Rebecca's apartment (p. 150). Over

dinner and drinks, discuss how your party compares with Rebecca's. Do outfits, accessories, or conversation topics seem drastically different? Do you feel a kinship with the women in the memoir, or do you feel like a member of a totally different species?

3. In chapter 6, Wednesday Martin contemplates the complexity of the relationships between mothers and nannies on the Upper East Side—relationships that can be very familiar to some and terribly foreign to others. In *Primates of Park Avenue*, Wednesday focuses only on the point of view of the mothers, the side of the relationship with which she is most familiar. For the nanny point of view, read *The Nanny Diaries* with your book club. Do the two books overlap in their consideration of this complicated relationship between mommies and nannies? Ultimately, do you agree with Wednesday that the nanny wields more power than the mom? Why or why not?

A CONVERSATION WITH
WEDNESDAY MARTIN

Q: *Primates of Park Avenue* is your second book. Discuss how this project compares with *Stepmonster*. Was one more difficult or challenging to write than the other? Did you have to be more vulnerable in telling one story over the other, or did both require a certain kind of vulnerability?

A: *Primates of Park Avenue* and *Stepmonster* were both very research-intensive blendings of memoir and social science. The difference is that *Primates* came to me very visually. I "saw" the story, not only as I had experienced it but as I wanted to tell it. I hope readers can visualize the story and characters as well!

Q: On page 52 you write that on the Upper East Side, "child's play was apparently a deadly serious business." Child's play—much like exercise or finding the perfect apartment, the perfect summer home, or the perfect handbag—seems to have heavy stakes attached for Upper East Side women. What strikes you as the *most* outrageous ritual you observed in this society?

A: The hiring of black-market Disney guides with access to disability passes so as to bypass lines really did take me by surprise. It said a lot about the pattern of "insider trading" at the heart of many tribal behaviors—I will give you this guide's number, and it establishes that we are one, we are people who do this. And it speaks to the tribe's impatience with doing things the way that "everybody else" has to.

Q: Why did you decide to tell this story from a female-only point of view? What is it about motherhood in particular that seems so distinct in this community?

A: I really had to do it that way. The sex segregation of the tribe I studied is remarkably pronounced. I didn't have access to the world of men. Men and women have very separate spheres in this tribe, and mixing is frowned upon for all kinds of reasons.

Q: In your introduction, you summarize this memoir as "a consideration of one narrow sliver of motherhood on one tiny island, and a meditation on what it might mean for everyone else" (p. 14). Will you answer your own question for us—what does this sliver of motherhood mean for us? Do you agree that ultimately your book is about the connection between women who are mothers, no matter where they live?

A: I think of the book as one contribution to the literature of motherhood. The themes that preoccupied me on my "quest" are pretty universal: the desire to be a good mother, to fit in, and to find and enjoy the perks of social support. It's the quest of every primate, actually. The cultural script of "intensive motherhood"—the belief that you should give every ounce of your energy and every minute of your time to enrich your kids' lives in every measure—intensifies with income. The richer you are, the more you're expected to do it. But the expectation that mothers are solely responsible for their children's well-being and that they do it on their own prevails in most industrialized settings. And it's really hard on kids and mothers alike.

Q: You've been compared to an urban Dian Fossey and to the anthropologist Jane Goodall. Who are some of your female heroes, women you look up to and perhaps channel as you write?

A: I grew up really admiring Jane Goodall, Margaret Mead, and Gloria Steinem, and I still do. I am a huge fan of the writing of evolutionary biologist and primatologist Sarah Blaffer Hrdy. If I met her, I would be utterly starstruck! In very real ways, all of these women remade the world, or established entirely new ways of thinking about it.

Q: Do you agree that loss is a major theme in *Primates of Park Avenue?* When you write, do you consciously choose themes, or do they arise organically from the writing?

A: The themes of *Primates of Park Avenue*—competition, anxiety, female aggression, social support, loss—presented themselves to me as I studied the women around me and mothered alongside them and had coffee with them. And yes, I do think that mothers everywhere, whether they are band foragers or mommies in Scarsdale or Madison or Cleveland, are processing the idea of loss, or of potentially losing a child, much of the time. Sadly, child loss has always been a big part of our experience as a species, and has been woven into human evolution.

Q: Along similar lines, you write on page 198 that part of the "script" for privileged motherhood is the belief that children will follow a certain path: go to school and college, marry, and, eventually, "bury us." Why do you suppose that these privileged mothers hold on so strongly to this belief in a set pattern for a life?

A: It's what parents everywhere hope for, isn't it? The tribe I studied is economically privileged in relative and absolute terms, and their rate of infant mortality is lower than that in many places in the world where resources and good prenatal care and medicine are not as accessible. They have come to expect that their children will outlive them. However, that does not shelter them from the realities of loss. Worldwide, being a fetus or a baby is risky, relative to other life stages.

Q: You share so much with readers that is personal; these things must have been painful memories for you to revisit. What was the most difficult part of writing *Primates of Park Avenue?* Did the act of writing work as a kind of catharsis for you?

A: Writing the chapter about the loss of my daughter, Daphne, was very sad, but also very helpful for me. It helped me understand and connect with other women who have experienced such losses. It was also surprisingly cathartic to write about the experience of being a playdate pariah. So many women had experienced it and wanted to talk to me about it. That was inspiring.

Q: It seems that your quest to obtain a Birkin bag was all-consuming and intense, and you spend an entire chapter describing for us the ins and outs of owning such a coveted item. What does the Birkin bag symbolize for you? Does it carry the same import now that you own it?

A: I wrote that part of the appeal of a Birkin bag is the "get" itself. Once the thrill of the hunt is done, you are left with a status object made of leather. I learned the hard way that such quests can backfire spectacularly: in my enthusiasm to get a Birkin in order to "play ball" with the other moms, I neglected to consider that it might actually injure me! Two different doctors told me that the bag was the likely cause of the neurological pain that made it hard for me to write!

Q: What news can you share with us about upcoming projects? Do you have plans for a new memoir?

A: I am now part of the tribe of fiction writers. They are very different from writers of nonfiction (well, at least that's what writers of nonfiction say). I love inventing a world and plots and characters entirely. It's very freeing, but I do feel a little crazy when I speak to my husband about what the characters are doing or how they feel or what they think. I mean, c'mon, they're characters. But I hope readers will enjoy the novel I'm working on. All the sex that the tribe of women I studied are not having, the main character of my novel is!